Teacher's Edition

SRA SPECTRUM MATH

FIFTH EDITION

gold

A Division of The McGraw·Hill Companies

Columbus, Ohio

www.sra4kids.com

SRA/McGraw-Hill
A Division of The McGraw·Hill Companies

Copyright © 2002 by SRA/McGraw-Hill.

All rights reserved. Except as permitted under the United States Copyright Act, no part of this publication may be reproduced or distributed in any form or by any means, or stored in a database or retrieval system, without the prior written permission of the publisher, unless otherwise indicated.

Send all inquiries to:
SRA/McGraw-Hill
8787 Orion Place
Columbus, OH 43240-4027

Printed in the United States of America.

ISBN 0-07-572338-7

1 2 3 4 5 6 7 8 9 MAZ 07 06 05 04 03 02 01

Contents

PROBLEM SOLVING STRATEGIES
Find the Facts 1
Find the Question 2
Choose the Operation 3
Draw a Picture 4
Look for a Pattern 5
Guess and Check 6

1 CHAPTER 1
Numeration
(0 through 10)
Lessons
1   Numbers 0 through 3 7
2   Numbers 4 through 7 8
3   Numbers 8 through 10 9
4   Numbers 0 through 10 10
5   Numbers 0 through 10 11
6   Order of Numbers 13
7   Order of Numbers 15
8   Number Patterns 16
9   Ordinal Numbers 17
CHAPTER 1 PRACTICE TEST 19

2 CHAPTER 2
Addition and Subtraction
(facts through 5)
CHAPTER 2 PRETEST 20
Lessons
1   Sums through 3 21
2   Sums of 4 and 5 22
3   Subtracting from 1, 2, and 3 23
4   Subtracting from 4 and 5 24
5   Number Families 25
6   Penny and Nickel 26
7   Problem Solving 27
CHAPTER 2 PRACTICE TEST 29

3 CHAPTER 3
Addition and Subtraction
(facts through 8)
CHAPTER 3 PRETEST 30
Lessons
1   Sums of 6 31
2   Subtracting from 6 32
3   Sums of 7 33
4   Subtracting from 7 34
5   Sums of 8 35
6   Subtracting from 8 36
7   Addition and Subtraction 37
8   Addition and Subtraction 39
9   Addition and Subtraction 41
10 Problem Solving 42
CHAPTER 3 PRACTICE TEST 43

4 CHAPTER 4
Addition and Subtraction
(facts through 10)
CHAPTER 4 PRETEST 44
Lessons
1   Sums of 9 45
2   Subtracting from 9 46
3   Sums of 10 47
4   Subtracting from 10 48
5   Practicing Addition 49
6   Practicing Subtraction 51
7   Addition and Subtraction 53
8   Money 55
9   Problem Solving 57
CHAPTER 4 PRACTICE TEST 59

5 CHAPTER 5
Numeration
(0 through 99)
CHAPTER 5 PRETEST 60
Lessons
1   Numbers 10 through 19 61
2   Numbers 20 through 29 62
3   Numbers 10 through 29 63
4   Tens 64
5   Numbers 30 through 49 65
6   Numbers 50 through 69 67
7   Numbers 70 through 99 68
8   Numbers 50 through 99 69
9   Numeration 71
10 Comparing Numbers 72
11 Skip Counting 73
CHAPTER 5 PRACTICE TEST 75

T3

6 CHAPTER 6
Measurement
CHAPTER 6 PRETEST 76
Lessons
1. Time—Hour 77
2. Time—Half Hour 79
3. Calendar 81
4. Charts 83
5. Bar Graphs 85
6. Picture Graphs 87
7. Centimeter 89
8. Inch 91
9. Measuring 93

CHAPTER 6 PRACTICE TEST 95

7 CHAPTER 7
Geometry
CHAPTER 7 PRETEST 96
Lessons
1. Plane Figures 97
2. Solid Figures 98
3. Geometric Patterns 100
4. Geometric Patterns 101
5. Symmetry 102

CHAPTER 7 PRACTICE TEST 103

8 CHAPTER 8
Addition and Subtraction
(2-digit with no renaming)
CHAPTER 8 PRETEST 104
Lessons
1. Addition and Subtraction Facts .. 105
2. Adding and Subtracting Tens 107
3. Addition (2-digit) 109
4. Addition (2-digit) 111
5. Subtraction (2-digit) 113
6. Subtraction (2-digit) 115
7. Adding 3 Numbers 117
8. Addition and Subtraction 119
9. Addition and Subtraction 121

CHAPTER 8 PRACTICE TEST 123

9 CHAPTER 9
Addition and Subtraction
(facts through 18)
CHAPTER 9 PRETEST 124
Lessons
1. Facts for 11 125
2. Facts for 12 127
3. Facts through 12 129
4. Facts for 13 131
5. Facts for 14 132
6. Facts through 14 133
7. Facts for 15 135
8. Facts for 16 136
9. Facts through 16 137
10. Facts through 18 139
11. Addition Facts through 18 141
12. Subtraction Facts through 18 ... 143

CHAPTER 9 PRACTICE TEST 145
MID-TEST Chapters 1–4 147
FINAL TEST Chapters 1–9 149–152
CUMULATIVE REVIEWS 153–162
SPECTRUM MATH Assessment 163
CHAPTER TESTS 1–9 165–173
Answers to CHAPTER TESTS 175–177
Evaluation 179

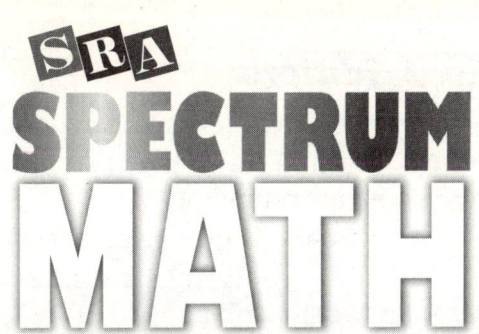

Twenty Years of
✔ **Straightforward** ✔ **Solid** ✔ **Comprehensive**

Mathematics Instruction and Practice that have led to student success in mathematics.

Proven effective in thousands of classrooms.

Eight levels provide thorough development of core mathematics skills and strategies.

The straightforward design and color level designations on the student books allow for flexible use **at grade level** or for **remediation** from second grade through adult education.

gold	Level 1
brown	Level 2
red	Level 3
orange	Level 4
yellow	Level 5
green	Level 6
blue	Level 7
purple	Level 8

Updated and Upgraded!

❶ New lessons teach the mathematics concepts in current national and state guidelines.

❷ Spectrum Math Software provides **extra practice** with immediate feedback for each skill, and printable extra practice pages.

❸ All NEW! Spectrum Math Achieve: Key Skills and Strategies

- **Research-Based Strategies** for rethinking and reteaching fundamental math skills that are crucial for further development in mathematics
- **Real-World Problem Solving Strategies** and mixed practice that teach students how to attack any math problem they encounter

T5

■ Student Editions

- Model **worked problems** to demonstrate math concepts
- Develop basic and **fundamental math concepts** step-by-step to promote understanding
- Provide readiness **diagnostic assessment** for skill assessment
- Include **problem solving strategies** and practice to develop mathematical reasoning
- Cover all major areas of mathematics including **geometry** and **algebra**
- Include **cumulative reviews** to maintain skills

■ Teacher Editions

- Provide **overprinted answers** and scoring for teacher convenience
- Identify **prerequisite skills** to ensure student understanding
- Suggest **Lesson Follow-up** tips to address student results
- Include **Chapter Tests** in blackline master form

■ Spectrum Software

- Complete and **comprehensive software math lessons** correlated to the Student Editions
- Offers **immediate feedback** and animated explanations for each skill
- Provides **timed flash cards** for **basic facts fluency**
- Includes complete **Teacher Management System** to track student progress

■ Spectrum Math Achieve: Key Skills and Strategies Workbook

NEW!

- For students who need **intensive reteaching and review of core math concepts** and **problem solving skills and strategies** that appear on math tests
- Systematically and explicitly leads students through math thinking processes to understand those **fundamental math skills** identified as causing students the most difficulty
- Uses **research-based strategies** for learning those skills and concepts that are most problematic for students
- Teaches **problem solving strategies** in a **real-world context**
- Includes **real-world mixed problem solving practice** to teach students how to handle any math problem

■ Spectrum Math Reference Books and Posters

Nonfiction books and posters that profile U. S. landmarks are filled with mathematical data.

Built-in program references reinforce study skills and find appropriate math information for real-world problem solving.

 For more information contact SRA at **888-SRA-4543**

www.sra4kids.com

Using SRA SPECTRUM MATH

A straightforward structure for a variety of classroom situations.

WHOLE CLASS
▶ *Spectrum Math* has been used successfully as a core math program with whole class instruction. The lessons added to this edition ensure that important content is covered.

SUPPLEMENTAL
▶ Many districts use *Spectrum Math* for extra practice of core mathematics to supplement other math instruction. *Spectrum Math* makes sure the basics are taught and practiced to ensure student achievement.

INTERVENTION
▶ Teachers have successfully used *Spectrum Math* to intensively reteach and practice crucial mathematics. The new *Spectrum Math Achieve: Key Skills and Strategies* components reteach key math skills and reinforce problem solving strategies to specifically address the needs of struggling students.

AFTER SCHOOL
▶ *Spectrum Math* is a perfect after school math reinforcement and practice program with its specific and concentrated lessons.

SUMMER SCHOOL
▶ *Spectrum Math's* focused and explicit lessons make it an ideal summer school program.

HOME SCHOOL
▶ *Spectrum Math* is frequently used as a comprehensive math curriculum in home school environments.

T7

Student Edition

Simple, direct, and explicit lessons

▶ Lesson title identifies the skill

▶ **Worked problems** model procedures and solutions

▶ Every lesson has plenty of practice opportunities with **computation** and **problem solving applications**.

▶ Includes instruction in **Problem Solving Strategies** at the beginning of every book.

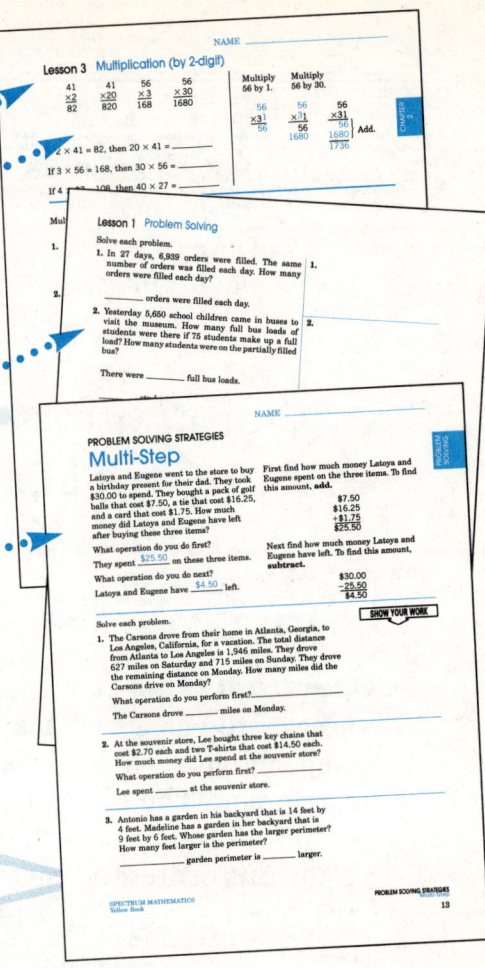

Teacher's Edition

Prerequisite skills are clearly identified.

◀ All answers are conveniently provided.

◀ References prompt appropriate use of the *Spectrum Math Achieve: Key Skills and Strategies* resources and when to use the **Mid-Test, Final-Test,** and **Cumulative Review.**

◀ **Lesson Follow-up and Error Analysis** gives suggestions for responding to different levels of student performance. Also references appropriate use of *Spectrum Math Software.*

✓ Also includes **Blackline Masters** of **Chapter Tests** for effective assessment.

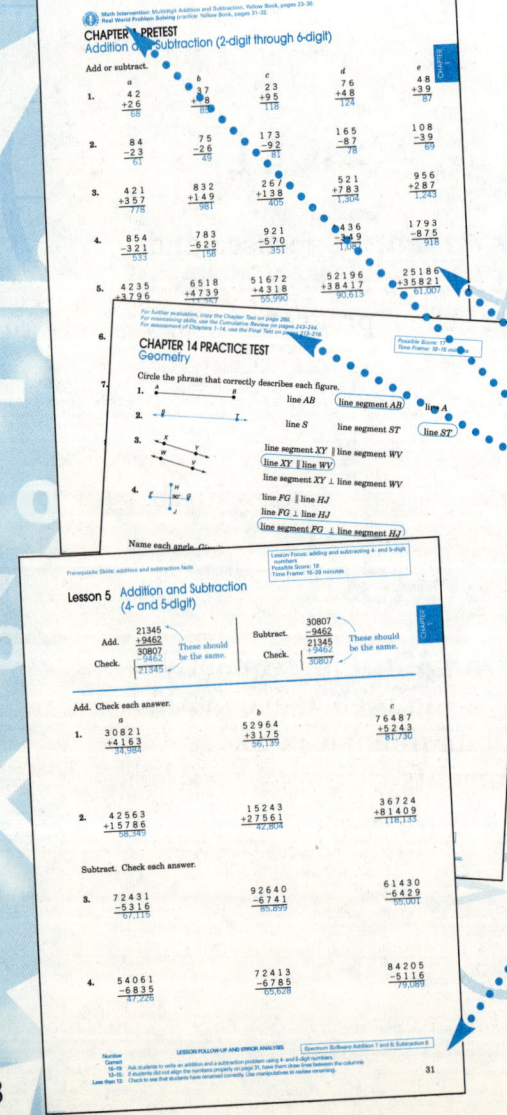

Spectrum Math Achieve: Key Skills and Strategies

Skills

Crucial problematic math skills are intensively and methodically taught step-by-step so that students understand how and why math works. Skills at each level are those on which students consistently score below proficiency on state and national tests. Research-based strategies facilitate student success.

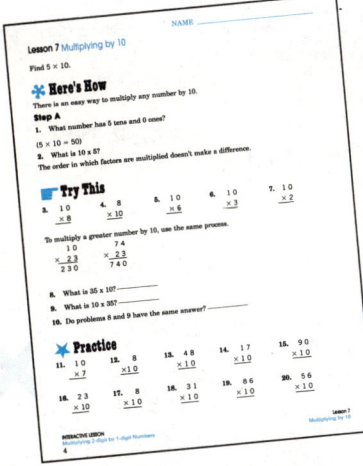

Interactive eight-page lessons focus on each critical skill. Some students may be able to work through the lessons on their own. Most remedial students will benefit from the support of a teacher, aide, or family member to guide them through the lesson.

✔ Each lesson begins with clear objectives and a **CheckUp** to assess whether students understand prerequisite skills.

✔ **Skills You Need to Know** are carefully taught.

✔ The lesson skill is developed **step-by-step** using problem solving strategies.

✔ **If You're Having Trouble** tips are included for struggling students.

✔ **Practice** is included to secure the skill.

✔ **Debugging** problems are included for student analysis of errors.

✔ Each lesson ends with a **Self-Check** for confidence.

Strategies

Spectrum Math Achieve: Key Skills and Strategies *teaches problem solving strategies in a real-world context and then provides distributed mixed practice to maintain student understanding and skill.*

Problem solving practice is tied to the math behind real-world landmarks. Engaging **Reference Books** and **Posters** provide the math data and context students need to solve the problems. Students practice **research skills** as they develop problem solving skills and strategies.

- California's Giant Sequoia – Gold, Level 1
- Pencil Factory – Brown, Level 2
- Madison Square Garden – Red, Level 3
- Denver Mint – Orange, Level 4
- The White House – Yellow, Level 5
- DFW 747 – Green, Level 6
- Atlanta's Olympic Stadium – Blue, Level 7
- Barging Through the Locks – Purple, Level 8

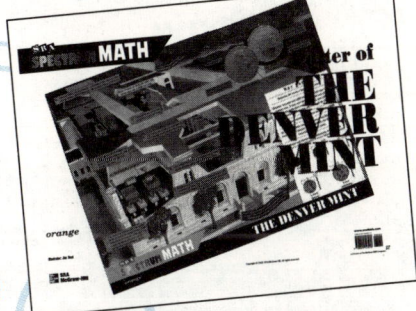

Answers and solutions are provided in the back of the **Spectrum Math Achieve: Key Skills and Strategies** workbook for convenient access during school, after school, or at home.

T9

	ADDITION (Whole Numbers)	ALGEBRA (Readiness)	DECIMALS and MONEY	DIVISION (Whole Numbers)	FRACTIONS	GEOMETRY	MEASUREMENT	MULTIPLICATION (Whole Numbers)
LEVEL 1 Gold Book	pages 21-22, 25, 27, 31, 33, 35, 37-47, 49-50, 53-54, 57-59, 105-112, 117-122, 125-127, 129-142 **25-32, 77-84, 87-94**		pages 26-28, 55-58, 61-65, 67-69			pages 97-102	pages 77-94	
LEVEL 2 Brown Book	pages 8-14, 29-30, 33, 35-36, 49-52, 57-58, 61-64, 69-70, 73-76, 79-82, 85-86, 89-92, 107-109, **15-22, 35-43, 66-73**		pages 17-19, 24, 67-88, 91	readiness pages 161-164	pages 45-48 **46-53**	pages 49-52	pages 55-70 **56-63**	readiness pages 155-160
LEVEL 3 Red Book	pages 23, 25-26, 29-32, 35-36, 49-52, 57-58, 61-64, 69-70, 73-76, 79-82, 85-86, 89-92, 107-108 **19-26, 41-48**		pages 102, 106, 107-108 **95-102**	pages 141-148, 151-158	pages 187-192 **127-134**	pages 195-202	pages 61-70, 73-82, 85-94, 135-138 **107-114, 117-124**	pages 121-128, 131-138 **65-72, 75-82, 85-92**
LEVEL 4 Orange Book	pages 23, 25-28, 33-38, 43-44, 47-54 **19-26, 29-36**		pages 97-102 **71-78**	pages 105-112, 115-126, 129-132, 135-136, 139-142, 145-146 **81-88, 91-98, 103-110**	pages 149-156 **113-120**	pages 159-168	pages 171-184, 187-202 **125-132**	pages 61-70, 73-82, 85-94, 135-138 **49-56, 59-66, 103-110**
LEVEL 5 Yellow Book	pages 24, 27-34, 89 **23-30**	pages 245-252	pages 87-98 **65-72**	pages 52-62, 65-74, 76-84, 95-96 **43-50, 53-60**	pages 139-148, 151-162, 165-180, 183-196 **97-104, 107-114, 117-124, 127-134**	pages 199-207 **137-144**	pages 113-124, 127-136 **85-92**	pages 39-50 **33-40**
LEVEL 6 Green Book	pages 25, 27-28, 31-34 **23-30**	pages 159-162, 237-250	pages 97-116, 119-126, 129-140 **73-80, 83-90, 93-100**	pages 38, 43-50 **33-40**	pages 53-68, 71-82, 85-94 **43-50, 53-60, 63-70**	pages 191-198 **135-142**	pages 143-152, 155-164 **103-110**	pages 37, 39-42, 47-50
LEVEL 7 Blue Book	pages 19-20, 23-26 **27-34**	pages 91-94, 97-100, 106, 117-126, 129-136, 171-184, 189-194, 245-262	pages 67-86, 109-112 **47-54**	pages 31-40	pages 43-64, 106-107 **37-44**	pages 156-168, 171-186 **109-116, 119-126, 129-136**	pages 138-144, 147-154, 171-186, 189-194 **89-96, 99-106**	pages 27, 39-40
LEVEL 8 Purple Book	pages 19-20, 27-28	pages 49-60, 63-70, 75-76, 79-82, 87-94, 97-100, 145-146, 151-156, 159-165, 169-176, 199-200, 239-262 **47-54**	pages 29-34, 84 **27-34**	pages 25-28	pages 37-46, 82, 84 **37-44**	pages 133-140, 159-175 **99-106, 109-116, 119-126**	pages 107-144, 117-130, 159-175 **79-86, 89-96**	pages 23-24, 27-28

T10 *bold represents page numbers in SPECTRUM MATH Achieve: Key Skills and Strategies   SPECTRUM MATH SCOPE AND SEQUENCE

NUMBER and NUMERATION	PATTERNS and RELATIONS	PROBABILITY	PROBLEM SOLVING and STRATEGIES	RATIO, PROPORTION and PERCENT	STATISTICS and GRAPHING	SUBTRACTION (Whole Numbers)
pages 7-18, 61-72 **15-22, 55-62**	pages 16, 73-74, 100-101		pages 1-6, 27-28, 38, 40, 42, 50, 52, 54, 57-58, 108, 110, 112, 114, 116, 118, 120, 126, 128, 130, 134, 138, 140 **1-6, 23-24, 33-34, 43-54, 63-64, 73-76, 85-86, 95-96**		pages 81-88 **65-80**	pages 23-25, 27-30, 32, 34, 36-44, 46, 48, 51-54, 56-59, 105-108, 113-116, 119-125, 127-140, 143-144 **35-42, 87-94**
pages 7, 17-26, 115-122 **25-32, 86-93**	pages 23-25, 51		pages 1-6, 14, 30, 32, 36, 38, 40, 42, 60, 80, 82, 84, 86, 88, 92, 94, 102, 104, 108, 110, 112, 124, 126, 128, 130, 132, 134 **1-6, 23-24, 33-34, 44-45, 54-55, 64-65, 74-75, 84-85, 94-95**		pages 71-74	pages 8-14, 31-32, 34, 37-42, 77-78, 85-88, 92-94, 97-98, 105-112, 129-134 **15-22, 76-83**
pages 39-46, 105 **29-36**	pages 43, 99-100	pages 211-212	pages 13-20, 26, 28, 30, 32, 34, 36, 40, 42, 46, 50, 52, 54, 56, 58, 62, 64, 66, 68, 70, 74, 76, 78, 80, 82, 84, 86, 90, 92, 94, 96, 98, 100, 108, 114, 116, 118, 122, 124, 126, 128, 132, 136, 138, 144, 146, 148, 152, 154, 156, 158, 162, 164, 166, 168, 172, 174, 176, 178, 180, 182-184, 200, 202, 212, **1-16, 27-28, 37-40, 49-52, 61-64, 73-74, 83-84, 93-94, 103-106, 115-116, 125-126, 135-138, 147-148**		pages 205-210 **139-146**	pages 24, 27, 29, 33-36, 53-58, 65-70, 73-74, 77-80, 83-86, 93-96 **19-26, 53-60**
pages 55-58, 143-146		pages 213-214	pages 13-20, 26, 28, 30, 34, 36, 38, 40, 42, 48, 50, 52, 54, 56, 58, 62, 64, 66, 68, 70, 74, 76, 78, 80, 82, 86, 88, 90, 92, 94, 100, 102, 106, 108, 110, 112, 116, 118, 120, 122, 124, 126, 132, 136, 138, 140, 142, 144, 146, 154, 156, 160, 162, 168, 174, 176, 182, 190, 192, 194, 196, 198, 201-202, 206, 207, 210, 212, 214 **1-16, 27-28, 37-38, 47-48, 57-58, 67-70, 79-80, 89-90, 99-102, 111-112, 121-124, 133-136, 145-146**		pages 205-212 **137-144**	pages 24-26, 29-30, 39-44, 47-50, 53-54 **19-26, 39-46**
pages 35-36, 49-50, 61-62, 141-142		pages 109-110	pages 13-22, 28, 30, 32, 34, 40, 42, 44, 46, 48, 50, 66, 68, 72, 80, 82, 88, 90, 92, 94, 104, 106, 108, 110, 112, 114, 116, 124, 126, 130, 132, 134, 136, 154, 156, 158, 160, 162, 174, 176, 178, 180, 186, 188, 190, 192, 194, 196 **1-20, 31-32, 41-42, 51-52, 61-64, 73-74, 83-84, 93-96, 105-106, 115-116, 125-126, 135-136, 145-146**		pages 101-108 **75-82**	pages 25-32, 35-36, 91-92 **23-30**
pages 33-34, 49-50, 58-61, 113-116		pages 183-186	pages 13-22, 28, 30, 32, 34, 40, 42, 44, 46, 48, 50, 64, 66, 68, 72, 80, 82, 88, 90, 92, 94, 104, 106, 108, 110, 112, 114, 116, 124, 126, 130, 132, 136, 138, 140, 146, 148, 156, 158, 160, 162, 170, 172, 174, 182, 184, 186, 188, **1-20, 31-32, 41-42, 51-52, 61-62, 71-72, 81-82, 91-92, 101-102, 111-114, 123-124, 133-134**	pages 167-174 **115-122**	pages 177-181, 187-188 **125-132**	pages 26, 29-34 **23-30**
pages 29-30, 44		pages 205-210	pages 5-16, 20, 22, 24, 26, 28, 32, 34, 36, 38, 40, 50, 54, 56, 60, 62, 64, 70, 72, 74, 78, 80, 82, 84, 86, 92, 94, 96-98, 100, 114, 118, 120, 122, 124, 126, 130, 132, 134, 136, 144, 150, 154, 172, 174, 176, 178, 180, 182, 184, 190, 192, 194, 204, 206, 208, 210-211 **1-24, 35-36, 45-46, 55-56, 65-66, 75-78, 87-88, 97-98, 107-108, 117-118, 127-128, 137-138, 147-148**	pages 89-100, 103-104, 117-125, 129-135 **57-64, 67-74, 79-86**	pages 197-211 **139-146**	pages 21-26 **27-34**
pages 128-130		pages 191-205 **139-146**	pages 5-16, 20, 22, 24, 26-28, 30, 32, 34, 40, 42, 44, 46, 52, 54, 56, 58, 60, 65-70, 78-80, 86, 88, 90, 92, 94, 98, 100, 102, 104, 113, 118, 120, 122, 124, 126, 146, 154, 156, 164, 172, 176, 192, 194, 196, 198, 200, 202, 204-205 **1-24, 35-36, 45-46, 55-58, 67-68, 77-78, 87-88, 97-98, 107-108, 117-118, 127-128, 137-138, 147-148**	pages 73-80 **59-66, 69-76**	pages 179-188 **129-136**	pages 21-22, 27–28

SPECTRUM MATH SCOPE AND SEQUENCE

T11

Error Analysis

As students develop math skills and understanding, they will invariably make mistakes. These errors provide important insight into student thinking and level of skill. All errors are not equal. Sometimes a student knows how to solve the problem but makes a simple mistake in copying the problem. Other times a student error can reveal that the student does not understand the fundamental skill necessary to solve a problem. In that case, error analysis can be used to identify the source of the problem and reteach the prerequisite skill.

The **Debugging** feature at the end of every lesson in the ***Achieve: Key Skills and Strategies*** workbook asks students to analyze errors as a way to truly understand the mathematical reasoning. It also provides a list of errors for students to avoid in their own work.

Below are some common errors that students make. Identifying the source of the error and then reteaching the skill will eliminate frustration and build confidence.

Choosing the Wrong Operation

8 + 4 = 4

Simple mistakes are made when students add instead of subtract or multiply instead of divide.

Misaligning Numbers in Computation

```
 895       34
 -24       ×7
 655       28
           21
           49
```

Many mistakes occur when students do not line up their numbers clearly, even when they understand the mathematics.

Regrouping

Regrouping is a very difficult concept for many students who do not have solid place value skills. When they are simply following a procedure rather than understanding why it works, errors occur.

- Subtracting the lower digit from the higher number regardless of whether it is the subtrahend.

```
 495
 -67
 432
```

- Subtracting from left to right before regrouping.

```
 495
 -67
 438
```

T12

Problem Solving Strategy practice:
Find the Facts, Gold Book, pages 1–2.

Lesson Focus: Problem Solving Strategy—Find the Facts
Possible Score: 6
Time Frame: 5–10 minutes

PROBLEM SOLVING STRATEGIES
Prerequisite Skills: addition and subtraction facts

Find the Facts

There are 4 .   What are the facts?

There are 2 .

How many in all?

Ring the facts.

There are 4 .

There are 2 .

How many in all?

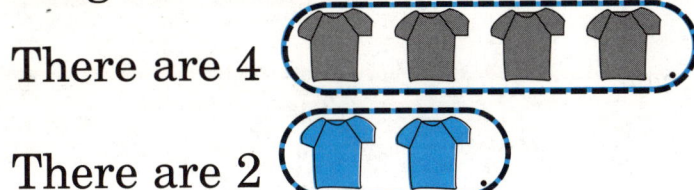

Ring the facts.

I have 5 little  .

I have 2 big  .

How many in all?

There are 6 .

4 fly away.

How many are left?

Cari has 3  .

Angie has 3  .

How many in all?

PROBLEM SOLVING STRATEGIES
Find the Facts

1

PROBLEM SOLVING STRATEGIES

Find the Question

There are 4  .   What is the question?
2 roll away.
How many are left?

Ring the question.

There are 4  .
3 roll away.
(How many are left?)

Ring the question.

Amy has 7  .
Mica has 2 more.
(How many in all?)

There were 5  .
Then 4 more came.
(Now how many in all?)

There were 4  .
2 flew away.
(How many are left?)

Problem Solving Strategy practice:
Choose the Correct Operation, Gold Book, pages 5–6.

PROBLEM SOLVING STRATEGIES
Prerequisite Skills: addition and subtraction facts

Lesson Focus: Problem Solving Strategy—
  Choose the Correct Operation
Possible Score: 4
Time Frame: 5–10 minutes

Choose the Correct Operation

Sara saw 4  .

Kyle saw 3 more.

How many in all?

There are __7__ birds.

Do you add or subtract?

To find out how many, **add**.

```
   4
 + 3
 ———
   7
```

Ring the correct operation. Then solve the problem.

There are 7  .

2 run away.

How many are left?

add or (subtract)

__5__ dogs are left.

SHOW YOUR WORK

```
   7
 - 2
 ———
   5
```

There are 5 little  .

There are 4 big  .

How many in all?

(add) or subtract

There are __9__ books.

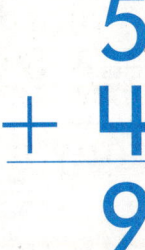

PROBLEM SOLVING STRATEGIES
Choose the Correct Operation

Problem Solving Strategy practice:
Draw a Picture, Gold Book, pages 7–8.

PROBLEM SOLVING STRATEGIES
Prerequisite Skills: addition and subtraction facts

Draw a Picture

Lesson Focus: Problem Solving Strategy—Draw a Picture
Possible Score: 2
Time Frame: 5–10 minutes

I saw 5 .

Barry saw 2 more.

How many in all?

There are __7__ in all.

What picture can you draw?

Draw a picture to add.

Draw a picture. Then solve the problem. SHOW YOUR WORK

There are 6 .

3 drive away.

How many are left?

There are __3__ left.

Jodi saw 4 .

Jarod saw 5 .

How many in all?

There are __9__ in all.

PROBLEM SOLVING STRATEGIES
Draw a Picture

4

Problem Solving Strategy practice:
Look for a Pattern, Gold Book, pages 9–10.

PROBLEM SOLVING STRATEGIES
Prerequisite Skills: pattern recognition

Look for a Pattern

Lesson Focus: Problem Solving Strategy—Look for a Pattern
Possible Score: 3
Time Frame: 5–10 minutes

What is the pattern?

Ring what comes next.

Ring what comes next.

PROBLEM SOLVING STRATEGIES
Look for a Pattern

5

Guess and Check

Ann has 2 ✏.

Tim has 4 ✏.

Kyle has 5 ✏.

Which two have 6 pencils in all?

(Ann and Tim)   Tim and Kyle

Ann and Kyle

Guess: Ann and Tim

Check:
$$\begin{array}{r} 2 \\ +\,4 \\ \hline 6 \end{array}$$

Solve each problem. Then ring the answer.

Anna has 3 .

Tom has 2 .

Jen has 1 .

Which two have 4 apples in all?

Anna and Tom   Tom and Jen

(Anna and Jen)

SHOW YOUR WORK

Guess: Anna and Jen

Check:
$$\begin{array}{r} 3 \\ +\,1 \\ \hline 4 \end{array}$$

Ed has 8 🎈.

Kim has 2 🎈.

Taylor has 1 🎈.

Which two have 10 balloons in all?

(Ed and Kim)   Kim and Taylor

Ed and Taylor

Guess: Ed and Kim

Check:
$$\begin{array}{r} 8 \\ +\,2 \\ \hline 10 \end{array}$$

Math Intervention: Numbers 0–10, Gold Book, pages 15–22.
Real World Problem Solving practice: Gold Book, pages 23–24.

Lesson Focus: counting objects
Possible Score: 6
Time Frame: 5 minutes

Lesson 1   Numbers 0 through 3
Prerequisite Skills: number recognition and counting

zero	one	two	three
0	1	2	3

Ring the numeral.

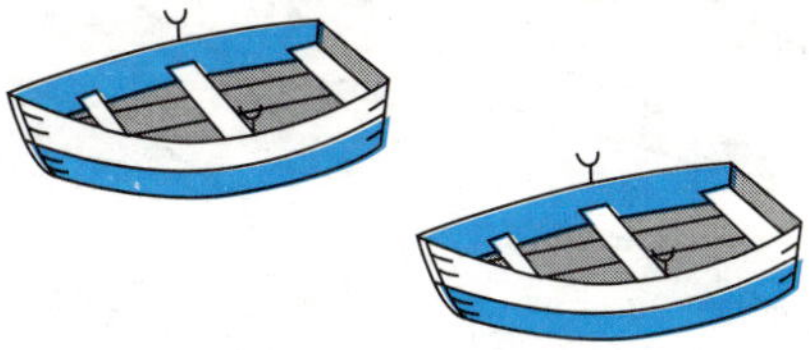

0 1 ② 3	0 ① 2 3
0 1 2 ③	0 1 ② 3
0 1 2 ③	⓪ 1 2 3

Number Correct
5–6: Have students draw sets of 3, 2, 1, and 0 objects.
3–4: Using manipulatives, ask students to count out a given number of objects.
Less than 3: Review the numbers 0, 1, 2, and 3 by showing sets of objects and writing the numerals for each set.

LESSON FOLLOW-UP AND ERROR ANALYSIS

Spectrum Software Whole Numbers 4

Prerequisite Skills: number recognition and counting

Lesson Focus: counting similar objects
Possible Score: 6
Time Frame: less than 5 minutes

Lesson 2 Numbers 4 through 7

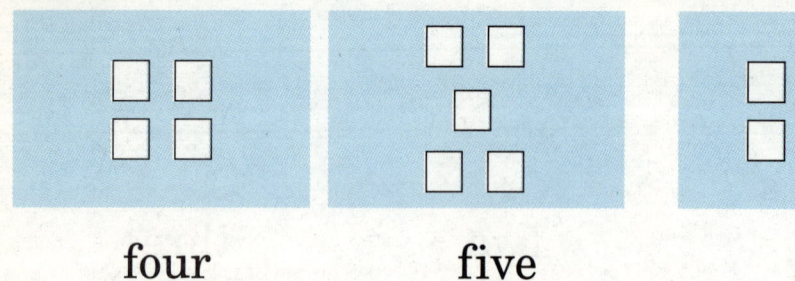

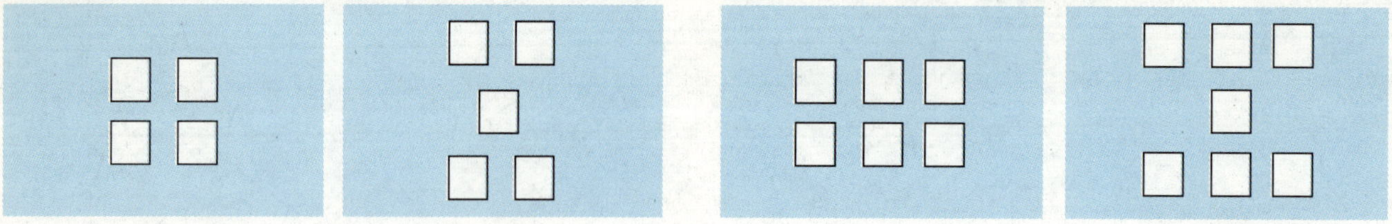

four	five	six	seven
4	5	6	7

Ring the numeral.

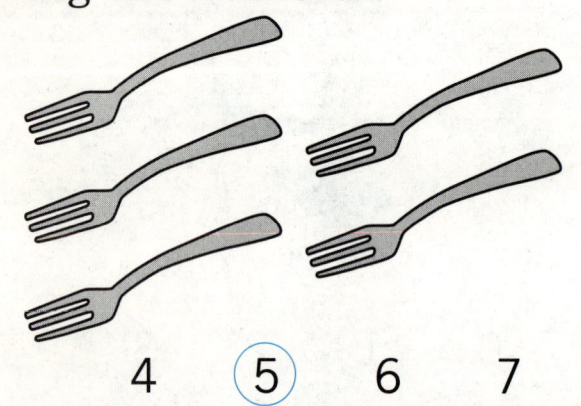

4 (5) 6 7

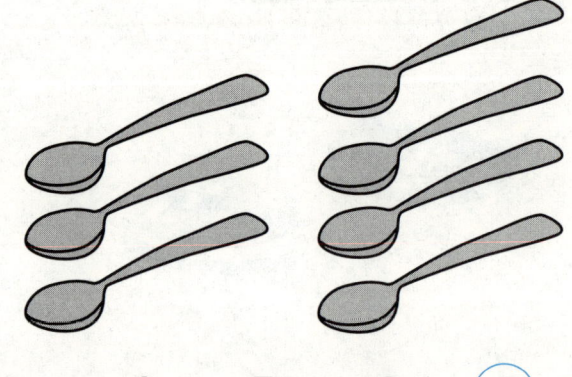

4 5 6 (7)

4 5 (6) 7

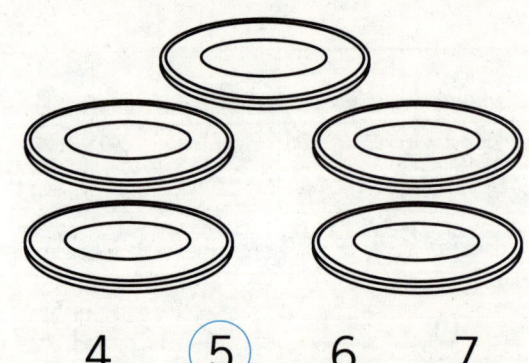

4 (5) 6 7

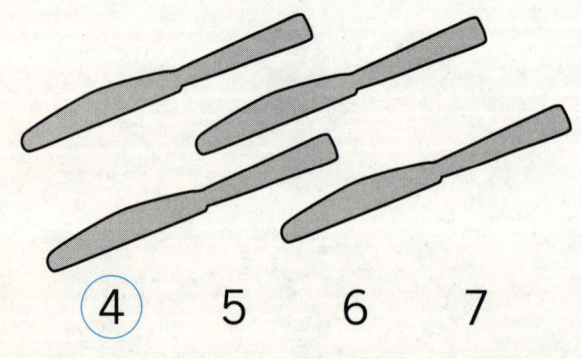

(4) 5 6 7

4 5 6 (7)

Number Correct

LESSON FOLLOW-UP AND ERROR ANALYSIS

Spectrum Software Whole Numbers 5

8
5–6: Have students draw sets of 7, 6, 5, and 4 objects.
3–4: If students are missing objects or counting them twice, suggest they mark each object as they count it aloud.
Less than 3: Review the numbers 4, 5, 6, and 7 by counting sets of objects and writing the numerals for each set.

Prerequisite Skills: number recognition and counting

Lesson Focus: counting similar objects
Possible Score: 6
Time Frame: less than 5 minutes

Lesson 3 Numbers 8 through 10

eight
8

nine
9

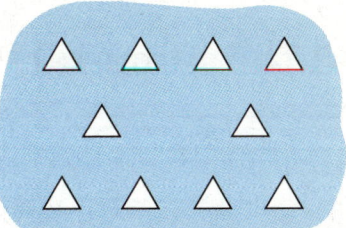
ten
10

Ring the numeral.

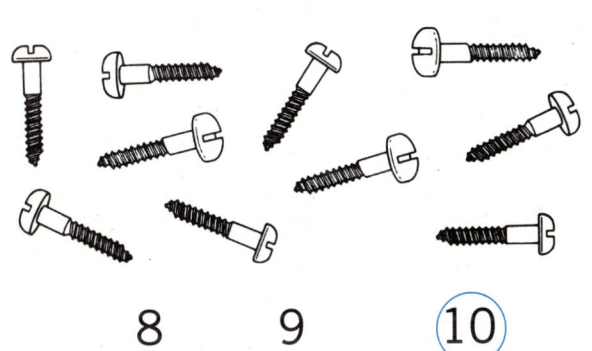

8　9　(10)

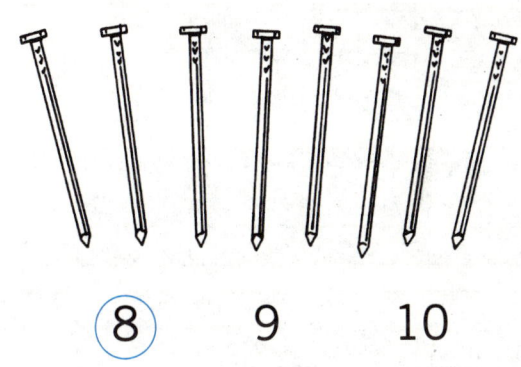

(8)　9　10

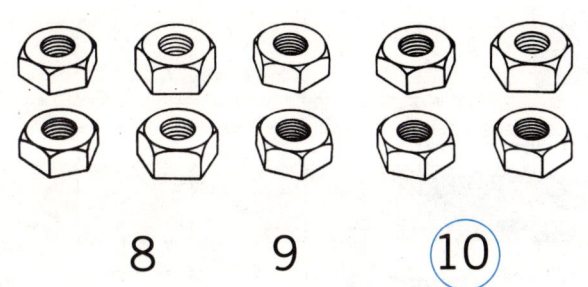

8　9　(10)

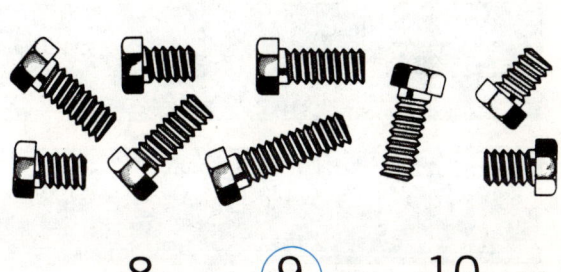

8　(9)　10

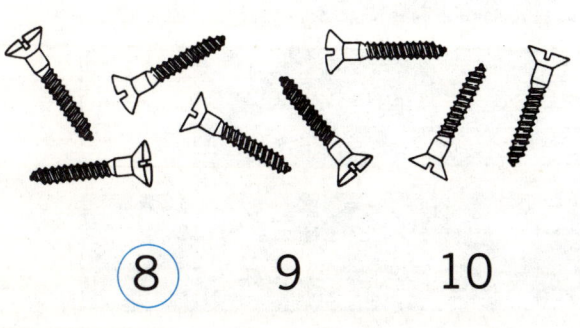

(8)　9　10

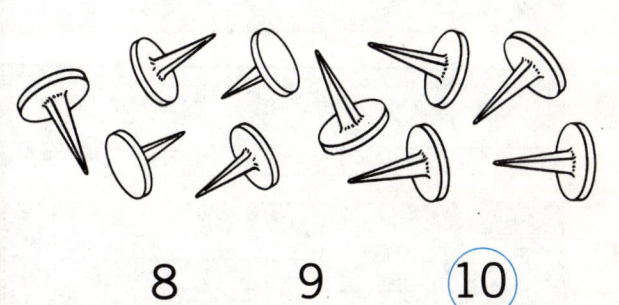

8　9　(10)

Number Correct

LESSON FOLLOW-UP AND ERROR ANALYSIS

Spectrum Software Whole Numbers 6 and 7

5–6: Have students draw sets of 10, 9, and 8 objects.
3–4: If students are missing objects or counting them twice, suggest they mark each object as they count it aloud.
Less than 3: Review the numbers 8, 9, and 10 by counting sets of objects and writing the numerals for each set.

Prerequisite Skills: number recognition and counting

Lesson Focus: coloring numbers of objects
Possible Score: 11
Time Frame: 5–10 minutes

Lesson 4   Numbers 0 through 10

Read the numeral. Color that many squares.

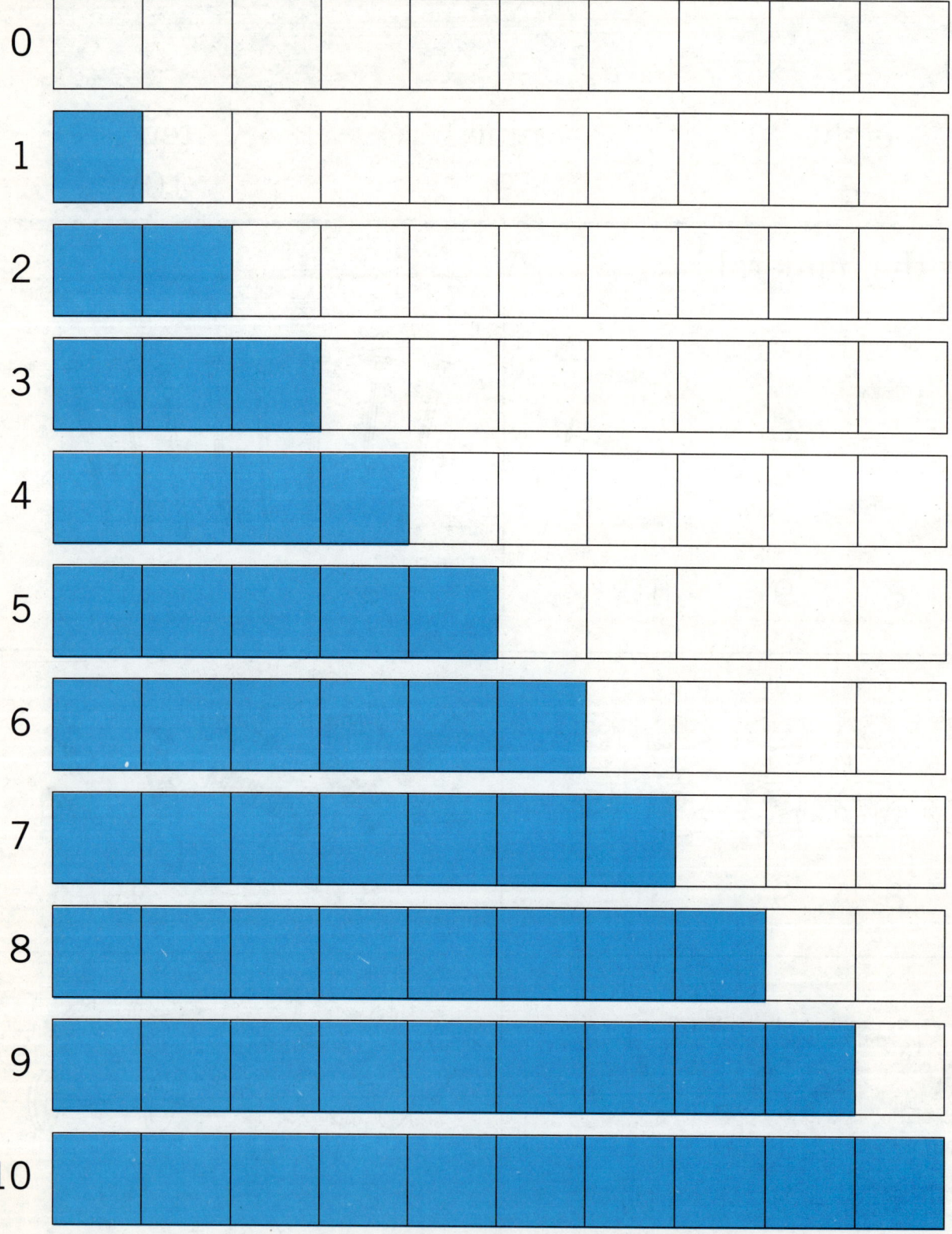

Number Correct	LESSON FOLLOW-UP AND ERROR ANALYSIS
	9–11: Have students count the number of squares not colored in each row and write that number on the right side of the row.
10	**7–8:** Have students write the counting numbers inside each colored square—1, 2, 3, 4, …10.
	Less than 7: Show students where to begin at the left. Then count and color that number of squares in each row.

Prerequisite Skills: number recognition and counting

Lesson Focus: creating number sets
Possible Score: 16
Time Frame: 5–10 minutes

Lesson 5 Numbers 0 through 10

Tell how many.

7

4

6

10

8

2

9

3

Number Correct	LESSON FOLLOW-UP AND ERROR ANALYSIS	*Spectrum Software* Whole Numbers 8 and 9
13–16:	Have students create and compare sets of objects using numbers 0 through 10.	
10–12:	If students are missing objects or counting them twice, suggest they mark each object as they count it aloud.	
Less than 10:	Review the numbers 0–10 by counting sets of objects and writing the numerals for each set.	

11

Lesson 5 Numbers 0 through 10

Read each name for the number.
Then draw that many ●s.

three 3

ten 10

five 5

seven 7

two 2

eight 8

one 1

nine 9

CHAPTER 1
Numeration (0 through 10)

Lesson 5
Numbers 0 through 10

Prerequisite Skills: number recognition

Lesson Focus: number recognition and sequencing
Possible Score: 41
Time Frame: 10–15 minutes

Lesson 6 Order of Numbers

Fill in each . Write numbers in order.

Count backward. Write a numeral on each _____.

10 9 8 7 6

5 4 3 2 1

Count forward. Write a numeral in each .

  8 9

Number Correct
- **34–41:** Have students make a set of number cards, mix them up, and place the cards in the correct order.
- **26–33:** If students automatically counted on instead of counting back, practice counting backward from 10.
- **Less than 26:** Have students practice counting forward and backward between 0 and 10.

LESSON FOLLOW-UP AND ERROR ANALYSIS

Spectrum Software Whole Numbers 10 and 11

Lesson 6 Order of Numbers

Count forward. Write the numerals in each ▱.
Then trace the number words on the ──.

	0	zero
●	1	one
●●	2	two
●●●	3	three
●●●●	4	four
●●●●●	5	five
●●●●●●	6	six
●●●●●●●	7	seven

CHAPTER 1
Numeration (0 through 10)

Prerequisite Skills: number recognition and counting

Lesson Focus: number recognition and sequencing (readiness for number lines)
Possible Score: 4
Time Frame: less than 5 minutes

Lesson 7 Order of Numbers

Connect the dots in order.

CHAPTER 1

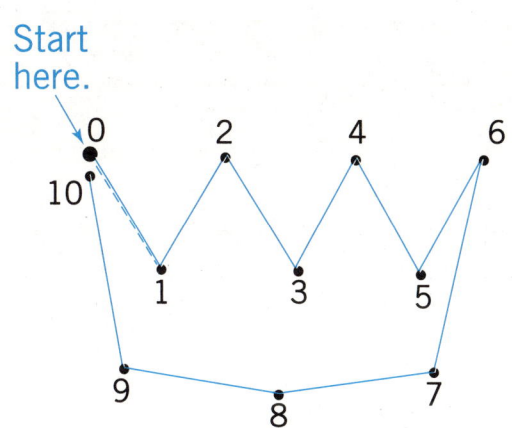

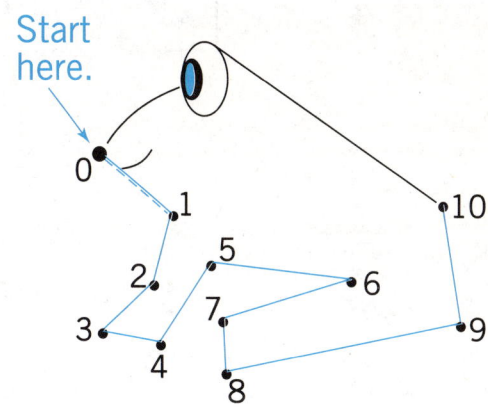

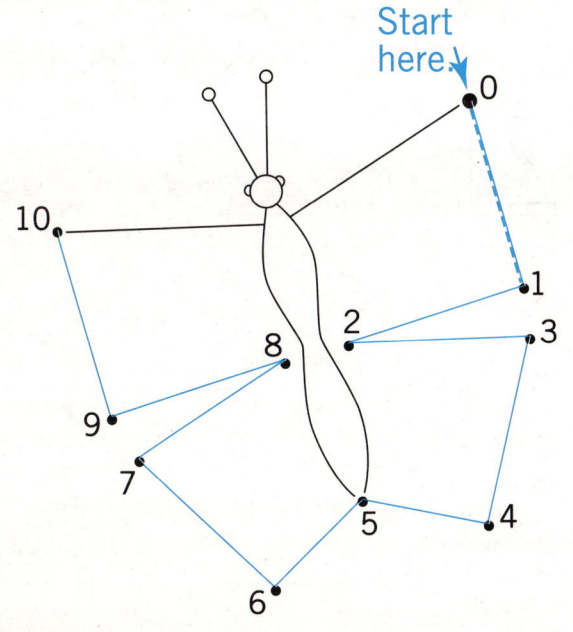

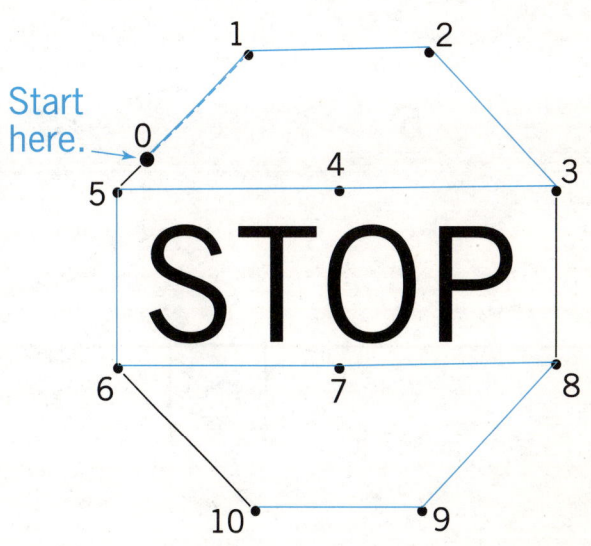

Number Correct

LESSON FOLLOW-UP AND ERROR ANALYSIS

3–4: Have students create their own dot-to-dot picture on a separate piece of paper.
2: If students begin at the wrong place, review the zero starting point in each of the four sections.
Less than 2: Review the ordering sequence and have students rework each picture using a different color.

15

Prerequisite Skills: number recognition and counting

Lesson Focus: number sequencing
Possible Score: 5
Time Frame: 5-10 minutes

Lesson 8   Number Patterns

Finish the pattern. Write a number in each ☐.

3   4   **5**   6   7

2   **3**   4   5   6

6   7   **8**   9   10

6   5   4   3   **2**

8   7   **6**   5   4

Number Correct

16

LESSON FOLLOW-UP AND ERROR ANALYSIS

4–5: Have students create their own number pattern.
3: Have students count from 1 to 10, or from 10 to 1, to help them complete the pattern.
Less than 3: Use numbered cards. Place them in ascending or descending order and have students lay them out to complete the pattern.

Prerequisite Skills: counting

Lesson Focus: ordinal numbers
Possible Score: 10
Time Frame: 5–10 minutes

Lesson 9 Ordinal Numbers

Ring the third 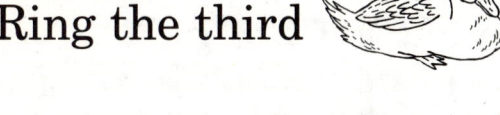.

Ring the fifth .

Ring the second .

 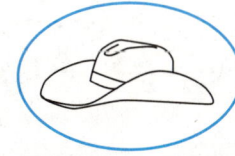  

Ring the eighth .

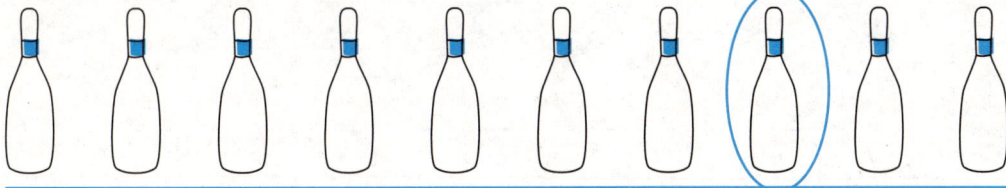

Ring the fourth .

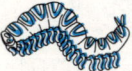     

Number Correct

LESSON FOLLOW-UP AND ERROR ANALYSIS

- **10:** Have students name the ordinal numbers up to 10.
- **8:** Have students write the ordinal numbers up to 10.
- **Less than 8:** Have students write the ordinal number under each picture in the problem.

17

Lesson 9 Ordinal Numbers

Ring the ninth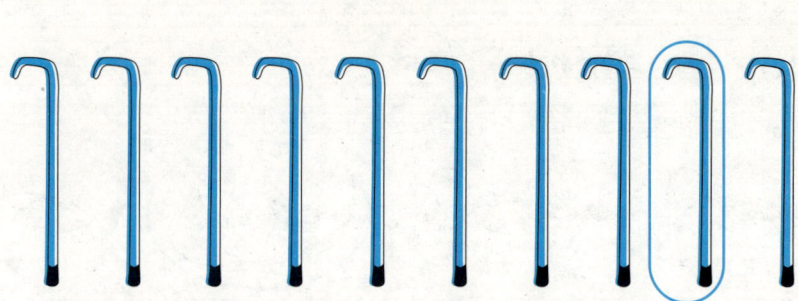

Ring the first .

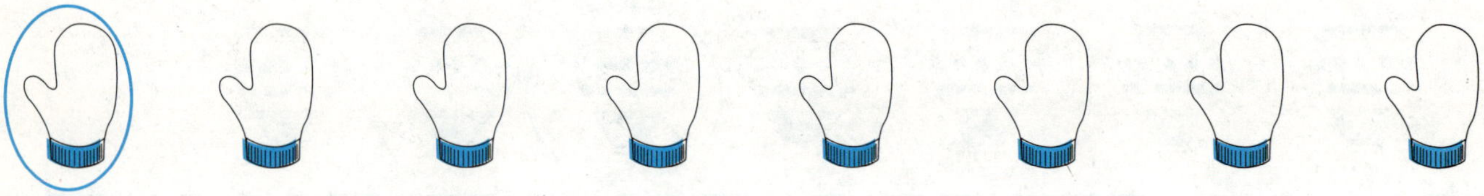

Ring the sixth  .

Ring the tenth .

Ring the seventh.

CHAPTER 1
Numeration (0 through 10)

Lesson 9
Ordinal Numbers

For further evaluation, copy the Chapter Test on page 165.
For maintaining skills, use the Cumulative Review on page 153.

Possible Score: 9
Time Frame: 10–15 minutes

CHAPTER 1 PRACTICE TEST
Numeration (0 through 10)

Tell how many.

$\underline{5}$

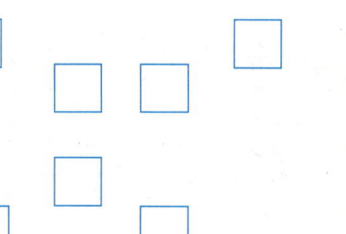

$\underline{7}$

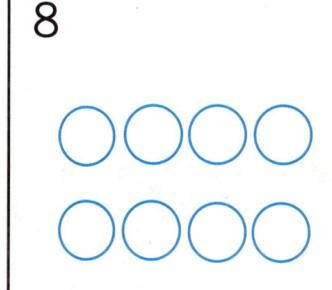

$\underline{1}$

Read the numeral. Draw that many ◯s.

10

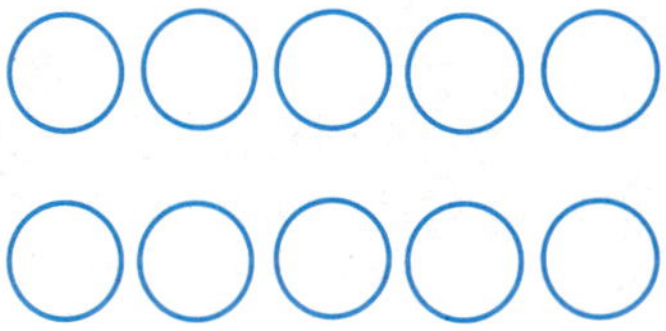

◯◯◯◯◯
◯◯◯◯◯

2

◯◯

8

◯◯◯◯
◯◯◯◯

Write a numeral in each ☐ to finish the pattern.

2 3 [4] 5 6

6 [7] 8 9 10

Ring the third  .

Number Correct
LESSON FOLLOW-UP AND ERROR ANALYSIS
Spectrum Software Whole Numbers 4–11

7–9: Help students make number cards and use them with the appropriate sections of the page.
5–6: Have students say the numbers out loud to find the answer.
Less than 4: Have students rework the page, marking each object or number as they count it out loud.

Math Intervention: Addition Facts, Gold Book, pages 25–32.
Real World Problem Solving practice: Gold Book, pages 33–34.

CHAPTER 2 PRETEST
Addition and Subtraction (facts through 5)

Add.

1 +2 = 3	0 +5 = 5	4 +1 = 5	2 +2 = 4	1 +0 = 1	2 +1 = 3
0 +2 = 2	4 +0 = 4	1 +3 = 4	3 +1 = 4	1 +4 = 5	3 +2 = 5
2 +0 = 2	0 +1 = 1	2 +3 = 5	5 +0 = 5	0 +4 = 4	2 +1 = 3

Subtract.

4 −1 = 3	5 −3 = 2	4 −2 = 2	5 −0 = 5	5 −1 = 4	3 −1 = 2
2 −0 = 2	5 −4 = 1	3 −2 = 1	3 −3 = 0	5 −2 = 3	4 −3 = 1
5 −5 = 0	4 −0 = 4	2 −2 = 0	3 −1 = 2	2 −1 = 1	4 −4 = 0

Prerequisite Skills: counting

Lesson Focus: adding through sums of 3
Possible Score: 20
Time Frame: 5–10 minutes

Lesson 1 Sums through 3
Add.

1 + 1 = __2__

$\begin{array}{r}1\\+1\\\hline 2\end{array}$

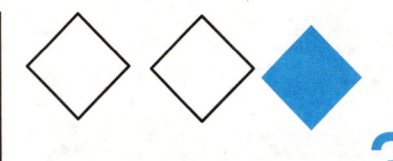

2 + 1 = __3__

$\begin{array}{r}2\\+1\\\hline 3\end{array}$

1 + 2 = __3__

$\begin{array}{r}1\\+2\\\hline 3\end{array}$

2 + 0 = __2__

0 + 2 = __2__

$\begin{array}{r}2\\+0\\\hline 2\end{array}$

$\begin{array}{r}0\\+2\\\hline 2\end{array}$

3 + 0 = __3__

0 + 3 = __3__

$\begin{array}{r}3\\+0\\\hline 3\end{array}$

$\begin{array}{r}0\\+3\\\hline 3\end{array}$

0 + 0 = __0__

$\begin{array}{r}0\\+0\\\hline 0\end{array}$

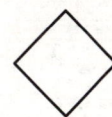

1 + 0 = __1__

0 + 1 = __1__

$\begin{array}{r}1\\+0\\\hline 1\end{array}$

$\begin{array}{r}0\\+1\\\hline 1\end{array}$

Number Correct	LESSON FOLLOW-UP AND ERROR ANALYSIS
17–20:	Have students draw their own picture stories showing addition through sums of 3.
13–16:	Have students count the number of each color. Then have them count the total number.
Less than 13:	Ask students to use two different manipulatives to make two groups and show sums of 1, 2, and 3.

Spectrum Software Addition 1

Prerequisite Skills: counting and adding through sums of 3

Lesson Focus: adding through sums of 5
Possible Score: 22
Time Frame: 5–10 minutes

Lesson 2 Sums of 4 and 5

Add.

⊙⊙⊙⊙⊙   4 + 1 = **5** $\begin{array}{r}4\\+1\\\hline 5\end{array}$

⊙⊙⊙⊙⊙   1 + 4 = **5** $\begin{array}{r}1\\+4\\\hline 5\end{array}$

⊙⊙⊙⊙   2 + 2 = **4** $\begin{array}{r}2\\+2\\\hline 4\end{array}$

⊙⊙⊙⊙⊙   0 + 5 = **5** $\begin{array}{r}0\\+5\\\hline 5\end{array}$

⊙⊙⊙⊙⊙   5 + 0 = **5** $\begin{array}{r}5\\+0\\\hline 5\end{array}$

⊙⊙⊙⊙⊙   2 + 3 = **5** $\begin{array}{r}2\\+3\\\hline 5\end{array}$

⊙⊙⊙⊙⊙   3 + 2 = **5** $\begin{array}{r}3\\+2\\\hline 5\end{array}$

⊙⊙⊙⊙   4 + 0 = **4** $\begin{array}{r}4\\+0\\\hline 4\end{array}$

⊙⊙⊙⊙   0 + 4 = **4** $\begin{array}{r}0\\+4\\\hline 4\end{array}$

⊙⊙⊙⊙   1 + 3 = **4** $\begin{array}{r}1\\+3\\\hline 4\end{array}$

⊙⊙⊙⊙   3 + 1 = **4** $\begin{array}{r}3\\+1\\\hline 4\end{array}$

Number Correct

LESSON FOLLOW-UP AND ERROR ANALYSIS

Spectrum Software Addition 2 and 3

22
- 19–22: Have students explain why 2 + 2 has only one set of buttons.
- 14–18: Have students tell how many are in each color. Then have them tell how many there are in all.
- Less than 14: Ask students to use two different manipulatives to make two groups and show sums of 4 and 5.

Prerequisite Skills: counting

Lesson Focus: subtracting from 1, 2, and 3
Possible Score: 16
Time Frame: 5–10 minutes

Lesson 3 Subtracting from 1, 2, and 3

Subtract.

$\begin{array}{r} 3 \\ -1 \\ \hline 2 \end{array}$
3 − 1 = **2**

$\begin{array}{r} 2 \\ -1 \\ \hline 1 \end{array}$
2 − 1 = **1**

$\begin{array}{r} 3 \\ -2 \\ \hline 1 \end{array}$
3 − 2 = **1**

$\begin{array}{r} 1 \\ -0 \\ \hline 1 \end{array}$
1 − 0 = **1**

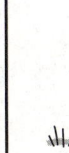
$\begin{array}{r} 3 \\ -0 \\ \hline 3 \end{array}$
3 − 0 = **3**

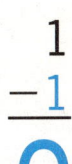
$\begin{array}{r} 1 \\ -1 \\ \hline 0 \end{array}$
1 − 1 = **0**

$\begin{array}{r} 2 \\ -2 \\ \hline 0 \end{array}$
2 − 2 = **0**

$\begin{array}{r} 3 \\ -3 \\ \hline 0 \end{array}$
3 − 3 = **0**

Number Correct

LESSON FOLLOW-UP AND ERROR ANALYSIS

Spectrum Software Subtraction 1

14–16: Have students draw their own picture stories showing subtraction from 1, 2, and 3.
10–13: Using three manipulatives, ask students to remove 1, 2, or 3 and count how many are left.
Less than 10: Have students count the number of objects pictured, cover the objects leaving, and count how many remain.

Prerequisite Skills: counting and subtracting from 3

Lesson Focus: subtracting from 4 and 5
Possible Score: 16
Time Frame: 5–10 minutes

Lesson 4 Subtracting from 4 and 5

Subtract.

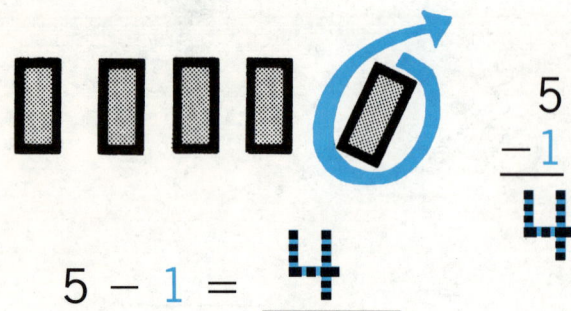

5 − 1 = 4

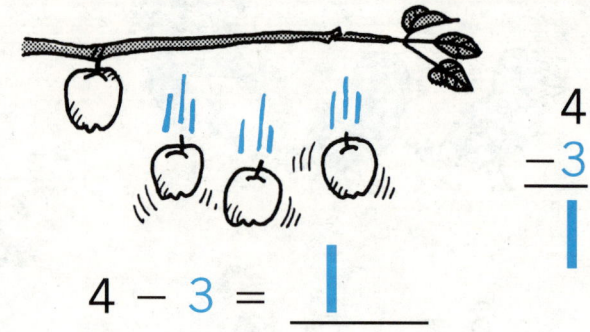

4 − 3 = 1

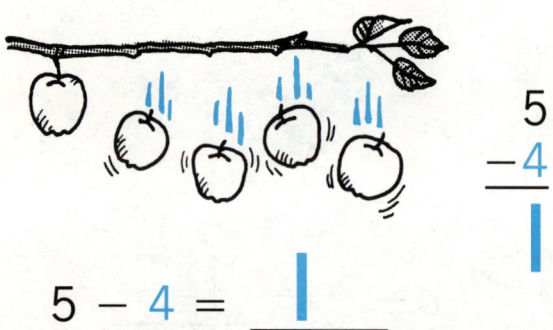

5 − 4 = 1

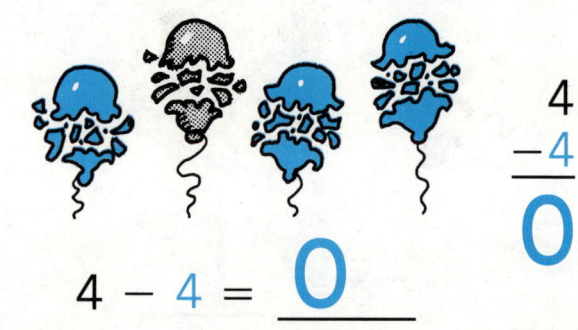

4 − 4 = 0

5 − 2 = 3

4 − 2 = 2

5 − 3 = 2

4 − 1 = 3

Number Correct
14–16: Have students draw their own picture stories showing subtraction from 4 and 5.
10–13: Using five manipulatives, ask students to remove 1, 2, 3, 4, or 5 and count how many are left.
Less than 10: Have students count the number of objects pictured, cover the objects subtracted, and count how many remain.

LESSON FOLLOW-UP AND ERROR ANALYSIS

Spectrum Software Subtraction 2 and 3

Prerequisite Skills: counting

Lesson Focus: fact families to 5
Possible Score: 28
Time Frame: 10–15 minutes

Lesson 5 Number Families

Add or subtract.

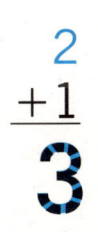

2	1	3	3	1	3	4	4
+1	+2	−2	−1	+3	+1	−1	−3
3	3	1	2	4	4	3	1

2	3	5	5	4	1	5	5
+3	+2	−2	−3	+1	+4	−4	−1
5	5	3	2	5	5	1	4

1	2			2	4		
+1	−1			+2	−2		
2	1			4	2		

2	0	2	2	5	0	5	5
+0	+2	−2	−0	+0	+5	−5	−0
2	2	0	2	5	5	0	5

Number Correct

LESSON FOLLOW-UP AND ERROR ANALYSIS

24–28: To reinforce numeration, have students ring each answer greater than 2.
18–23: If students have not performed the correct operation, have them rework the problem.
Less than 18: Have students use manipulatives to determine each sum or difference.

Prerequisite Skills: counting

Lesson Focus: using pennies and nickels
Possible Score: 8
Time Frame: less than 5 minutes

Lesson 6 Penny and Nickel

1 penny
1¢

5 pennies
5¢

1 nickel
5¢

Tell how much money.

_5_ ¢

_2_ ¢

_1_ ¢

_3_ ¢

_4_ ¢

_5_ ¢

_5_ ¢

_3_ ¢

Number Correct

LESSON FOLLOW-UP AND ERROR ANALYSIS

Spectrum Software Decimals 1 and 2

7–8: Have students add one penny to each group and tell how much money is in each new group.
5–6: If students are counting pennies twice, suggest they mark each penny as they count it.
Less than 5: Review the numbers 0 through 5 by counting sets of objects and writing the numerals for each set.

Prerequisite Skills: adding and subtracting through 5

Lesson Focus: using pictures to solve problems
Possible Score: 12
Time Frame: 10–15 minutes

Lesson 7 Problem Solving

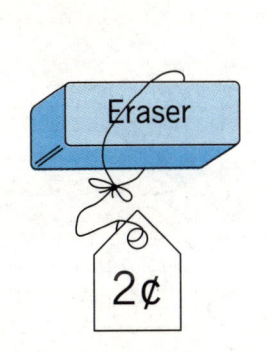

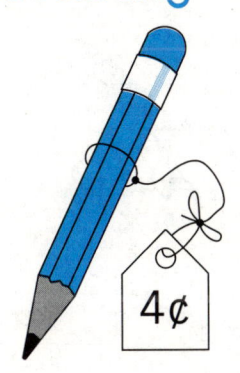

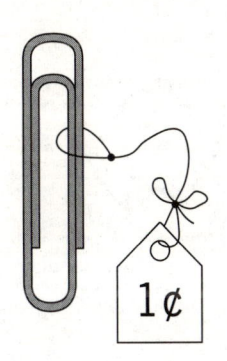

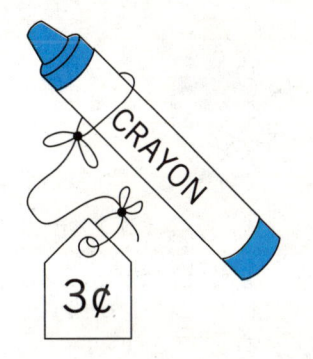

Eraser 2¢   Pencil 4¢   Paper clip 1¢   CRAYON 3¢

Add or subtract.

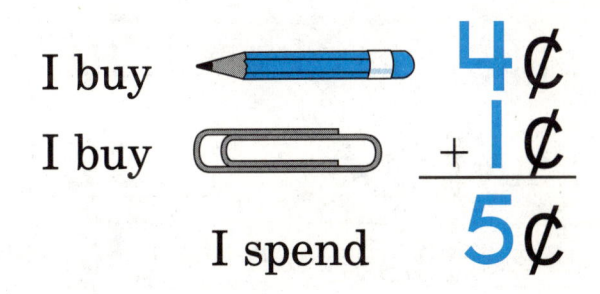

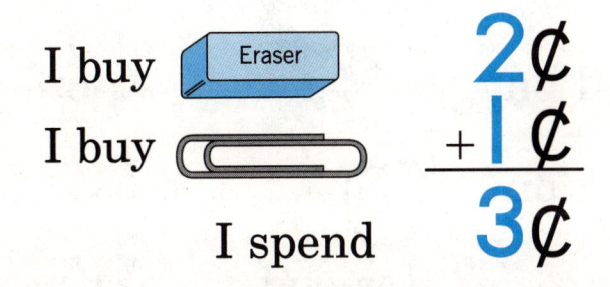

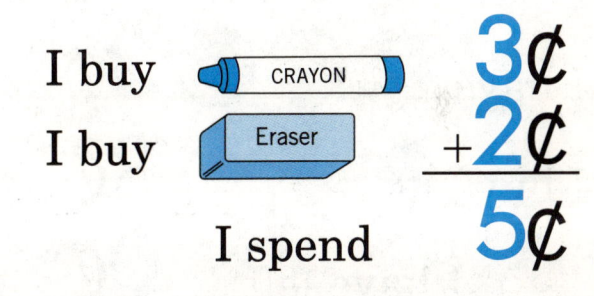

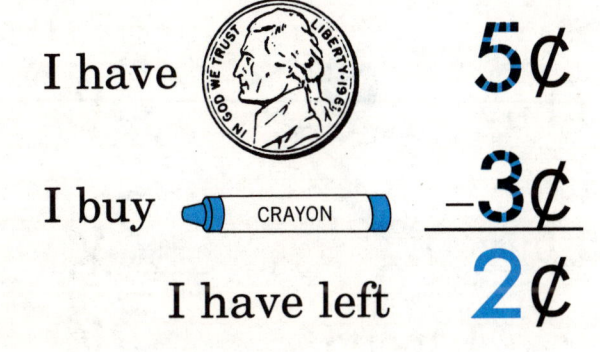

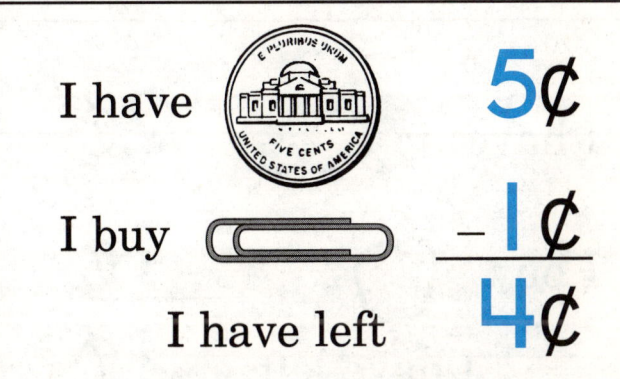

I buy (paper clip)   1¢
I buy CRAYON   +3¢
I spend   4¢

I buy (pencil)   4¢
I buy (paper clip) +1¢
I spend   5¢

I buy Eraser   2¢
I buy (paper clip) +1¢
I spend   3¢

I buy CRAYON   3¢
I buy Eraser   +2¢
I spend   5¢

I have (nickel)   5¢
I buy CRAYON   −3¢
I have left   2¢

I have (nickel)   5¢
I buy (paper clip) −1¢
I have left   4¢

Number Correct
10–12: Have students tell which combinations of objects on the page they cannot buy with a nickel.
7–9: If students have not performed the correct operation, have them rework the answer.
Less than 7: Have students use manipulatives to help them rework each incorrect answer.

LESSON FOLLOW-UP AND ERROR ANALYSIS   *Spectrum Software* Addition 2 and 3; Subtraction 2 and 3

Lesson 7 Problem Solving

3¢   1¢   2¢   5¢

Add or subtract.

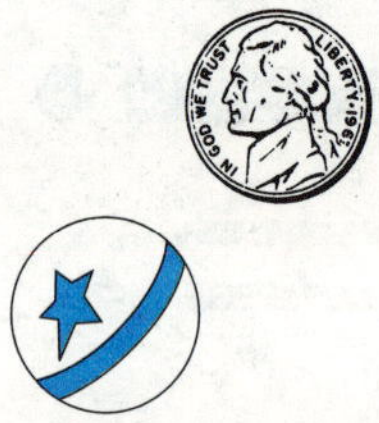

I have   5¢
I buy   −5¢
I have left 0¢

I buy   3¢
I buy   +1¢
I spend 4¢

I have   3¢
I buy   −3¢
I have left 0¢

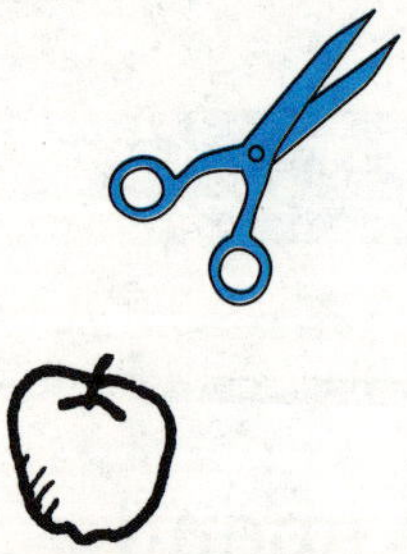

I buy   2¢
I buy   +1¢
I spend 3¢

I have   2¢
I buy   −1¢
I have left 1¢

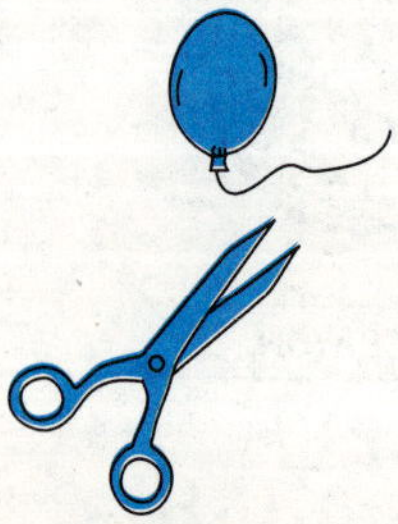

I buy   3¢
I buy   +2¢
I spend 5¢

CHAPTER 2
Addition and Subtraction (facts through 5)

Lesson 7
Problem Solving

28

For further evaluation, copy the Chapter Test on page 166.
For maintaining skills, use the Cumulative Review on page 154.

Possible Score: 36
Time Frame: 10–15 minutes

CHAPTER 2 PRACTICE TEST
Addition and Subtraction (facts through 5)

Add.

3	1	0	2	5	1
+1	+1	+0	+1	+0	+0
4	2	0	3	5	1

0	2	1	0	1	3
+3	+2	+2	+1	+4	+2
3	4	3	1	5	5

1	4	0	2	4	2
+3	+0	+5	+0	+1	+3
4	4	5	2	5	5

Subtract.

2	4	5	3	5	4
−1	−1	−0	−2	−4	−4
1	3	5	1	1	0

4	5	0	4	3	5
−0	−1	−0	−2	−0	−2
4	4	0	2	3	3

2	4	5	3	3	1
−0	−3	−3	−1	−3	−1
2	1	2	2	0	0

Number Correct   LESSON FOLLOW-UP AND ERROR ANALYSIS   *Spectrum Software* Addition 1–3; Subtraction 1–3

- **31–36:** To reinforce numeration, have students ring each answer greater than 2.
- **23–30:** Have students draw squares for each incorrect answer in a row they select to illustrate the problem.
- **Less than 23:** Have students use manipulatives to rework each incorrect answer.

Math Intervention: Subtraction Facts, Gold Book, pages 35–42.
Real World Problem Solving practice: Gold Book, pages 43–44.

CHAPTER 3 PRETEST
Addition and Subtraction (facts through 8)

Add.

5	3	6	4	1
+3	+4	+0	+4	+5
8	**7**	**6**	**8**	**6**

2	1	2	3	6
+6	+7	+4	+3	+1
8	**8**	**6**	**6**	**7**

7	4	5	2	6
+0	+3	+2	+5	+2
7	**7**	**7**	**7**	**8**

Subtract.

6	8	7	6	7
−3	−4	−4	−0	−1
3	**4**	**3**	**6**	**6**

8	6	8	6	8
−6	−5	−3	−4	−7
2	**1**	**5**	**2**	**1**

7	7	7	7	8
−0	−3	−2	−5	−2
7	**4**	**5**	**2**	**6**

Prerequisite Skills: adding through sums of 5

Lesson Focus: adding through sums of 6
Possible Score: 20
Time Frame: 5–10 minutes

Lesson 1 Sums of 6

Add.

$1 + 5 = \underline{6}$

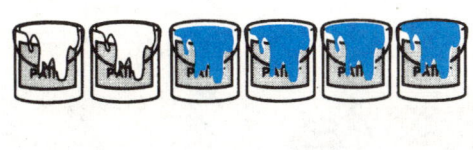

$\begin{array}{r} 1 \\ +5 \\ \hline 6 \end{array}$

$5 + 1 = \underline{6}$

$\begin{array}{r} 5 \\ +1 \\ \hline 6 \end{array}$

$2 + 4 = \underline{6}$

$\begin{array}{r} 2 \\ +4 \\ \hline 6 \end{array}$

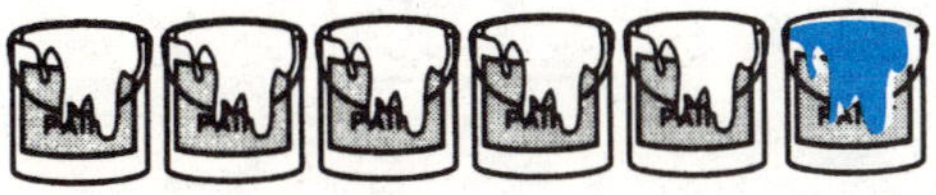

$4 + 2 = \underline{6}$

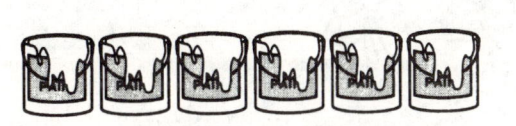

$\begin{array}{r} 4 \\ +2 \\ \hline 6 \end{array}$

$6 + 0 = \underline{6}$

$\begin{array}{r} 6 \\ +0 \\ \hline 6 \end{array}$

$0 + 6 = \underline{6}$

$\begin{array}{r} 0 \\ +6 \\ \hline 6 \end{array}$

$3 + 3 = \underline{6}$

$\begin{array}{r} 3 \\ +3 \\ \hline 6 \end{array}$

| $\begin{array}{r}2\\+4\\\hline 6\end{array}$ | $\begin{array}{r}1\\+3\\\hline 4\end{array}$ | $\begin{array}{r}5\\+1\\\hline 6\end{array}$ | $\begin{array}{r}3\\+3\\\hline 6\end{array}$ | $\begin{array}{r}2\\+2\\\hline 4\end{array}$ | $\begin{array}{r}3\\+2\\\hline 5\end{array}$ |

CHAPTER 3

Number Correct
17–20:
13–16:
Less than 13:

LESSON FOLLOW-UP AND ERROR ANALYSIS
To reinforce numeration, have students ring each answer of 5.
Have students count the number in each color. Then have them count the total number.
Have students use manipulatives to rework each incorrect answer.

Spectrum Software Addition 4 and 5

Prerequisite Skills: subtracting from 5

Lesson Focus: subtracting from 6
Possible Score: 18
Time Frame: 5–10 minutes

Lesson 2   Subtracting from 6

Subtract.

$6 - 1 = \underline{5}$ $\begin{array}{r}6\\-1\\\hline 5\end{array}$

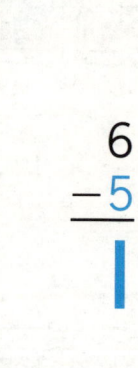

$6 - 5 = \underline{1}$ $\begin{array}{r}6\\-5\\\hline 1\end{array}$

$6 - 4 = \underline{2}$ $\begin{array}{r}6\\-4\\\hline 2\end{array}$

$6 - 2 = \underline{4}$ $\begin{array}{r}6\\-2\\\hline 4\end{array}$

$6 - 3 = \underline{3}$ $\begin{array}{r}6\\-3\\\hline 3\end{array}$

$6 - 0 = \underline{6}$ $\begin{array}{r}6\\-0\\\hline 6\end{array}$

$\begin{array}{r}6\\-3\\\hline 3\end{array}$ $\begin{array}{r}6\\-6\\\hline 0\end{array}$ $\begin{array}{r}6\\-1\\\hline 5\end{array}$ $\begin{array}{r}6\\-4\\\hline 2\end{array}$ $\begin{array}{r}6\\-2\\\hline 4\end{array}$ $\begin{array}{r}6\\-5\\\hline 1\end{array}$

Number Correct   LESSON FOLLOW-UP AND ERROR ANALYSIS   *Spectrum Software* Subtraction 4 and 5

15–18: Have students draw their own picture stories showing subtracting from 6.
12–14: Using six manipulatives, ask students to remove 1, 2, 3, 4, 5, or 6 and count how many are left.
Less than 12: Have students count the number of objects pictured, cover the ones flying away, and verbalize the entire fact.

Prerequisite Skills: adding through sums of 6

Lesson Focus: adding through sums of 7
Possible Score: 22
Time Frame: 5–10 minutes

Lesson 3   Sums of 7

Add.

$3 + 4 = \underline{7}$ 　　$\begin{array}{r}3\\+4\\\hline 7\end{array}$

$6 + 1 = \underline{7}$ 　　$\begin{array}{r}6\\+1\\\hline 7\end{array}$

$4 + 3 = \underline{7}$ 　　$\begin{array}{r}4\\+3\\\hline 7\end{array}$

$1 + 6 = \underline{7}$ 　　$\begin{array}{r}1\\+6\\\hline 7\end{array}$

$7 + 0 = \underline{7}$ 　　$\begin{array}{r}7\\+0\\\hline 7\end{array}$

$2 + 5 = \underline{7}$ 　　$\begin{array}{r}2\\+5\\\hline 7\end{array}$

$0 + 7 = \underline{7}$ 　　$\begin{array}{r}0\\+7\\\hline 7\end{array}$

$5 + 2 = \underline{7}$ 　　$\begin{array}{r}5\\+2\\\hline 7\end{array}$

$\begin{array}{r}5\\+2\\\hline 7\end{array}$ 　$\begin{array}{r}3\\+3\\\hline 6\end{array}$ 　$\begin{array}{r}4\\+3\\\hline 7\end{array}$ 　$\begin{array}{r}1\\+6\\\hline 7\end{array}$ 　$\begin{array}{r}3\\+4\\\hline 7\end{array}$ 　$\begin{array}{r}6\\+0\\\hline 6\end{array}$

Number Correct
19–22: Have students draw their own number stories.
14–18: Have students use manipulatives to rework each incorrect answer on the page.
Less than 14: Have students rework each incorrect answer using manipulatives and explain each step.

LESSON FOLLOW-UP AND ERROR ANALYSIS

Spectrum Software Addition 4 and 5

33

Prerequisite Skills: subtracting from 6

Lesson Focus: subtracting from 7
Possible Score: 16
Time Frame: less than 5 minutes

Lesson 4 Subtracting from 7

Subtract.

$$\begin{array}{r}7\\-6\\\hline 1\end{array}$$

7 − 6 = __1__

$$\begin{array}{r}7\\-1\\\hline 6\end{array}$$

7 − 1 = __6__

$$\begin{array}{r}7\\-3\\\hline 4\end{array}$$

7 − 3 = __4__

$$\begin{array}{r}7\\-4\\\hline 3\end{array}$$

7 − 4 = __3__

$$\begin{array}{r}7\\-7\\\hline 0\end{array}$$

7 − 7 = __0__

$$\begin{array}{r}7\\-0\\\hline 7\end{array}$$

7 − 0 = __7__

$$\begin{array}{r}7\\-2\\\hline 5\end{array}$$

7 − 2 = __5__

$$\begin{array}{r}7\\-5\\\hline 2\end{array}$$

7 − 5 = __2__

Number Correct

LESSON FOLLOW-UP AND ERROR ANALYSIS

Spectrum Software Subtraction 4 and 5

14–16: Have students draw their own picture stories showing subtracting from 7.
10–13: Be sure sudents count the number of dots, not the number of dominoes.
Less than 10: Have students count the number of dots on each domino, cover the part falling off, and count how many dots remain.

Prerequisite Skills: adding through sums of 7

Lesson Focus: adding through sums of 8
Possible Score: 20
Time Frame: 5–10 minutes

Lesson 5 Sums of 8

Add.

$\begin{array}{r}5\\+3\\\hline 8\end{array}$

$5 + 3 = \underline{8}$

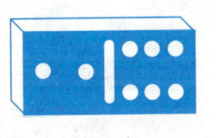

$\begin{array}{r}3\\+5\\\hline 8\end{array}$

$3 + 5 = \underline{8}$

$\begin{array}{r}2\\+6\\\hline 8\end{array}$

$2 + 6 = \underline{8}$

$\begin{array}{r}6\\+2\\\hline 8\end{array}$

$6 + 2 = \underline{8}$

$\begin{array}{r}7\\+1\\\hline 8\end{array}$

$7 + 1 = \underline{8}$

$\begin{array}{r}1\\+7\\\hline 8\end{array}$

$1 + 7 = \underline{8}$

$\begin{array}{r}4\\+4\\\hline 8\end{array}$

$4 + 4 = \underline{8}$

CHAPTER 3

$\begin{array}{r}3\\+3\\\hline 6\end{array}$ $\begin{array}{r}5\\+3\\\hline 8\end{array}$ $\begin{array}{r}2\\+6\\\hline 8\end{array}$ $\begin{array}{r}8\\+0\\\hline 8\end{array}$ $\begin{array}{r}4\\+3\\\hline 7\end{array}$ $\begin{array}{r}0\\+8\\\hline 8\end{array}$

Number Correct LESSON FOLLOW-UP AND ERROR ANALYSIS | *Spectrum Software* Addition 4 and 5; Word Problems 1–3

17–20: Have students draw or write the four number combinations that make 8.
13–16: Have students use manipulatives to rework each incorrect answer on the page.
Less than 13: Have students count the domino dots remaining to help them rework each incorrect answer.

Prerequisite Skills: subtracting from 7

Lesson Focus: subtracting from 8
Possible Score: 16
Time Frame: less than 5 minutes

Lesson 6 Subtracting from 8

Subtract.

$\begin{array}{r} 8 \\ -7 \\ \hline 1 \end{array}$

8 − 7 = 1

$\begin{array}{r} 8 \\ -1 \\ \hline 7 \end{array}$

8 − 1 = 7

$\begin{array}{r} 8 \\ -2 \\ \hline 6 \end{array}$

8 − 2 = 6

$\begin{array}{r} 8 \\ -6 \\ \hline 2 \end{array}$

8 − 6 = 2

$\begin{array}{r} 8 \\ -4 \\ \hline 4 \end{array}$

8 − 4 = 4

$\begin{array}{r} 8 \\ -8 \\ \hline 0 \end{array}$

8 − 8 = 0

$\begin{array}{r} 8 \\ -3 \\ \hline 5 \end{array}$

8 − 3 = 5

$\begin{array}{r} 8 \\ -5 \\ \hline 3 \end{array}$

8 − 5 = 3

Number Correct **LESSON FOLLOW-UP AND ERROR ANALYSIS** *Spectrum Software* Subtraction 4 and 5; Word Problems 4 and 5

14–16: Have students draw their own picture stories showing subtracting from 8.
10–13: Have students count and record all the dots, count how many are taken away, and finally how many are left.
Less than 10: Have students use manipulatives to rework each incorrect answer and explain each step.

Prerequisite Skills: adding and subtracting through 8

> Lesson Focus: addition and subtraction
> Possible Score: 41
> Time Frame: 15–20 minutes

Lesson 7 Addition and Subtraction

Add.

5 +3 **8**	1 +6 **7**	3 +3 **6**	2 +6 **8**	1 +7 **8**	5 +1 **6**
0 +7 **7**	4 +2 **6**	4 +4 **8**	6 +0 **6**	3 +4 **7**	6 +1 **7**
3 +5 **8**	8 +0 **8**	5 +2 **7**	2 +4 **6**	6 +2 **8**	0 +8 **8**

Subtract.

8 −3 **5**	6 −5 **1**	8 −4 **4**	7 −3 **4**	6 −2 **4**	6 −6 **0**
8 −5 **3**	7 −0 **7**	8 −1 **7**	7 −6 **1**	8 −6 **2**	7 −5 **2**
8 −8 **0**	6 −3 **3**	7 −1 **6**	8 −2 **6**	6 −1 **5**	7 −2 **5**

Number LESSON FOLLOW-UP AND ERROR ANALYSIS   *Spectrum Software* Addition 4 and 5; Subtraction 4 and 5; Word Problems 6 and 7
Correct
34–41: To reinforce numeration, have students ring each answer that is the same number as their age.
26–33: If students have not performed the correct operation, have them rework the answer.
Less than 26: Have students use manipulatives to rework each incorrect answer and explain each step.

Lesson 7 Problem Solving

Solve each problem.

There are 6 blue 👕.
There are 2 white 👕.
How many in all?

$$\begin{array}{r} 6 \\ +2 \\ \hline 8 \end{array}$$

There are 7 🚁.
4 🚁 fly away.
How many are left?

$$\begin{array}{r} 7 \\ -4 \\ \hline 3 \end{array}$$

I saw 2 big ☕.
I saw 3 little ☕.
How many in all?

$$\begin{array}{r} 2 \\ +3 \\ \hline 5 \end{array}$$

Bob has 8 ✏️.
Ann has 5 ✏️.
How many more does Bob have?

$$\begin{array}{r} 8 \\ -5 \\ \hline 3 \end{array}$$

There is 1 🐟.
Then 5 more come.
Now how many in all?

$$\begin{array}{r} 1 \\ +5 \\ \hline 6 \end{array}$$

CHAPTER 3
Addition and Subtraction (facts through 8)

Lesson 7
Addition and Subtraction

Prerequisite Skills: adding and subtracting through 8

Lesson Focus: addition and subtraction
Possible Score: 41
Time Frame: 15–20 minutes

Lesson 8 Addition and Subtraction

Add or subtract. STOP! Watch the + and −.

2 +5 ― 7	8 −3 ― 5	7 +0 ― 7	8 −4 ― 4	6 +1 ― 7	7 −2 ― 5
7 −5 ― 2	3 +3 ― 6	4 +2 ― 6	0 +6 ― 6	8 −0 ― 8	8 −6 ― 2
8 −1 ― 7	7 −1 ― 6	1 +6 ― 7	6 −5 ― 1	3 +4 ― 7	5 +1 ― 6
6 −6 ― 0	2 +4 ― 6	5 +2 ― 7	6 −0 ― 6	1 +7 ― 8	7 −3 ― 4
1 +5 ― 6	6 −3 ― 3	7 −4 ― 3	4 +3 ― 7	8 −2 ― 6	4 +4 ― 8
7 −6 ― 1	5 +3 ― 8	6 −2 ― 4	0 +8 ― 8	2 +6 ― 8	8 −8 ― 0

CHAPTER 3

Number Correct   LESSON FOLLOW-UP AND ERROR ANALYSIS   *Spectrum Software* Addition 4 and 5; Subtraction 4 and 5

34–41: To reinforce numeration, have students choose a row and write each answer using a number word. Use page 14 for guidance.
26–33: If students have not performed the correct operation, have them rework the answer.
Less than 26: Have students use manipulatives to rework each incorrect answer and explain each step.

39

Lesson 8 Problem Solving

Solve each problem.

There are 8 🐰.
Then 7 ran away.
How many are left?

$$\begin{array}{r}8\\-7\\\hline 1\end{array}$$

There are 4 white ☂.
There are 3 blue ☂.
How many in all?

$$\begin{array}{r}4\\+3\\\hline 7\end{array}$$

Rob saw 7 🐦 flying.
He saw 1 🐦 sitting.
How many did he see in all?

$$\begin{array}{r}7\\+1\\\hline 8\end{array}$$

Cal has 6 🤖.
He gave Meg 4 🤖.
How many does he have left?

$$\begin{array}{r}6\\-4\\\hline 2\end{array}$$

There are 7 🎈.
7 of the 🎈 broke.
How many are left?

$$\begin{array}{r}7\\-7\\\hline 0\end{array}$$

CHAPTER 3
Addition and Subtraction (facts through 8)

Lesson 8
Addition and Subtraction

Prerequisite Skills: adding and subtracting through 8

Lesson Focus: adding and subtracting
Possible Score: 30
Time Frame: 15–20 minutes

Lesson 9 Addition and Subtraction

Add or subtract. Check students' work before they color.
If you get 6, color that part orange.

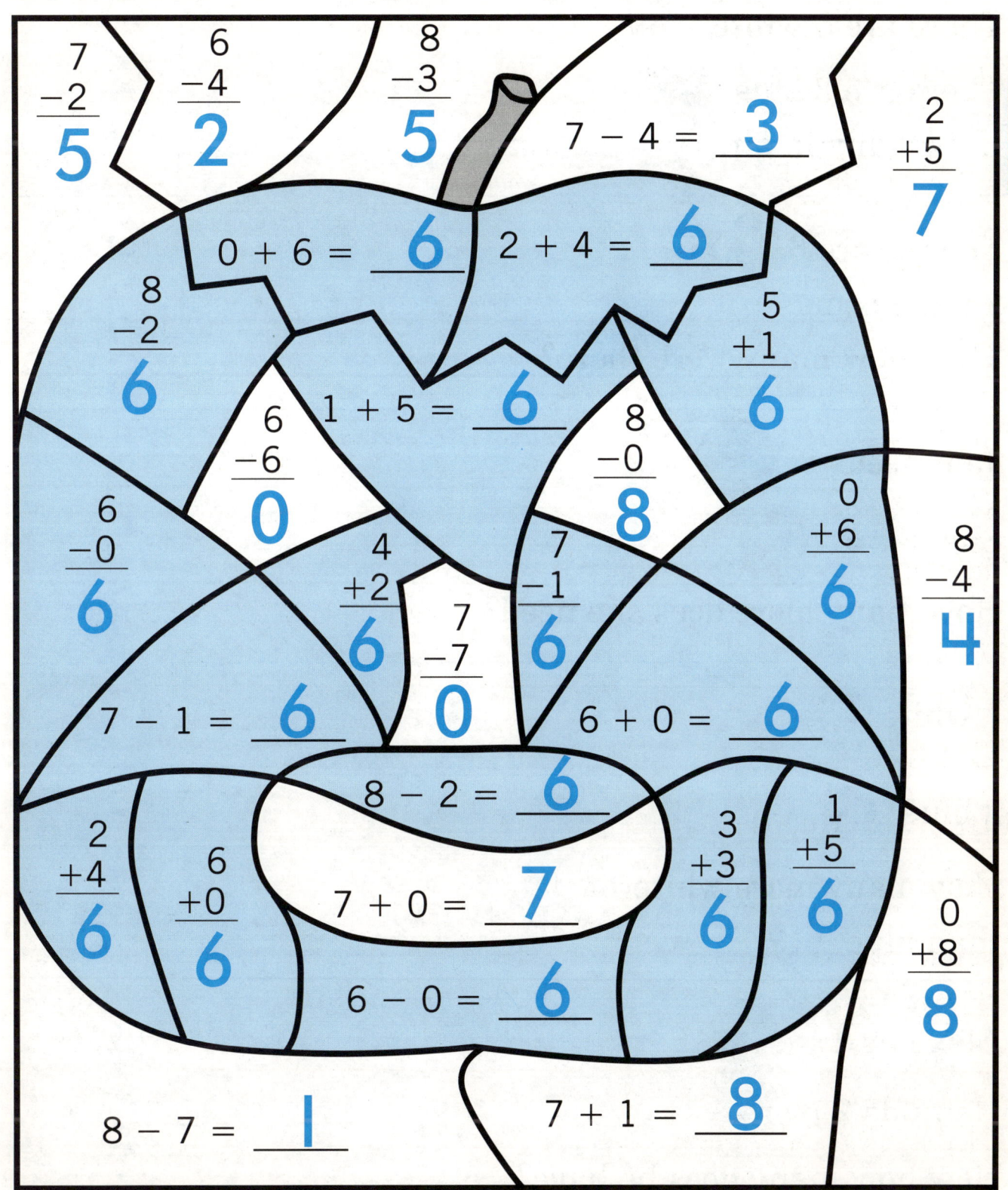

$\begin{array}{r}7\\-2\\\hline 5\end{array}$ $\begin{array}{r}6\\-4\\\hline 2\end{array}$ $\begin{array}{r}8\\-3\\\hline 5\end{array}$

$7 - 4 = \underline{\ 3\ }$

$\begin{array}{r}2\\+5\\\hline 7\end{array}$

$0 + 6 = \underline{\ 6\ }$ $2 + 4 = \underline{\ 6\ }$

$\begin{array}{r}8\\-2\\\hline 6\end{array}$

$1 + 5 = \underline{\ 6\ }$

$\begin{array}{r}5\\+1\\\hline 6\end{array}$

$\begin{array}{r}6\\-6\\\hline 0\end{array}$ $\begin{array}{r}8\\-0\\\hline 8\end{array}$

$\begin{array}{r}6\\-0\\\hline 6\end{array}$ $\begin{array}{r}4\\+2\\\hline 6\end{array}$ $\begin{array}{r}7\\-1\\\hline 6\end{array}$ $\begin{array}{r}0\\+6\\\hline 6\end{array}$ $\begin{array}{r}8\\-4\\\hline 4\end{array}$

$\begin{array}{r}7\\-7\\\hline 0\end{array}$

$7 - 1 = \underline{\ 6\ }$ $6 + 0 = \underline{\ 6\ }$

$8 - 2 = \underline{\ 6\ }$

$\begin{array}{r}2\\+4\\\hline 6\end{array}$ $\begin{array}{r}6\\+0\\\hline 6\end{array}$

$7 + 0 = \underline{\ 7\ }$

$\begin{array}{r}3\\+3\\\hline 6\end{array}$ $\begin{array}{r}1\\+5\\\hline 6\end{array}$ $\begin{array}{r}0\\+8\\\hline 8\end{array}$

$6 - 0 = \underline{\ 6\ }$

$8 - 7 = \underline{\ 1\ }$ $7 + 1 = \underline{\ 8\ }$

Number Correct
- **26–30:** Have students color the parts of the picture that do not have 6 for an answer.
- **20–25:** If students have not performed the correct operation, have them rework the answer.
- **Less than 20:** Have students use manipulatives to rework each incorrect answer and explain each step.

LESSON FOLLOW-UP AND ERROR ANALYSIS

Spectrum Software Addition 4 and 5; Subtraction 4 and 5

CHAPTER 3

41

Prerequisite Skills: addition and subtraction facts through 8

Lesson Focus: problem solving
Possible Score: 5
Time Frame: 10–15 minutes

Lesson 10 Problem Solving

Solve each problem.

There are 5 white 🦋.
There are 3 blue 🦋.
How many in all?

$$\begin{array}{r} 5 \\ +3 \\ \hline 8 \end{array}$$

There were 6 🐕.
2 more came.
Then how many were there?

$$\begin{array}{r} 6 \\ +2 \\ \hline 8 \end{array}$$

Joni needs 8 🪙.
She has 5 🪙.
How many more does she need?

$$\begin{array}{r} 8 \\ -5 \\ \hline 3 \end{array}$$

7 white 🎈.
3 blue 🎈.
How many more white than blue 🎈?

$$\begin{array}{r} 7 \\ -3 \\ \hline 4 \end{array}$$

Alex has 4 🍁.
He finds 2 more.
Now how many does he have?

$$\begin{array}{r} 4 \\ +2 \\ \hline 6 \end{array}$$

Number Correct

LESSON FOLLOW-UP AND ERROR ANALYSIS

5: Have students write several problems of their own.
4: Have students read the problems aloud and then write the necessary fact.
Less than 4: Have students write down the numbers in the problem and then use them to write the necessary fact.

Spectrum Software Word Problems 1–7

42

For further evaluation, use the Chapter Test on page 167.
For maintaining skills, use the Cumulative Review on page 155.

Possible Score: 30
Time Frame: 10–15 minutes

CHAPTER 3 PRACTICE TEST
Addition and Subtraction (facts through 8)

Add.

3	0	4	2	2
+5	+6	+3	+5	+6
8	6	7	7	8

5	4	4	1	7
+1	+4	+2	+6	+1
6	8	6	7	8

Subtract.

6	7	8	6	8
−4	−2	−6	−3	−0
2	5	2	3	8

8	7	6	6	8
−1	−5	−2	−0	−3
7	2	4	6	5

Add or subtract. STOP! Watch the + and −.

3	6	7	3	8
+3	−1	−4	+4	−7
6	5	3	7	1

7	5	8	7	6
−7	+2	−4	+0	+2
0	7	4	7	8

Number Correct — **LESSON FOLLOW-UP AND ERROR ANALYSIS**   *Spectrum Software* Addition 4 and 5; Subtraction 4 and 5; Word Problems 1–7

26–30: To reinforce numeration, have students ring each answer of 8 in red and ring each answer of 7 in blue.
20–25: If students have not performed the correct operation, have them rework the answer.
Less than 20: Have students use manipulatives to rework each incorrect answer and explain each step.

Math Intervention: Word Problems, Gold Book, pages 45–52.
Real World Problem Solving practice: Gold Book, pages 53–54.

CHAPTER 4 PRETEST
Addition and Subtraction (facts through 10)

Add.

2 + 6 **8**	1 + 8 **9**	3 + 7 **10**	8 + 2 **10**	3 + 6 **9**
0 + 8 **8**	2 + 7 **9**	6 + 4 **10**	9 + 1 **10**	0 + 9 **9**
5 + 5 **10**	4 + 5 **9**	7 + 3 **10**	6 + 4 **10**	2 + 8 **10**

Subtract.

10 − 3 **7**	9 − 4 **5**	10 − 4 **6**	9 − 0 **9**	9 − 1 **8**
10 − 6 **4**	10 − 5 **5**	9 − 3 **6**	9 − 5 **4**	9 − 7 **2**
9 − 0 **9**	9 − 6 **3**	9 − 2 **7**	9 − 6 **3**	10 − 1 **9**

Prerequisite Skills: adding through sums of 8

Lesson Focus: adding through sums of 9
Possible Score: 26
Time Frame: 5–10 minutes

Lesson 1   Sums of 9

Add.

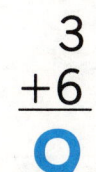

$2 + 7 = \underline{9}$ $\begin{array}{r}2\\+7\\\hline 9\end{array}$ $5 + 4 = \underline{9}$ $\begin{array}{r}5\\+4\\\hline 9\end{array}$

$7 + 2 = \underline{9}$ $\begin{array}{r}7\\+2\\\hline 9\end{array}$ $4 + 5 = \underline{9}$ $\begin{array}{r}4\\+5\\\hline 9\end{array}$

$1 + 8 = \underline{9}$ $\begin{array}{r}1\\+8\\\hline 9\end{array}$ $3 + 6 = \underline{9}$ $\begin{array}{r}3\\+6\\\hline 9\end{array}$

$8 + 1 = \underline{9}$ $\begin{array}{r}8\\+1\\\hline 9\end{array}$ $6 + 3 = \underline{9}$ $\begin{array}{r}6\\+3\\\hline 9\end{array}$

$0 + 9 = \underline{9}$ $\begin{array}{r}0\\+9\\\hline 9\end{array}$ $9 + 0 = \underline{9}$ $\begin{array}{r}9\\+0\\\hline 9\end{array}$

$\begin{array}{r}5\\+4\\\hline 9\end{array}$ $\begin{array}{r}3\\+6\\\hline 9\end{array}$ $\begin{array}{r}8\\+1\\\hline 9\end{array}$ $\begin{array}{r}4\\+5\\\hline 9\end{array}$ $\begin{array}{r}7\\+2\\\hline 9\end{array}$ $\begin{array}{r}0\\+9\\\hline 9\end{array}$

Number Correct

LESSON FOLLOW-UP AND ERROR ANALYSIS

22–26: Have students draw a picture story for each exercise in the bottom row.
17–21: Have students use manipulatives to rework each incorrect answer on the page.
Less than 17: Have students count the domino dots to help them rework each incorrect answer.

Spectrum Software Addition 4 and 5

Prerequisite Skills: subtracting from 8

Lesson Focus: subtracting from 9
Possible Score: 20
Time Frame: 5–10 minutes

Lesson 2   Subtracting from 9

Subtract.

9 − 6 = **3** $\begin{array}{r}9\\-6\\\hline 3\end{array}$ 9 − 3 = **6** $\begin{array}{r}9\\-3\\\hline 6\end{array}$

9 − 0 = **9** $\begin{array}{r}9\\-0\\\hline 9\end{array}$ 9 − 9 = **0** $\begin{array}{r}9\\-9\\\hline 0\end{array}$

9 − 5 = **4** $\begin{array}{r}9\\-5\\\hline 4\end{array}$ 9 − 4 = **5** $\begin{array}{r}9\\-4\\\hline 5\end{array}$

9 − 8 = **1** $\begin{array}{r}9\\-8\\\hline 1\end{array}$ 9 − 1 = **8** $\begin{array}{r}9\\-1\\\hline 8\end{array}$

9 − 2 = **7** $\begin{array}{r}9\\-2\\\hline 7\end{array}$ 9 − 7 = **2** $\begin{array}{r}9\\-7\\\hline 2\end{array}$

Number Correct

LESSON FOLLOW-UP AND ERROR ANALYSIS

Spectrum Software Subtraction 4 and 5

17–20: Have students draw their own picture stories to show subtracting from 9.
13–16: Have students cross out the ones taken away, and count the dots that remain.
Less than 13: Have students count all the dots, cover the ones taken away, and finally count the dots that remain.

Prerequisite Skills: adding through sums of 9

Lesson Focus: adding through sums of 10
Possible Score: 26
Time Frame: 5–10 minutes

Lesson 3 Sums of 10

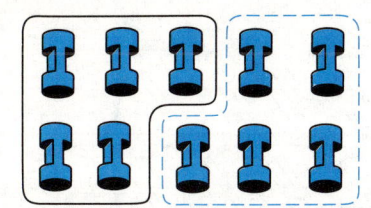

$5 + 5 = \underline{10}$

$\begin{array}{r}5\\+5\\\hline 10\end{array}$

Add.

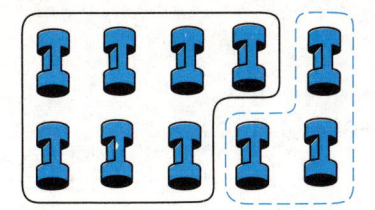

$7 + 3 = \underline{10}$ $\quad \begin{array}{r}7\\+3\\\hline 10\end{array}$ $\qquad 3 + 7 = \underline{10}$ $\quad \begin{array}{r}3\\+7\\\hline 10\end{array}$

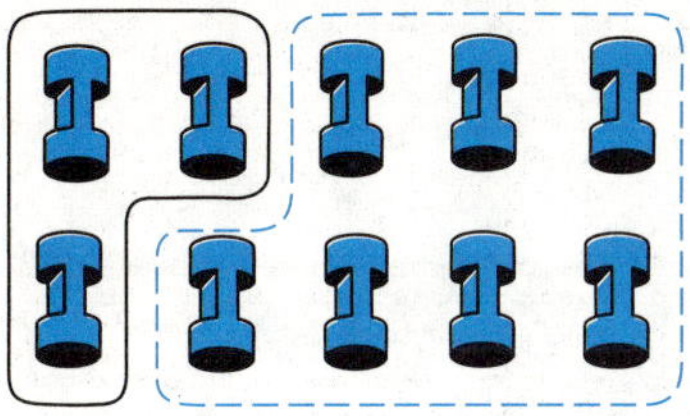

$1 + 9 = \underline{10}$ $\quad \begin{array}{r}1\\+9\\\hline 10\end{array} \begin{array}{r}9\\+1\\\hline 10\end{array}$ $\qquad 2 + 8 = \underline{10}$ $\quad \begin{array}{r}2\\+8\\\hline 10\end{array} \begin{array}{r}8\\+2\\\hline 10\end{array}$

$9 + 1 = \underline{10}$ $\qquad\qquad\qquad 8 + 2 = \underline{10}$

$6 + 4 = \underline{10}$ $\quad \begin{array}{r}6\\+4\\\hline 10\end{array} \begin{array}{r}4\\+6\\\hline 10\end{array}$ $\qquad 10 + 0 = \underline{10}$ $\quad \begin{array}{r}10\\+0\\\hline 10\end{array} \begin{array}{r}0\\+10\\\hline 10\end{array}$

$4 + 6 = \underline{10}$ $\qquad\qquad\qquad 0 + 10 = \underline{10}$

$\begin{array}{r}3\\+7\\\hline 10\end{array} \quad \begin{array}{r}6\\+4\\\hline 10\end{array} \quad \begin{array}{r}5\\+5\\\hline 10\end{array} \quad \begin{array}{r}1\\+9\\\hline 10\end{array} \quad \begin{array}{r}2\\+8\\\hline 10\end{array} \quad \begin{array}{r}7\\+3\\\hline 10\end{array}$

Number Correct

LESSON FOLLOW-UP AND ERROR ANALYSIS

Spectrum Software Addition 4 and 5

22–26: Have students make dot pictures illustrating various combinations for sums of 10. (○●●●●●●●●●)
17–21: Have students use manipulatives to rework each incorrect answer.
Less than 17: Have students use manipulatives and count aloud as they rework each incorrect answer.

47

Prerequisite Skills: subtracting from 9

Lesson Focus: subtracting from 10
Possible Score: 24
Time Frame: 5–10 minutes

Lesson 4 Subtracting from 10

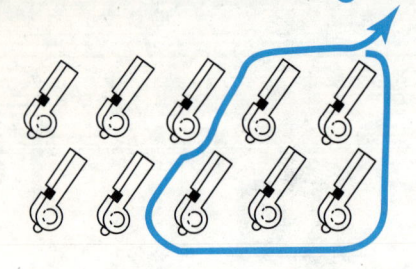

$\begin{array}{r}10\\-5\\\hline 5\end{array}$

10 − 5 = __5__

$\begin{array}{r}10\\-10\\\hline 0\end{array}$

10 − 10 = __0__

Subtract.

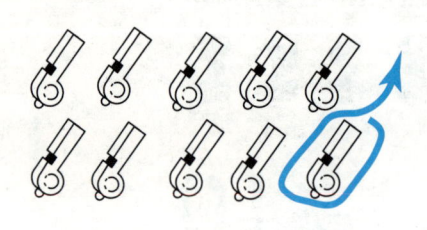

$\begin{array}{r}10\\-1\\\hline 9\end{array}$

10 − 1 = __9__

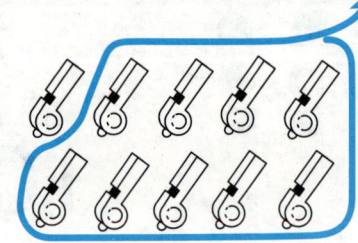

$\begin{array}{r}10\\-9\\\hline 1\end{array}$

10 − 9 = __1__

10 − 7 = __3__ $\begin{array}{r}10\\-7\\\hline 3\end{array}$ $\begin{array}{r}10\\-3\\\hline 7\end{array}$ 10 − 4 = __6__ $\begin{array}{r}10\\-4\\\hline 6\end{array}$ $\begin{array}{r}10\\-6\\\hline 4\end{array}$

10 − 3 = __7__   10 − 6 = __4__

10 − 8 = __2__ $\begin{array}{r}10\\-8\\\hline 2\end{array}$ $\begin{array}{r}10\\-2\\\hline 8\end{array}$ 10 − 0 = __10__ $\begin{array}{r}10\\-0\\\hline 10\end{array}$

10 − 2 = __8__

$\begin{array}{r}10\\-7\\\hline 3\end{array}$ $\begin{array}{r}10\\-1\\\hline 9\end{array}$ $\begin{array}{r}10\\-5\\\hline 5\end{array}$ $\begin{array}{r}10\\-10\\\hline 0\end{array}$ $\begin{array}{r}10\\-2\\\hline 8\end{array}$ $\begin{array}{r}10\\-6\\\hline 4\end{array}$

LESSON FOLLOW-UP AND ERROR ANALYSIS

Spectrum Software Subtraction 4 and 5

Number Correct
- **20–24:** Have students draw their own picture stories to show subtracting from 10.
- **16–19:** Have students count the total number of whistles, cover the whistles removed, and count the remaining whistles.
- **Less than 16:** Have students use manipulatives to rework each incorrect answer.

Prerequisite Skills: adding through sums of 10

Lesson Focus: practicing addition
Possible Score: 41
Time Frame: 10–15 minutes

Lesson 5 Practicing Addition

Add.

6 +4 **10**	7 +2 **9**	4 +4 **8**	4 +5 **9**	9 +1 **10**	3 +2 **5**
2 +7 **9**	6 +2 **8**	9 +0 **9**	2 +5 **7**	1 +4 **5**	4 +6 **10**
8 +1 **9**	2 +2 **4**	3 +6 **9**	1 +7 **8**	7 +3 **10**	1 +8 **9**
2 +3 **5**	2 +8 **10**	3 +5 **8**	8 +2 **10**	6 +1 **7**	0 +9 **9**
1 +9 **10**	6 +3 **9**	3 +4 **7**	5 +2 **7**	5 +4 **9**	4 +3 **7**
5 +3 **8**	8 +0 **8**	5 +5 **10**	3 +7 **10**	2 +6 **8**	3 +3 **6**

CHAPTER 4

Number Correct

LESSON FOLLOW-UP AND ERROR ANALYSIS

Spectrum Software Addition 4 and 5

34–41: Have students choose two problems on page 50 and write a new picture story for each.
26–33: Check to see that students have written the vertical addition correctly on page 50.
Less than 26: Have students use manipulatives to rework each incorrect answer and explain each step.

Lesson 5   Problem Solving

Solve each problem.

There are 5 white 🦋.
There are 4 blue 🦋.
How many in all?

$\begin{array}{r}5\\+4\\\hline 9\end{array}$

There are 3 🐑.
7 more 🐑 come.
How many are there now?

$\begin{array}{r}3\\+7\\\hline 10\end{array}$

Beth has 9 👕.
She buys 1 more.
Now how many does she have?

$\begin{array}{r}9\\+1\\\hline 10\end{array}$

There are 6 🕯.
There are 3 🕯.
How many in all?

$\begin{array}{r}6\\+3\\\hline 9\end{array}$

There were 8 🐕.
2 more came.
Then how many were there?

$\begin{array}{r}8\\+2\\\hline 10\end{array}$

CHAPTER 4
Addition and Subtraction (facts through 10)

Lesson 5
Practicing Addition

Prerequisite Skills: subtracting from 10

Lesson Focus: practicing subtraction
Possible Score: 41
Time Frame: 10–15 minutes

Lesson 6 Practicing Subtraction

Subtract.

$9 - 4 = 5$	$7 - 6 = 1$	$10 - 5 = 5$	$9 - 7 = 2$	$8 - 5 = 3$	$10 - 9 = 1$
$10 - 4 = 6$	$6 - 3 = 3$	$9 - 6 = 3$	$10 - 3 = 7$	$9 - 0 = 9$	$5 - 1 = 4$
$3 - 1 = 2$	$9 - 1 = 8$	$10 - 8 = 2$	$7 - 2 = 5$	$9 - 5 = 4$	$2 - 2 = 0$
$10 - 1 = 9$	$7 - 0 = 7$	$5 - 3 = 2$	$8 - 7 = 1$	$10 - 2 = 8$	$6 - 4 = 2$
$9 - 8 = 1$	$7 - 4 = 3$	$10 - 0 = 10$	$4 - 2 = 2$	$8 - 4 = 4$	$9 - 3 = 6$
$10 - 6 = 4$	$8 - 6 = 2$	$9 - 2 = 7$	$8 - 1 = 7$	$9 - 9 = 0$	$10 - 7 = 3$

Number Correct
34–41: Have students use the same exercises on page 52 and write new problems to solve.
26–33: Check to see that students have written the vertical subtraction correctly on page 52.
Less than 26: Have students use manipulatives to rework each incorrect answer and explain each step.

LESSON FOLLOW-UP AND ERROR ANALYSIS

Spectrum Software Subtraction 4 and 5; Word Problems 8 and 9

CHAPTER 4

51

Lesson 6 Problem Solving

Solve each problem.

There are 10 white 🌼.
There are 4 blue 🌼.
How many more white 🌼 than blue 🌼 are there?

$$\begin{array}{r}10\\-4\\\hline 6\end{array}$$

10 🖍 are on the table.
2 are broken.
How many are not broken?

$$\begin{array}{r}10\\-2\\\hline 8\end{array}$$

There are 9 🐟.
6 swim away.
How many 🐟 are left?

$$\begin{array}{r}9\\-6\\\hline 3\end{array}$$

Joni wants 9 🪙.
She has 5 🪙.
How many more does she need?

$$\begin{array}{r}9\\-5\\\hline 4\end{array}$$

There were 10 ⛄.
5 ⛄ melted.
How many did not melt?

$$\begin{array}{r}10\\-5\\\hline 5\end{array}$$

Lesson 6
Practicing Subtraction

Prerequisite Skills: adding and subtracting through 10

Lesson Focus: addition and subtraction
Possible Score: 41
Time Frame: 15–20 minutes

Lesson 7 Addition and Subtraction

Add or subtract. STOP! Watch the + and −.

5 +2 = **7**	10 −6 = **4**	7 +1 = **8**	9 −4 = **5**	1 +9 = **10**	9 −8 = **1**
9 +0 = **9**	8 −0 = **8**	10 −9 = **1**	1 +8 = **9**	2 +7 = **9**	9 −1 = **8**
10 −1 = **9**	2 +8 = **10**	1 +6 = **7**	8 −3 = **5**	6 +3 = **9**	10 −3 = **7**
9 −9 = **0**	4 +5 = **9**	8 +1 = **9**	10 −8 = **2**	9 −0 = **9**	5 +5 = **10**
4 +4 = **8**	9 −3 = **6**	7 +3 = **10**	9 −7 = **2**	3 +6 = **9**	10 −7 = **3**
7 +2 = **9**	8 −7 = **1**	0 +8 = **8**	9 −2 = **7**	10 −5 = **5**	4 +6 = **10**

CHAPTER 4

Number Correct
34–41:
26–33:
Less than 26:

LESSON FOLLOW-UP AND ERROR ANALYSIS

Have students choose a row of problems on page 53 and write a picture story for each.
If students have not performed the correct operation, have them rework the answer.
Have students use manipulatives to rework each incorrect answer and explain each step.

Spectrum Software Addition 4 and 5; Subtraction 4 and 5

Lesson 7 Problem Solving

Solve each problem.

There are 9 white ◯.
There are 4 blue ●.
How many more white ◯ than blue ●?

$$\begin{array}{r}9\\-4\\\hline 5\end{array}$$

Alex has 7 🍁.
He finds 2 more.
Now how many does he have?

$$\begin{array}{r}7\\+2\\\hline 9\end{array}$$

There are 5 ◻.
There are 5 ◼.
How many in all?

$$\begin{array}{r}5\\+5\\\hline 10\end{array}$$

There were 10 🐱.
6 ran away.
Then how many were left?

$$\begin{array}{r}10\\-6\\\hline 4\end{array}$$

There were 9 🍞.
8 were eaten.
How many were not eaten?

$$\begin{array}{r}9\\-8\\\hline 1\end{array}$$

CHAPTER 4
Addition and Subtraction (facts through 10)
54

Lesson 7
Addition and Subtraction

Prerequisite Skills: using pennies, nickels, and dimes

Lesson Focus: using pennies, nickels, and dimes
Possible Score: 12
Time Frame: 15–20 minutes

Lesson 8 Money

1 penny
1¢

1 nickel
5¢

1 dime
10¢

Tell how much money.

<u>10</u> ¢

<u>6</u> ¢

<u>6</u> ¢

<u>8</u> ¢

<u>10</u> ¢

<u>5</u> ¢

<u>10</u> ¢

<u>9</u> ¢

Number Correct

LESSON FOLLOW-UP AND ERROR ANALYSIS

10–12: Have students change the prices on page 56 to 7¢, 5¢, 6¢, and 3¢ and find the new answers.
7–9: Have students use real coins with page 56 to help them rework each incorrect answer.
Less than 7: Have students use coins and count them aloud as they subtract to rework each incorrect answer.

Spectrum Software Decimals 1–3

55

Lesson 8 Problem Solving

10 pennies   10¢    1 dime 1 nickel
                     10¢   5¢

I have	I buy	I have left
	 5¢	9¢ − 5¢ 4¢
	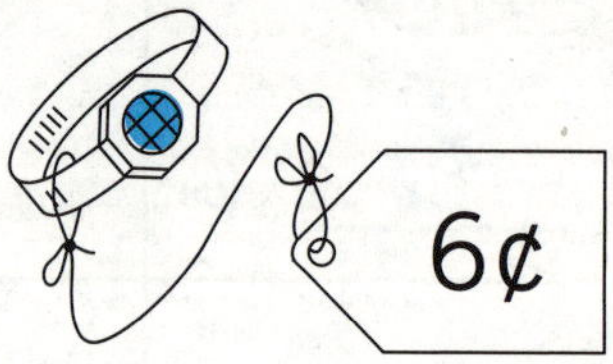 6¢	8¢ − 6¢ 2¢
	 8¢	10¢ − 8¢ 2¢
	 5¢	10¢ − 5¢ 5¢

CHAPTER 4
Addition and Subtraction (facts through 10)

Lesson 8
Money

Prerequisite Skills: adding and subtracting through 10

Lesson 9 Problem Solving

Lesson Focus: solving problems
Possible Score: 12
Time Frame: 15–20 minutes

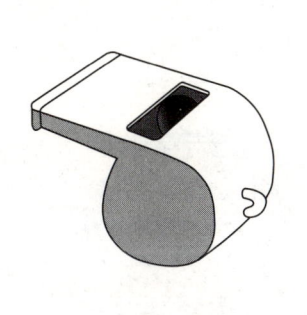

3¢    4¢   5¢   6¢

CHAPTER 4

Add or subtract.

I buy
I buy
I spent

$3¢$
$+4¢$
$7¢$

I buy
I buy
I spent

$4¢$
$+6¢$
$10¢$

I have
I buy
I have left

$10¢$
$-6¢$
$4¢$

I have
I buy
I have left

$9¢$
$-3¢$
$6¢$

I have
I buy
I have left

$8¢$
$-5¢$
$3¢$

I have
I buy
I have left

$10¢$
$-4¢$
$6¢$

Number Correct

LESSON FOLLOW-UP AND ERROR ANALYSIS

Spectrum Software Addition 4 and 5; Subtraction 4 and 5

10–12: Have students make up their own problems like the ones on the page and solve them.
7–9: If students have not performed the correct operation, have them rework the answer.
Less than 7: Have students read the sentences aloud and record the prices. Have pennies or counters available.

57

Lesson 9 **Problem Solving**

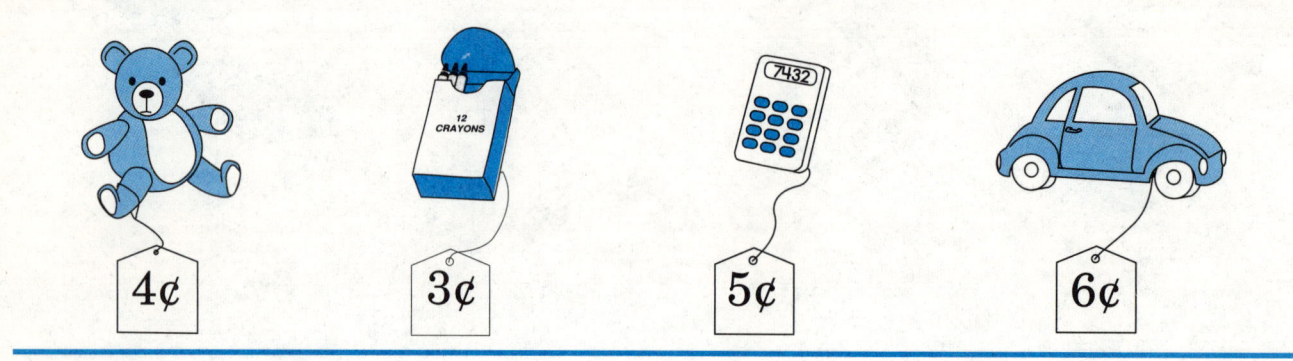

Items with prices: teddy bear 4¢, crayons 3¢, calculator 5¢, car 6¢.

Add or subtract.

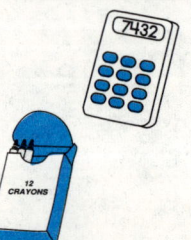

I buy (bear)
I buy (crayons)
I spent
4¢
+ 3¢
7¢

I buy (car)
I buy (crayons)
I spent
6¢
+ 3¢
9¢

I have
I buy (car)
I have left
8¢
− 6¢
2¢

I have
I buy (bear)
I have left
10¢
− 4¢
6¢

I have
I buy (calculator)
I have left
7¢
− 5¢
2¢

I buy (calculator)
I buy (crayons)
I spent
5¢
+ 3¢
8¢

CHAPTER 4
Addition and Subtraction (facts through 10)
58

Lesson 9
Problem Solving

For further evaluation, copy the Chapter Test on page 168.
For maintaining skills, use the Cumulative Review on page 156.

Possible Score: 30
Time Frame: 5–10 minutes

CHAPTER 4 PRACTICE TEST
Addition and Subtraction (facts through 10)
For assessment of Chapters 1–4, use the Mid-Test on pages 147–148.

Add.

6	8	4	7	2
+2	+1	+6	+3	+8
8	**9**	**10**	**10**	**10**

5	6	1	3	9
+4	+3	+9	+6	+0
9	**9**	**10**	**9**	**9**

Subtract.

10	9	9	10	10
−4	−2	−6	−3	−1
6	**7**	**3**	**7**	**9**

9	9	10	9	10
−1	−5	−9	−7	−5
8	**4**	**1**	**2**	**5**

Add or subtract. STOP! Watch the + and −.

0	10	9	2	9
+8	−8	−0	+7	−9
8	**2**	**9**	**9**	**0**

10	8	10	3	5
−2	+2	−6	+7	+5
8	**10**	**4**	**10**	**10**

Number Correct — **LESSON FOLLOW-UP** — *Spectrum Software* Addition 4 and 5; Subtraction 4 and 5; Word Problems 8 and 9; Decimals 1–3

26–30: To reinforce numeration, have students ring each answer less than 3 and □ each answer greater than 5.
20–25: If students have not performed the correct operation, have them rework the answer.
Less than 20: Have students use manipulatives to rework each incorrect answer.

Math Intervention: Subtraction Facts, Gold Book, pages 35–42.
Real World Problem Solving practice: Gold Book, pages 43–44.

CHAPTER 5 PRETEST
Numeration (0 through 99)

Complete.

1 ten 5 ones = __15__	5 tens 0 ones = __50__
2 tens 2 ones = __22__	3 tens 4 ones = __34__
6 tens 1 one = __61__	4 tens 8 ones = __48__
9 tens 6 ones = __96__	3 tens 9 ones = __39__
5 tens 5 ones = __55__	8 tens 4 ones = __84__
7 tens 4 ones = __74__	6 tens 7 ones = __67__
4 tens 2 ones = __42__	5 tens 3 ones = __53__

Write the numbers in order for each row.

12	13	14	15	16	17	18	19	20

32	33	34	35	36	37	38	39	40

60	61	62	63	64	65	66	67	68

Prerequisite Skills: numbers through 10; counting ones and tens

Lesson Focus: numbers through 19
Possible Score: 24
Time Frame: 5–10 minutes

Lesson 1 Numbers 10 through 19

<u> 1 </u> ten <u> 0 </u> ones = <u> 10 </u>

<u> 1 </u> ten <u> 1 </u> one = <u> 11 </u>

Complete.

<u> 1 </u> ten <u> 2 </u> ones = <u> 12 </u>

<u> 1 </u> ten <u> 3 </u> ones = <u> 13 </u>

<u> 1 </u> ten <u> 4 </u> ones = <u> 14 </u>

<u> 1 </u> ten <u> 5 </u> ones = <u> 15 </u>

<u> 1 </u> ten <u> 6 </u> ones = <u> 16 </u>

<u> 1 </u> ten <u> 7 </u> ones = <u> 17 </u>

<u> 1 </u> ten <u> 8 </u> ones = <u> 18 </u>

<u> 1 </u> ten <u> 9 </u> ones = <u> 19 </u>

CHAPTER 5

Number Correct
LESSON FOLLOW-UP AND ERROR ANALYSIS
Spectrum Software Whole Numbers 12

20–24: Have students use a real dime and pennies to create problems like the ones on the page.
16–19: Have students count aloud before they write the number on each blank.
Less than 16: Help students understand that a dime has a value of 10 even though it is only one coin.

Prerequisite Skills: numbers through 19; counting ones and tens

Lesson Focus: numbers 20 through 29
Possible Score: 24
Time Frame: 5–10 minutes

Lesson 2 Numbers 20 through 29

$\underline{\ 2\ }$ tens $\underline{\ 0\ }$ ones = $\underline{\ 20\ }$

$\underline{\ 2\ }$ tens $\underline{\ 1\ }$ one = $\underline{\ 21\ }$

Complete.

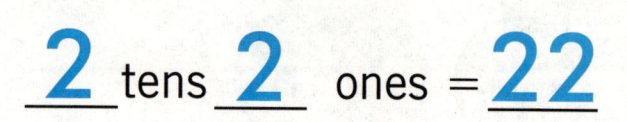

$\underline{\ 2\ }$ tens $\underline{\ 2\ }$ ones = $\underline{22}$

$\underline{\ 2\ }$ tens $\underline{\ 3\ }$ ones = $\underline{23}$

$\underline{\ 2\ }$ tens $\underline{\ 4\ }$ ones = $\underline{24}$

$\underline{\ 2\ }$ tens $\underline{\ 5\ }$ ones = $\underline{25}$

$\underline{\ 2\ }$ tens $\underline{\ 6\ }$ ones = $\underline{26}$

$\underline{\ 2\ }$ tens $\underline{\ 7\ }$ ones = $\underline{27}$

$\underline{\ 2\ }$ tens $\underline{\ 8\ }$ ones = $\underline{28}$

$\underline{\ 2\ }$ tens $\underline{\ 9\ }$ ones = $\underline{29}$

LESSON FOLLOW-UP AND ERROR ANALYSIS

Number Correct
- **20–24:** Have students choose an amount and write a picture story using that amount.
- **16–19:** Explain that two dimes equal 20 cents, so students should start counting from 20.
- **Less than 16:** Have students count aloud as they write the numbers on each blank.

Spectrum Software Whole Numbers 13

Prerequisite Skills: numbers 10 through 29; counting ones and tens

Lesson Focus: numbers 10 through 29
Possible Score: 24
Time Frame: 5–10 minutes

Lesson 3 Numbers 10 through 29

Complete.

__2__ tens __3__ ones = __23__

__2__ tens __0__ ones = __20__

__1__ ten __5__ ones = __15__

__2__ tens __6__ ones = __26__

__2__ tens __2__ ones = __22__

__1__ ten __7__ ones = __17__

__1__ ten __3__ ones = __13__

__2__ tens __4__ ones = __24__

Number Correct
20–24: Have students use real dimes and pennies to create problems like the ones on the page.
16–19: Remind students to count on from 10 when there is one dime and from 20 when there are two dimes.
Less than 16: Have students count aloud as they write the numbers on each blank.

LESSON FOLLOW-UP AND ERROR ANALYSIS

Spectrum Software Whole Numbers 13

Prerequisite Skills: one dime equals 10 cents

Lesson Focus: using dimes to count by tens
Possible Score: 14
Time Frame: 5–10 minutes

Lesson 4 Tens

1 ten = 10

2 tens = 20

Complete.

3 tens = 30

4 tens = 40

5 tens = 50

6 tens = 60

7 tens = 70

8 tens = 80

9 tens = 90

Number Correct
12–14: Have students use real dimes to create problems like those on the page.
9–11: Check to see that students have counted the number of dimes correctly.
Less than 9: Help students realize that even though the coins are dimes, they are counting by tens.

LESSON FOLLOW-UP AND ERROR ANALYSIS

Spectrum Software Whole Numbers 12 and 13

Prerequisite Skills: counting; value of ones and tens

Lesson Focus: numbers through 49
Possible Score: 73
Time Frame: 10–15 minutes

Lesson 5 Numbers 30 through 49

Complete.

__3__ tens __2__ ones = __32__

__3__ tens __4__ ones = __34__

__3__ tens __9__ ones = __39__

__4__ tens __0__ ones = __40__

3 tens 7 ones = __37__

4 tens 1 one = __41__

4 tens 9 ones = __49__

3 tens 5 ones = __35__

4 tens 3 ones = __43__

4 tens 2 ones = __42__

3 tens 3 ones = __33__

4 tens 4 ones = __44__

4 tens 6 ones = __46__

3 tens 8 ones = __38__

Number Correct
62–73: Have students write a picture story for any two answers on page 65.
47–61: Help students see the connection between the coins at the top of the page and the problems as written.
Less than 47: Have students use manipulatives or coins to help them rework each incorrect answer.

LESSON FOLLOW-UP AND ERROR ANALYSIS

Spectrum Software Whole Numbers 12 and 13

CHAPTER 5

65

Lesson 5 Numbers 0 through 49

Complete the table.

0	1	2	3	4	5	6	7	8	9
10	11	12	13	14	15	16	17	18	19
20	21	22	23	24	25	26	27	28	29
30	31	32	33	34	35	36	37	38	39
40	41	42	43	44	45	46	47	48	49

Connect the dots in order.

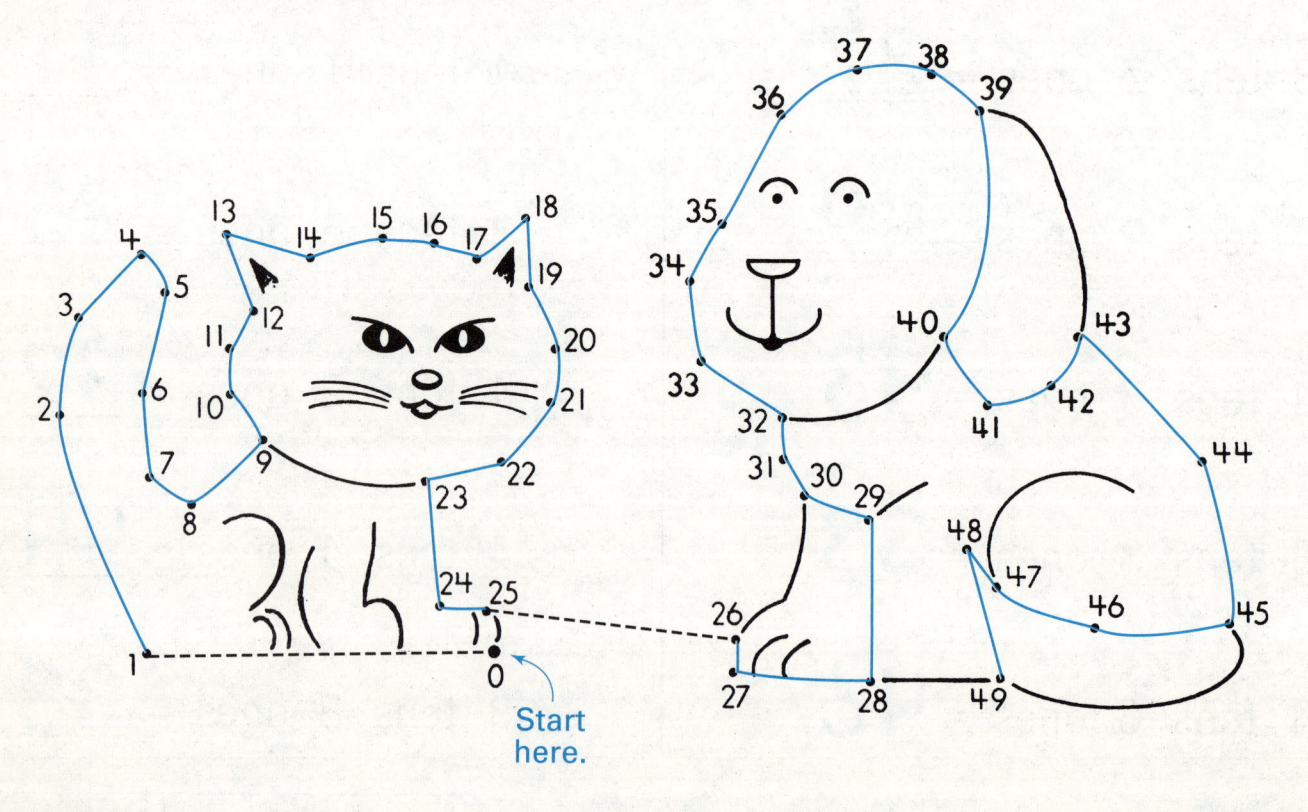

Start here.

CHAPTER 5
Numeration (0 through 99)

Prerequisite Skills: numbers through 49

Lesson Focus: numbers 50 through 69
Possible Score: 20
Time Frame: less than 5 minutes

Lesson 6 Numbers 50 through 69

6 tens 4 ones = __64__

Complete.

5 tens 0 ones = __50__	6 tens 0 ones = __60__
5 tens 1 one = __51__	6 tens 1 one = __61__
5 tens 2 ones = __52__	6 tens 2 ones = __62__
5 tens 3 ones = __53__	6 tens 3 ones = __63__
5 tens 4 ones = __54__	6 tens 4 ones = __64__
5 tens 5 ones = __55__	6 tens 5 ones = __65__
5 tens 6 ones = __56__	6 tens 6 ones = __66__
5 tens 7 ones = __57__	6 tens 7 ones = __67__
5 tens 8 ones = __58__	6 tens 8 ones = __68__
5 tens 9 ones = __59__	6 tens 9 ones = __69__

CHAPTER 5

Number Correct
17–20: Ask students to write the numbers from 40 to 70.
13–16: Students may easily detect the pattern. Help them grasp the connection between each problem and its answer.
Less than 13: Have students use manipulatives to help them rework each incorrect answer.

LESSON FOLLOW-UP AND ERROR ANALYSIS

Spectrum Software Whole Numbers 12 and 13

Prerequisite Skills: numbers through 69

Lesson Focus: numbers 70 through 99
Possible Score: 14
Time Frame: 5–10 minutes

Lesson 7 Numbers 70 through 99

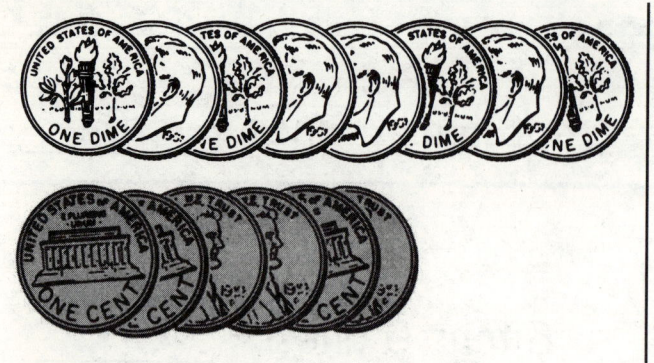

8 tens 6 ones = __86__

9 tens 4 ones = __94__

Complete.

7 tens 4 ones = __74__

9 tens 1 one = __91__

7 tens 8 ones = __78__

9 tens 8 ones = __98__

8 tens 5 ones = __85__

9 tens 9 ones = __99__

7 tens 0 ones = __70__

8 tens 8 ones = __88__

7 tens 9 ones = __79__

8 tens 7 ones = __87__

8 tens 9 ones = __89__

9 tens 2 ones = __92__

7 tens 3 ones = __73__

9 tens 6 ones = __96__

Number Correct

LESSON FOLLOW-UP AND ERROR ANALYSIS

Spectrum Software Whole Numbers 12 and 13

12–14: Have students increase each answer by one and write that number.
9–11: Because students sometimes transpose numbers, be sure they have written the numbers in the correct order.
Less than 9: Ask students to write above each number the sum it represents, such as 80 + 6 above 86.

Prerequisite Skills: numbers through 99

Lesson Focus: value of dimes and pennies
Possible Score: 59
Time Frame: 15–20 minutes

Lesson 8 Numbers 50 through 99

Tell how many cents.

58 ¢

93 ¢

60 ¢

84 ¢

72 ¢

55 ¢

69 ¢

96 ¢

Number Correct
50–59: To reinforce place value, have students write their answers on page 69 in order from least to greatest.
38–49: Have students write the value of dimes and the number of pennies before writing their answers (50 + 8).
Less than 38: Have students count the dimes and pennies aloud before they write their answers.

LESSON FOLLOW-UP AND ERROR ANALYSIS

Spectrum Software Whole Numbers 14; Word Problems 10

69

Lesson 8 Numbers 50 through 99

Complete the table.

50	51	52	53	54	55	56	57	58	59
60	61	62	63	64	65	66	67	68	69
70	71	72	73	74	75	76	77	78	79
80	81	82	83	84	85	86	87	88	89
90	91	92	93	94	95	96	97	98	99

Connect the dots in order.

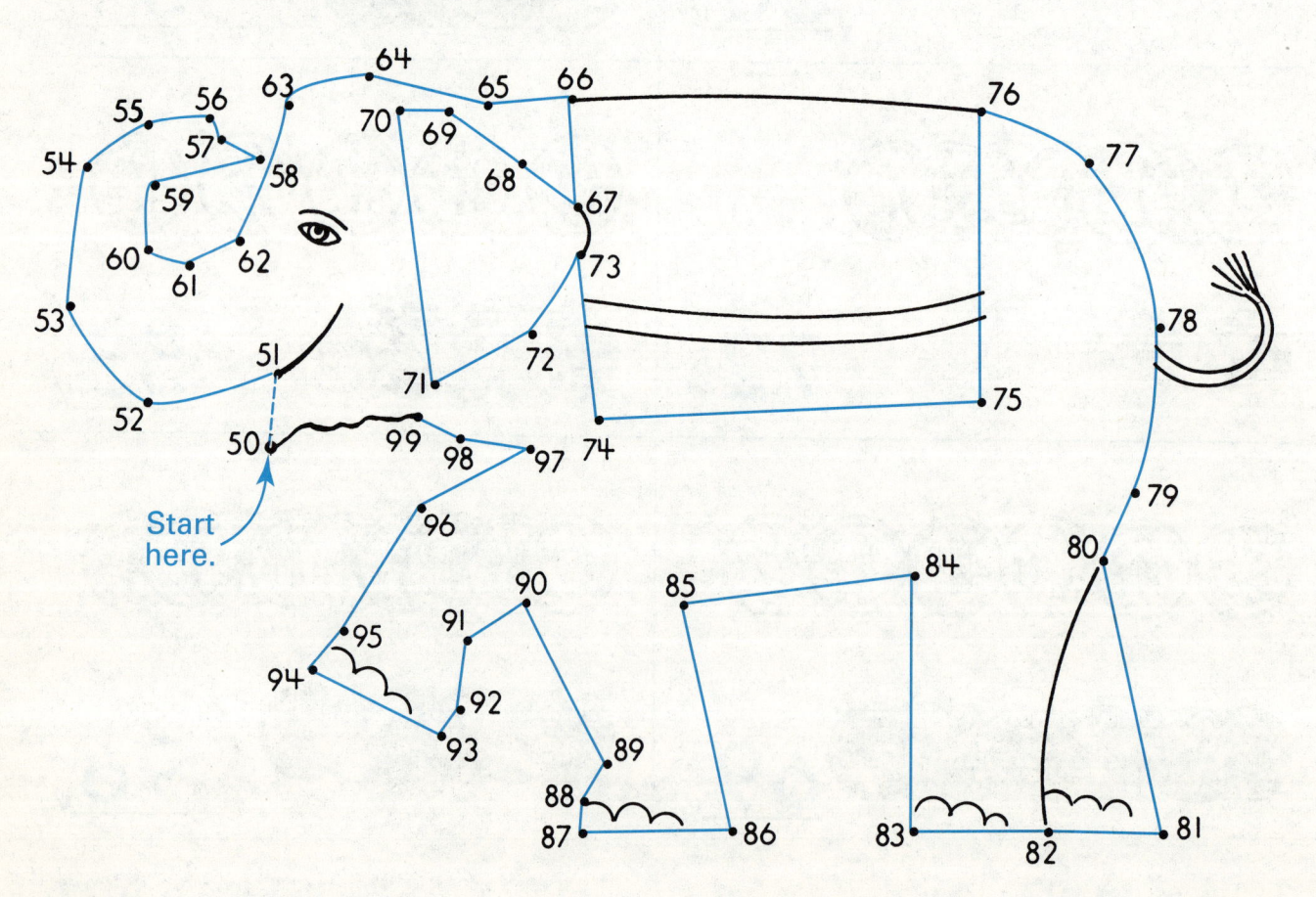

Start here.

CHAPTER 5
Numeration (0 through 99)

Lesson 8
Numbers 50 through 99

Prerequisite Skills: ordering numbers; recognizing the value of numbers through 99

Lesson Focus: ordering numbers
Possible Score: 30
Time Frame: 5–10 minutes

Lesson 9   Numeration

Ring the greatest and ▢ the least.

26 [15] (31)	[53] (71) 68	[40] 70 (90)
(32) [23] 30	85 [65] (95)	(64) 46 [42]
[36] (92) 67	(91) 57 [19]	78 (94) [29]

Complete.

Before	Between	After
18, 19, 20	36, **37**, 38	91, 92, **93**
63, 64, 65	29, **30**, 31	87, 88, **89**
69, 70, 71	53, **54**, 55	48, 49, **50**
33, 34, 35	20, **21**, 22	66, 67, **68**

Number Correct
26–30: For the bottom four rows, have students write the numbers that come before and after the sequence.
20–25: Ask students to underline the tens digit in each number before they rework any incorrect answers.
Less than 20: Have students use dimes and pennies or base-ten blocks when deciding the greatest and least.

LESSON FOLLOW-UP AND ERROR ANALYSIS

Spectrum Software Whole Numbers 15–17

Prerequisite Skills: ordering numbers; recognizing the value of numbers through 99

Lesson Focus: comparing numbers
Possible Score: 24
Time Frame: 5–10 minutes

Lesson 10 Comparing Numbers

Ring the number that is greater.

10	(22)	37	25	28	(38)
25	(28)	(49)	43	33	(37)
95	(97)	74	(76)	(58)	50
20	(30)	21	(23)	42	(47)

Ring the number that is least.

35	(24)	73	(53)	24	(17)
(22)	29	46	(40)	53	(52)
68	(64)	(92)	98	36	(35)
(43)	49	(25)	31	(39)	51

Number Correct — LESSON FOLLOW-UP AND ERROR ANALYSIS
- **22–24:** Have students write several problems of their own and exchange with each other to solve.
- **19–21:** Ask students to underline the tens digit in each number before they rework any incorrect answers.
- **Less than 19:** Have students use dimes and pennies or base-ten blocks when deciding the greatest and least.

Prerequisite Skills: counting

Lesson Focus: skip counting by 2s, 5s, 10s
Possible Score: 53
Time Frame: 10–15 minutes

Lesson 11 Skip Counting

Count by 2s. Write the missing numbers.

2, 4, 6, __8__, 10, 12, 14

6, 8, 10, __12__, 14, 16, 18

22, 24, __26__, 28, 30, __32__, 34

12, 14, __16__, 18, 20, __22__, 24

__30__, 32, 34, __36__, 38, __40__, 42

62, __64__, 66, __68__, 70, __72__, 74

28, 30, __32__, __34__, 36, 38, 40, 42

50, __52__, 54, 56, __58__, __60__, 62

84, __86__, __88__, 90, 92, __94__, 96

46, 48, __50__, 52, __54__, __56__, 58, 60

76, 78, 80, __82__, __84__, __86__, 88

38, __40__, __42__, 44, __46__, 48, 50

Number Correct — **LESSON FOLLOW-UP AND ERROR ANALYSIS**

49–53: Have students write a rule for skip counting 2s, 5s, and 10s.
40–48: Have students start at 2, 5, or 10 and count up by 1s.
Less than 40: Have students start at 1, write out the consecutive numbers, and circle the correct numbers as they count by 2.

Lesson 11   Skip Counting

Count by 5s. Write the missing numbers.

5, 10, __15__, 20, 25, 30

25, 30, __35__, 40, 45, 50

60, 65, 70, 75, 80, __85__, 90, __95__

__35__, 40, 45, __50__, 55, 60, __65__

50, __55__, 60, 65, __70__, __75__, 80

15, 20, 25, __30__, __35__, __40__, 45

Count by 10s. Write the missing numbers.

10, 20, __30__, 40, 50, 60

20, 30, 40, __50__, 60, __70__, 80

50, __60__, 70, 80, 90, __100__

30, 40, __50__, __60__, 70, __80__

0, 10, __20__, 30, __40__, __50__

CHAPTER 5
Numeration (0 through 99)
74

Lesson 11
Skip Counting

For further evaluation, copy the Chapter Test on page 169.
For maintaining skills, use the Cumulative Review on page 157.

Possible Score: 27
Time Frame: 5–10 minutes

CHAPTER 5 PRACTICE TEST
Numeration (0 through 99)

Complete.

3 tens   7 ones = **37**   9 tens   9 ones = **99**

2 tens   8 ones = **28**   3 tens   1 one = **31**

7 tens   0 ones = **70**   5 tens   4 ones = **54**

Name the numbers in order for each row.

16	**17**	**18**	**19**	**20**	**21**	**22**	**23**	24
79	**80**	**81**	**82**	**83**	**84**	**85**	**86**	87

Ring the number that is greater.

16   (19) | (35)   31 | (76)   72

Count by 2s. Write the missing numbers.

4, 6, **8**, 10, **12**, 14

26, 28, 30, **32**, 34, **36**, 38

Number LESSON FOLLOW-UP AND ERROR ANALYSIS
Correct
24–27: Have students ring the greatest number on the pages and square the least number.
20–23: Remind students to think of dimes and then pennies when reworking each incorrect answer.
Less than 20: Remind students to write the tens number first, then the ones. They may first need to write the number as a sum (10 + 4).

Spectrum Software Whole Numbers 12–17; Word Problems 10

Math Intervention: Reading a Graph, Green Book, pages 65–72.
Real World Problem Solving practice: Green Book, pages 73–74.

CHAPTER 6 PRETEST
Measurement

Write the time for each clock.

6:30 | |
__six__ thirty  | __2__ : __30__  | __8__ : __30__

Use a centimeter ruler.

How long is each object?

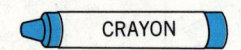

__3__ centimeters 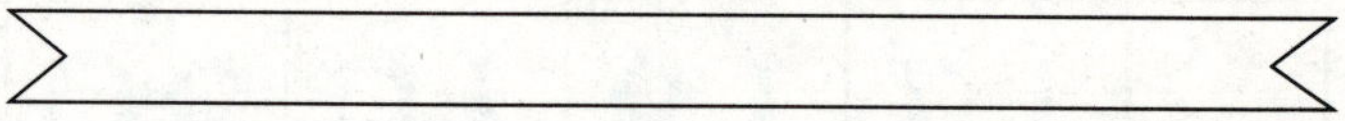   __9__ centimeters

Use an inch ruler.

How long is each object?

__4__ inches

__3__ inches

Prerequisite Skills: recognizing hour/minute hands; experience with analog and digital clocks

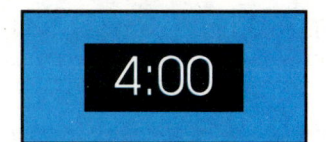

Lesson 1 Time—Hour

Lesson Focus: telling time by the hour
Possible Score: 24
Time Frame: 5–10 minutes

4:00   4 o'clock
          4:00

Both clocks show the same time.

Write the time for each clock.

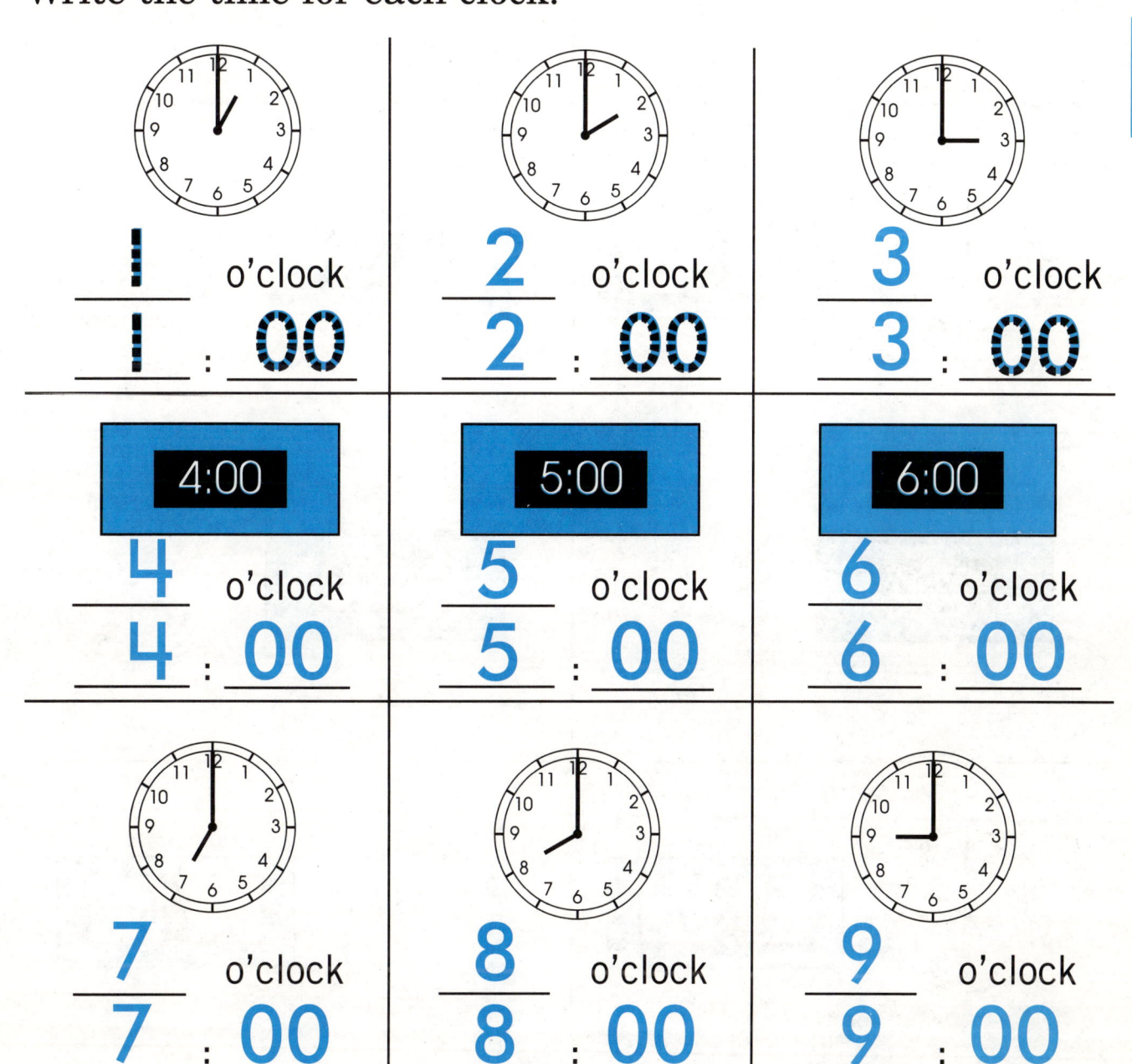

1 o'clock
1 : 00

2 o'clock
2 : 00

3 o'clock
3 : 00

4:00
4 o'clock
4 : 00

5:00
5 o'clock
5 : 00

6:00
6 o'clock
6 : 00

7 o'clock
7 : 00

8 o'clock
8 : 00

9 o'clock
9 : 00

CHAPTER 6

Number Correct
LESSON FOLLOW-UP AND ERROR ANALYSIS
Spectrum Software Measurement 1

20–24: Ask students to ring the hour (closest to the time) they get up and □ the hour (closest to the time) they go to bed.
15–19: Point out that a clock with hands (analog) shows the same time but in a different manner than a digital clock.
Less than 15: Review that the hour is shown by the shorter hand on a clock and by the first number on a digital clock.

Lesson 1 *Time—Hour*

Show this time on this clock.   Show this time on this clock.

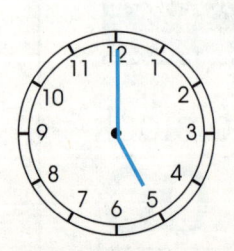

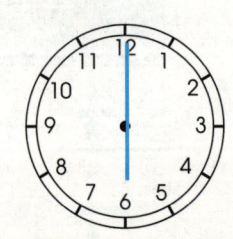

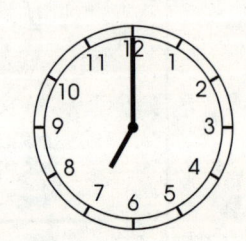

9:00

10:00

12:00

11:00

5:00

6:00

2:00

7:00

CHAPTER 6
Measurement
78

Lesson 1
Time—Hour

Prerequisite Skills: telling time by the hour

Lesson Focus: telling time by the half hour
Possible Score: 24
Time Frame: 10–15 minutes

Lesson 2 Time—Half Hour

1 o'clock
1:00

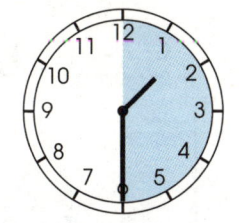

one thirty
1:30

2 o'clock
2:00

Write the time for each clock.

two thirty 2:30	three thirty 3:30	four thirty 4:30
11:30 eleven thirty 11:30	12:30 twelve thirty 12:30	5:30 five thirty 5:30
six thirty 6:30	ten thirty 10:30	eight thirty 8:30

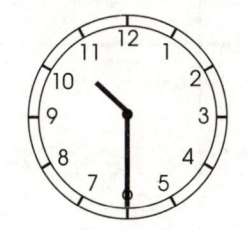

Number Correct

LESSON FOLLOW-UP AND ERROR ANALYSIS

Spectrum Software Measurement 2

20–24: Ask students to ring the time (closest to the time) school starts and ☐ the time (closest to the time) school ends.
15–19: Remind students that the shorter hand always points to the hour and the longer hand points to the half hour.
Less than 15: Point out that when the longer hand points to 6, it is the half hour and is read as "thirty."

Lesson 2 Time—Half Hour

Show this time on this clock. **Show this time on this clock.**

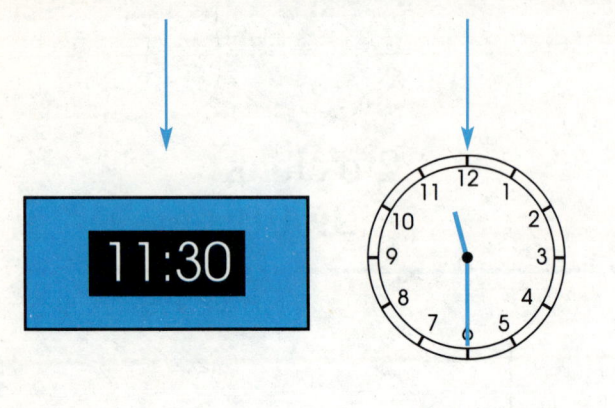

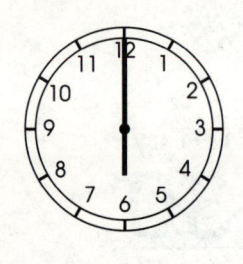

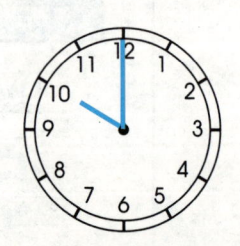

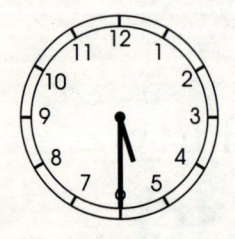

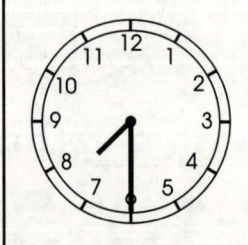

11:30	12:30
6:00	9:30
10:00	10:30
5:30	7:30

CHAPTER 6
Measurement

Prerequisite Skills: number recognition and counting

Lesson Focus: reading a calendar
Possible Score: 19
Time Frame: 15–20 minutes

Lesson 3   Calendar

September						
S	M	T	W	Th	F	S
	1	2	3	4	5	6
7	8	9	10	11	12	13
14	15	16	17	18	19	20
21	22	23	24	25	26	27
28	29	30				

There are 12 months in a year.
September has 30 days.
September 1 is on Monday.
There are 5 Mondays in September.
There are 4 Saturdays in September.

September 19 is on __Friday__.

Complete.

How many days are in a week? __7__

What day comes after Thursday? __Friday__

September 30 is on __Tuesday__.

There are __5__ Tuesdays in September.

Days of the Week

Sunday
Monday
Tuesday
Wednesday
Thursday
Friday
Saturday

October						
S	M	T	W	Th	F	S
			1	2	3	4
5	6	7	8	9	10	11
12	13	14	15	16	17	18
19	20	21	22	23	24	25
26	27	28	29	30	31	

October has __31__ days.

October 1 is on __Wednesday__.

There are __5__ Wednesdays in October.

October 31 is on __Friday__.

There are __4__ Sundays in October.

Number Correct

LESSON FOLLOW-UP AND ERROR ANALYSIS

Spectrum Software Measurement 3

15–19: Have students make a calendar for the current month or the month in which they were born.
11–14: Review the abbreviations for the days of the week used on calendars.
Less than 11: Encourage students to connect the days and the dates on the calendars with their pencils when necessary.

Lesson 3 Calendar

January						
Sun.	Mon.	Tues.	Wed.	Thurs.	Fri.	Sat.
				1	2	3
4	5	6	7	8	9	10
11	12	13	14	15	16	17
18	19	20	21	22	23	24
25	26	27	28	29	30	31

Months of the Year	Number of Days
January	31
February	28
March	31
April	30
May	31
June	30
July	31
August	31
September	30
October	31
November	30
December	31

Complete.

> Thirty days have September,
> April, June, and __November__.
> All the rest have thirty-one,
> Except __February__, which has only 28.

The first month of the year is __January__.

The last month of the year is __December__.

January has __31__ days.

January 3 is on __Saturday__.

In what month is your birthday? __Answers will vary.__

What month is it today? __Answers will vary.__

In what month is Valentine's Day? __February__

CHAPTER 6
Measurement
82

Lesson 3
Calendar

Prerequisite Skills: counting; reading a calendar

Lesson Focus: reading a chart
Possible Score: 30
Time Frame: 15–20 minutes

Lesson 4 Charts

Our Weather Calendar — March

Sun.	Mon.	Tues.	Wed.	Thurs.	Fri.	Sat.
				1 snowy	2 sunny	3 snowy
4 snowy	5 sunny	6 cloudy	7 sunny	8 sunny	9 cloudy	10 sunny
11 sunny	12 sunny	13 sunny	14 cloudy	15 rainy	16 sunny	17 sunny
18 sunny	19 cloudy	20 cloudy	21 stormy	22 sunny	23 cloudy	24 sunny
25 cloudy	26 rainy	27 sunny	28 stormy	29 cloudy	30 cloudy	31 rainy

Legend: sunny, rainy, cloudy, snowy, stormy

Complete.

What was the weather on

March 4? **snowy**   March 10? **sunny**

March 15? **rainy**   March 21? **stormy**

March 30? **cloudy**   March 31? **rainy**

How many days did it rain ☂ ? **4**

How many days did it storm ⚡ ? **2**

How many days did it snow ☃ ? **3**

How many days was it cloudy ☁ ? **8**

How many days was it sunny ☺ ? **14**

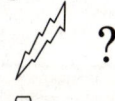

Number Correct
LESSON FOLLOW-UP AND ERROR ANALYSIS
25–30: Ask students to ring the weather symbols that best describe the weather on the day they complete the page.
19–24: Have students cross out each symbol as they count it and write the number on the correct blank.
Less than 19: Point out that the weather calendar has three parts: the day, the date, and the symbol.

Lesson 4   Charts

Make a weather calendar for one week.

Write the numbers to show the dates.

Draw to show the weather.

sunny    cloudy    rainy    snowy 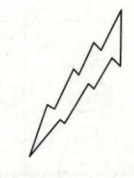   stormy

Sunday	Monday	Tuesday	Wednesday	Thursday	Friday	Saturday

Use your weather calendar.   Answers will vary.

How many days was it

cloudy ? _____   sunny ? _____

snowy ? _____   stormy ? _____

rainy ? _____

Complete.

Write today's date.   _____ _____ , _____
                         Month   Date   Year

What day of the week is it today? _____

When were you born?   _____ _____ , _____
                         Month   Date   Year

CHAPTER 6
Measurement
84

Lesson 4
Charts

Prerequisite Skills: counting

Lesson 5 Bar Graphs

Look at the bar graph.

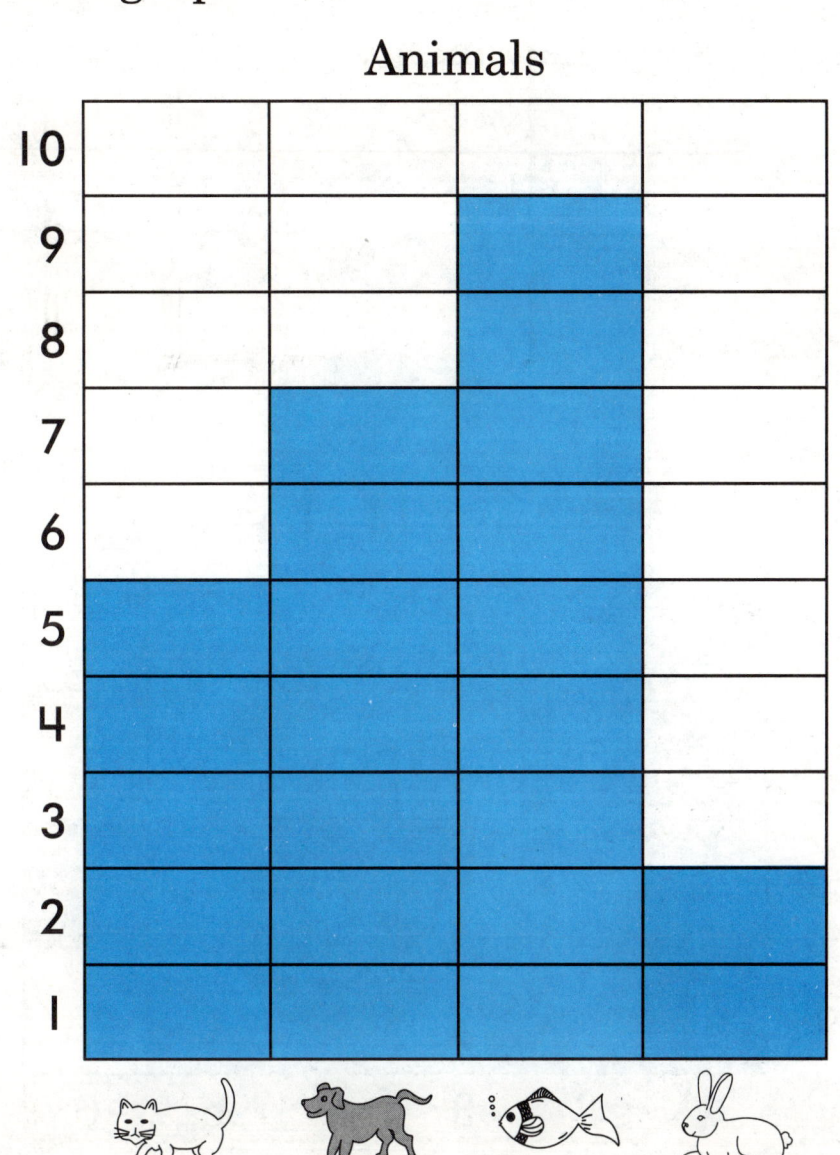

Lesson Focus: reading and making a bar graph
Possible Score: 11
Time Frame: 5–10 minutes

Animals

How many cats? 5

How many fish? 9

How many dogs? 7

How many rabbits? 2

Number Correct
LESSON FOLLOW-UP AND ERROR ANALYSIS
9–11: Have students make their own graph.
7–8: Have students count one square at a time.
Less than 7: Have students count a square and then write the number in the square.

Lesson 5 Bar Graphs

Count each kind.
Color squares to show how many.

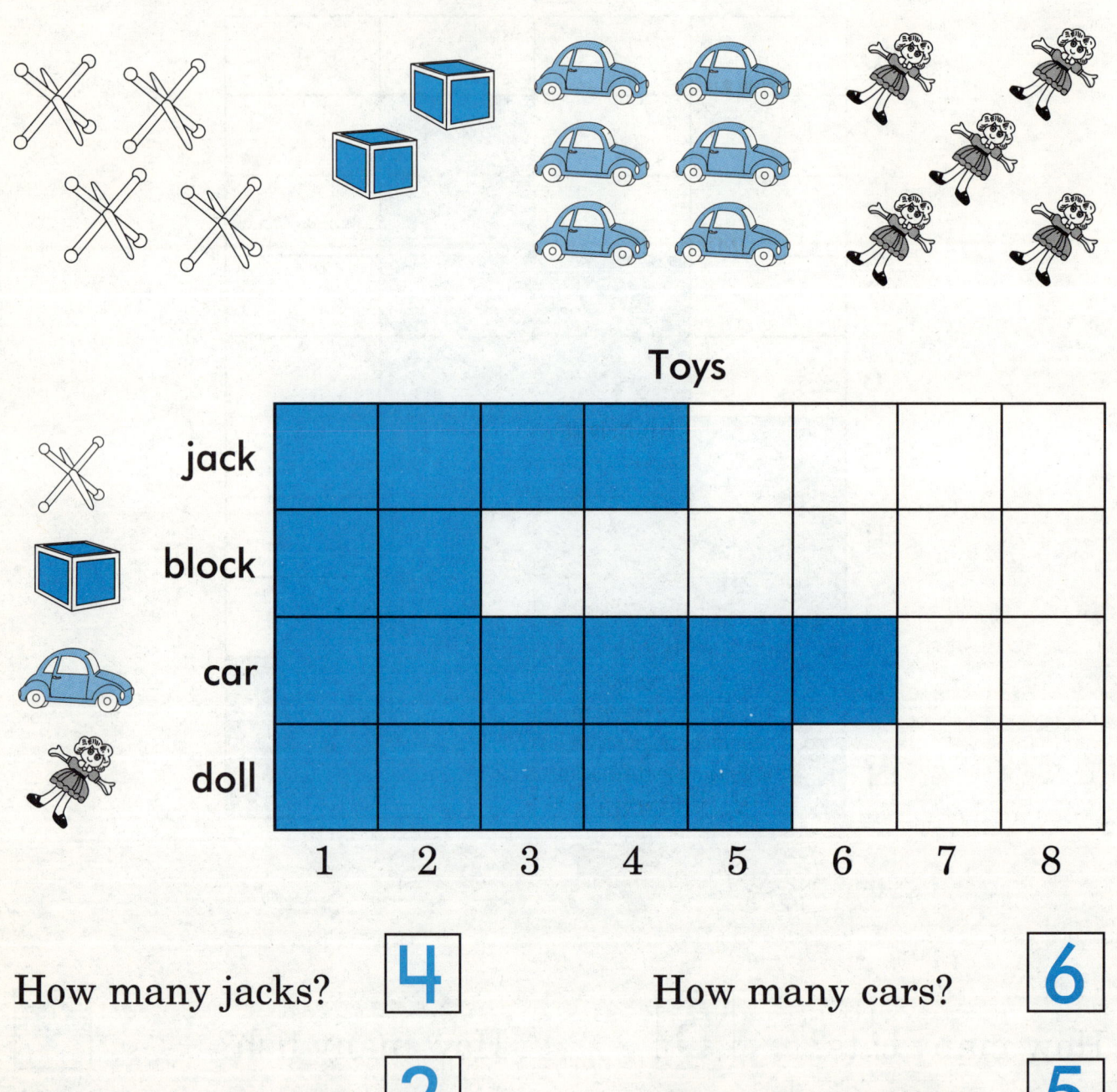

Toys

	jack								
	block								
	car								
	doll								

1 2 3 4 5 6 7 8

How many jacks? 4   How many cars? 6

How many blocks? 2   How many dolls? 5

Prerequisite Skills: counting

Lesson Focus: reading picture graphs
Possible Score: 6
Time Frame: 15–20 minutes

Lesson 6 Picture Graphs

Look at the picture graph.

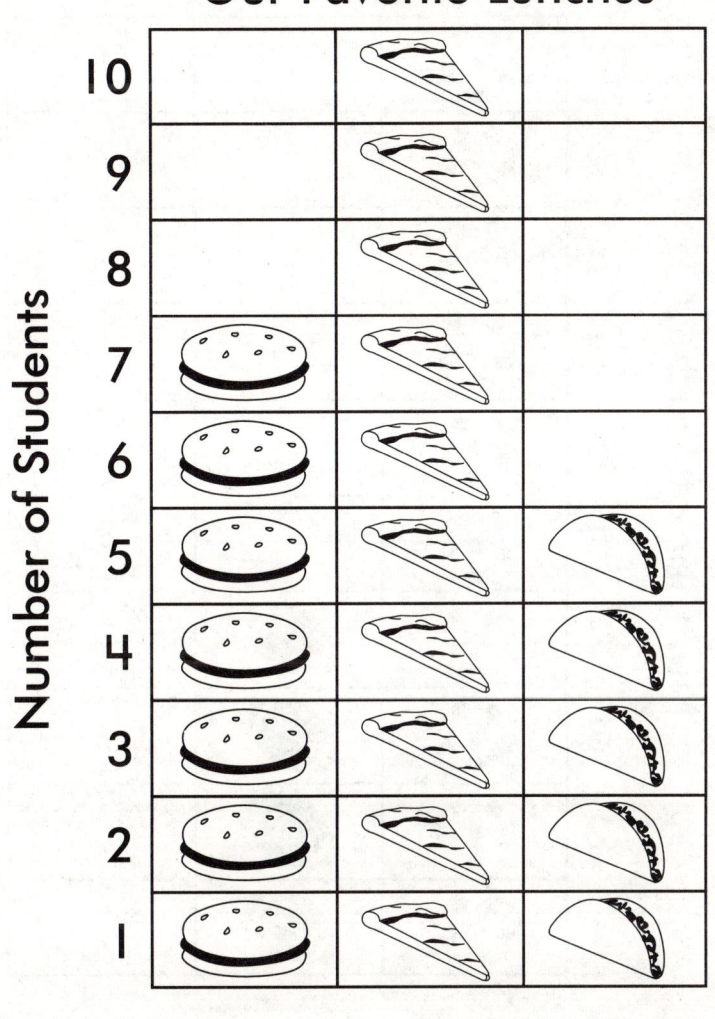

Our Favorite Lunches

(Number of Students: 1–10)

How many students like 🍔ʔ **7**

How many students like 🍕ʔ **10**

How many students like 🌮ʔ **5**

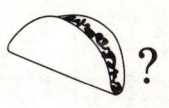

Number Correct

LESSON FOLLOW-UP AND ERROR ANALYSIS

6: Have students make their own graph.
4: Have students write the correct number next to each name on the graph.
Less than 3: Have students draw the correct number of items next to the statements at the top of page and then redraw them on the graph.

87

Lesson 6 Picture Graphs

Look at the picture graph.

Our Favorite Sport

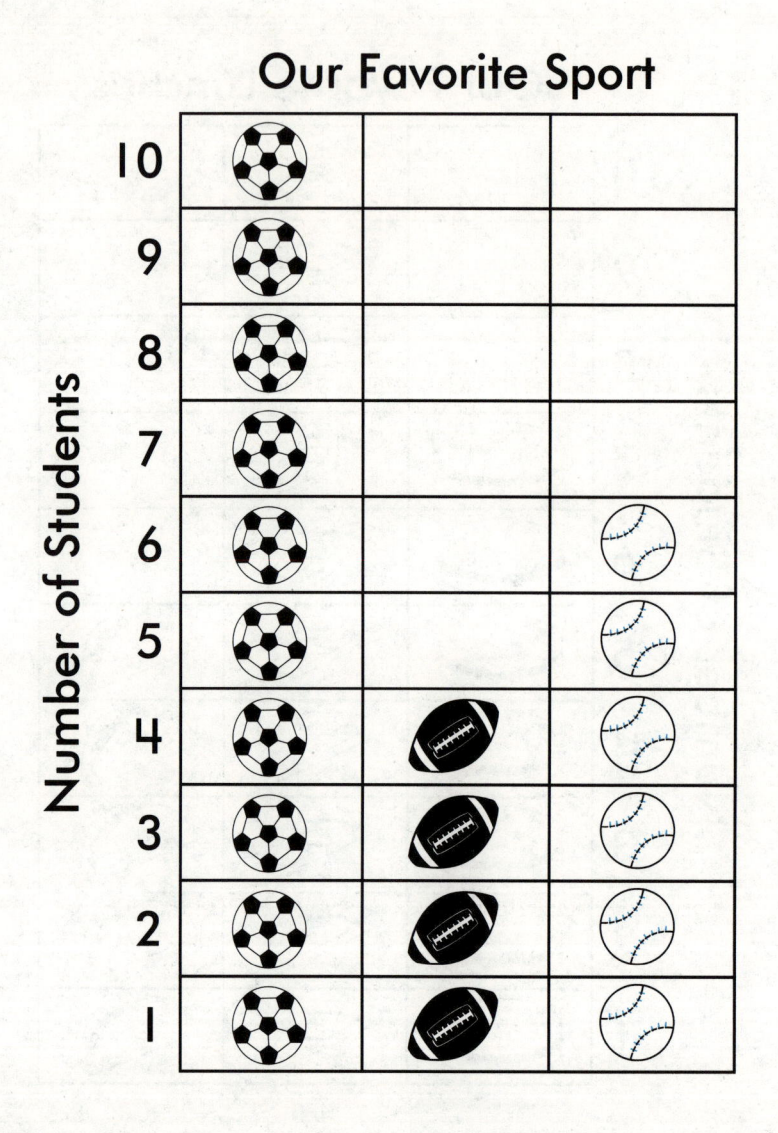

How many students like  ⚽? 10

How many students like 🏈? 4

How many students like ⚾? 6

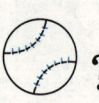

CHAPTER 6
Measurement
88

Lesson 6
Picture Graphs

Prerequisite Skills: counting

Lesson Focus: measuring in centimeters
Possible Score: 12
Time Frame: 10–15 minutes

Lesson 7 Centimeter

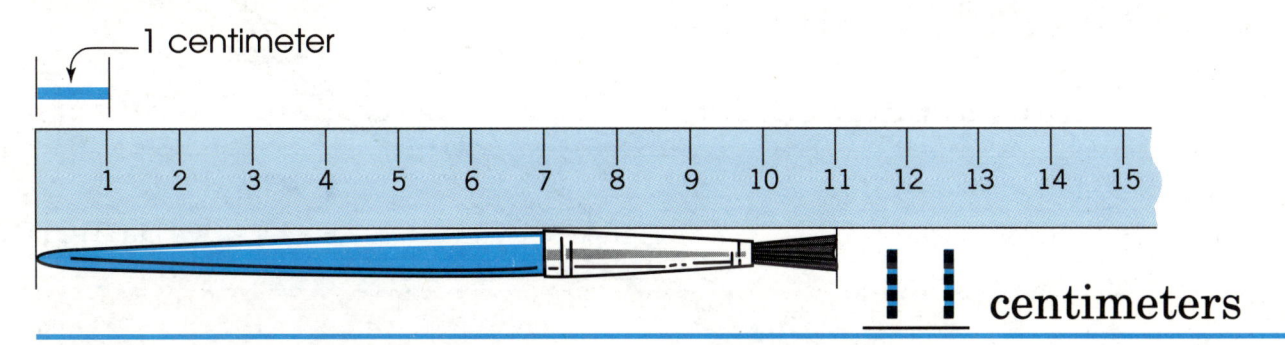

11 centimeters

How long is each object?

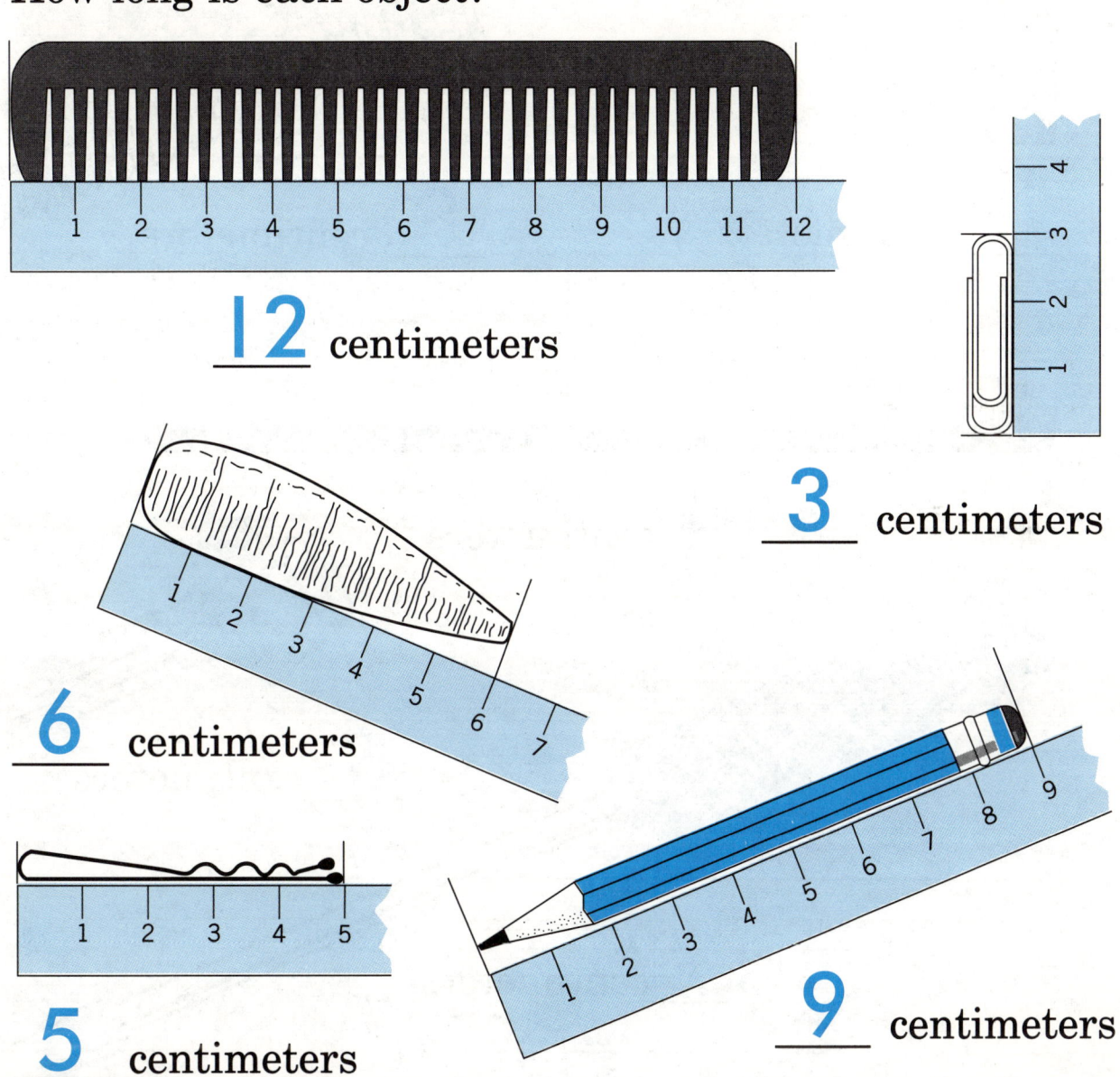

12 centimeters

3 centimeters

6 centimeters

5 centimeters

9 centimeters

Number Correct

LESSON FOLLOW-UP AND ERROR ANALYSIS

Spectrum Software Measurement 4

10–12: Have students use the centimeter ruler to measure at least two other objects and record the measurements.
7–9: Point out that zero is the starting point on the ruler even though it is not marked on the ruler.
Less than 7: Have students count each mark on the ruler until they reach the end of the object.

89

Lesson 7 Centimeter

←Cut off and save this ruler.

How long is each object?

__12__ centimeters

__4__ centimeters

__8__ centimeters

__14__ centimeters

__6__ centimeters

__17__ centimeters

__3__ centimeters

CHAPTER 6
Measurement
90

Lesson 7
Centimeter

Prerequisite Skills: counting

Lesson Focus: measuring in inches
Possible Score: 12
Time Frame: 10–15 minutes

Lesson 8   Inch

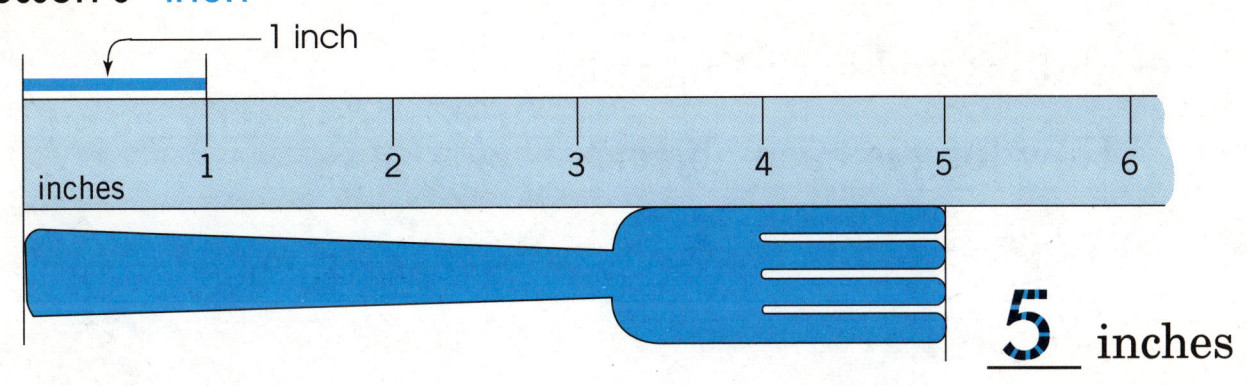

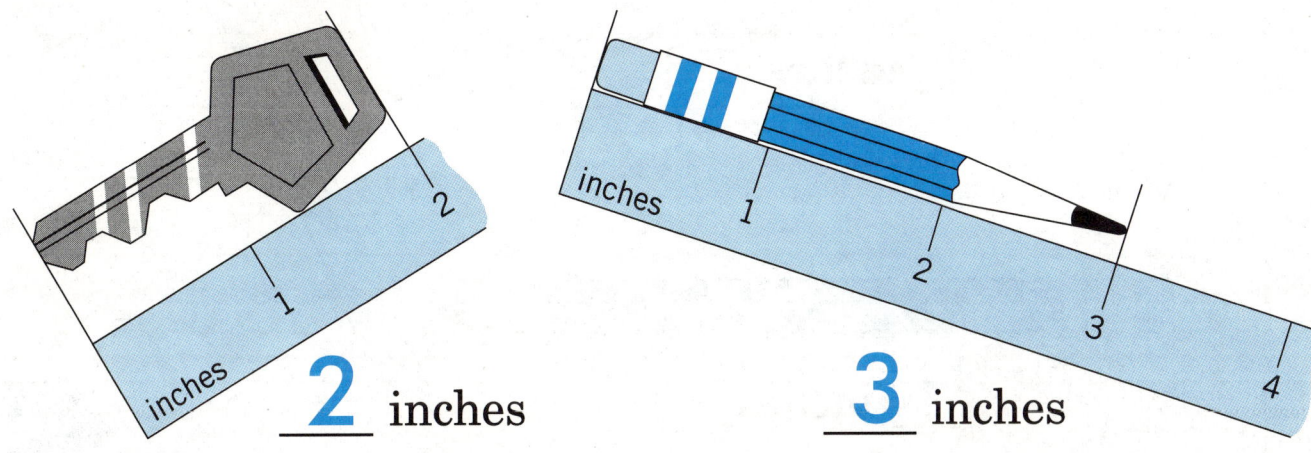

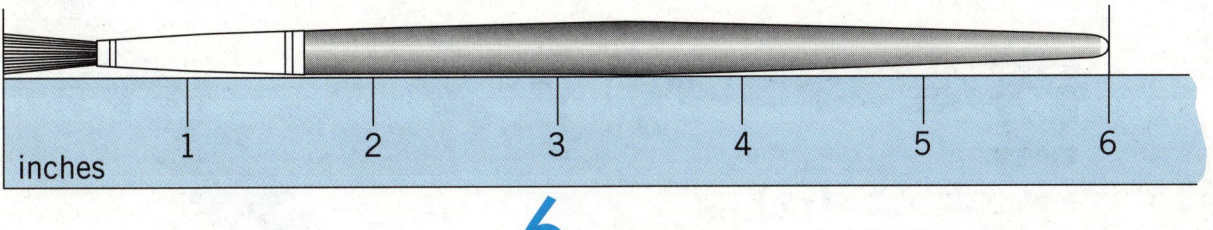

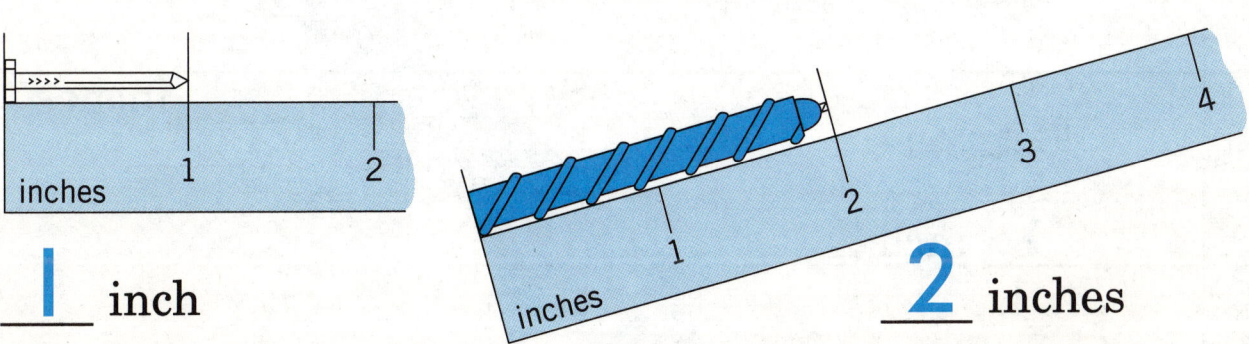

How long is each object?

__5__ inches

__2__ inches

__3__ inches

__6__ inches

__1__ inch

__2__ inches

Number Correct	LESSON FOLLOW-UP AND ERROR ANALYSIS	Spectrum Software Measurement 5
10–12:	Have students ring a measurement on the page and find something else that measures the same length.	
7–9:	Point out that zero is the starting point on the ruler even though it is not marked on the ruler.	
Less than 7:	Have students count each mark on the ruler until they reach the end of the object.	

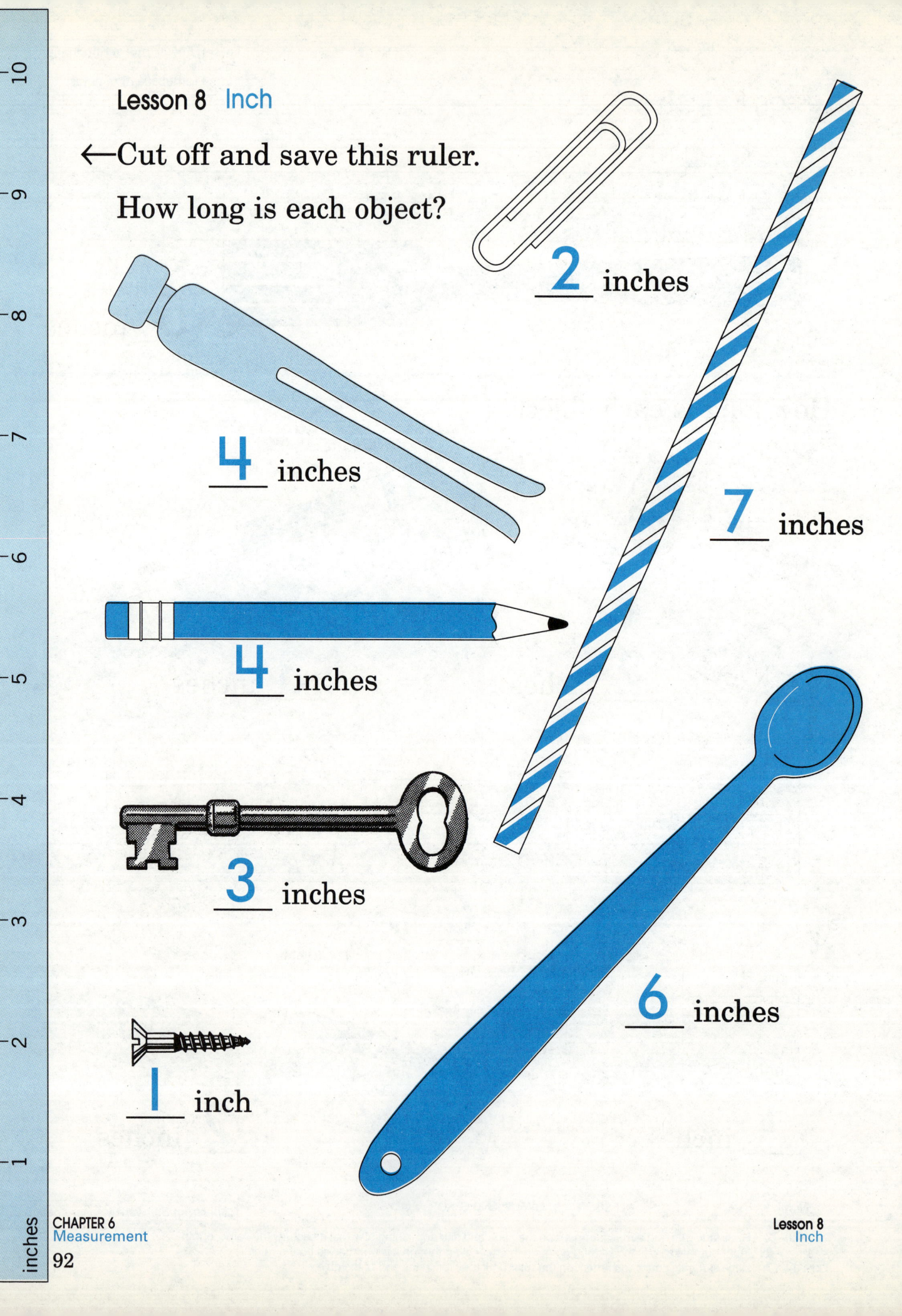

Lesson 8 Inch

←Cut off and save this ruler.

How long is each object?

_2_ inches

_4_ inches

_7_ inches

_4_ inches

_3_ inches

_6_ inches

_1_ inch

CHAPTER 6
Measurement

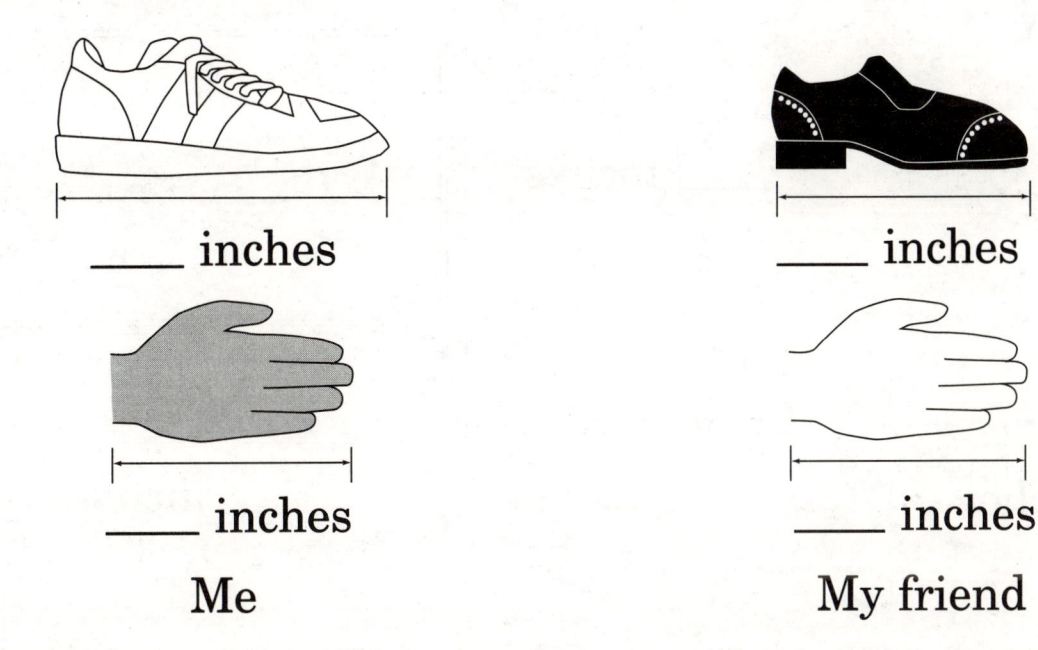

Prerequisite Skills: reading centimeter and inch rulers

Lesson Focus: measuring with rulers
Possible Score: 10
Time Frame: 15–20 minutes

Lesson 9 Measuring

Work with a friend.
Use a centimeter ruler.
Measure each other. **Answers will vary.**

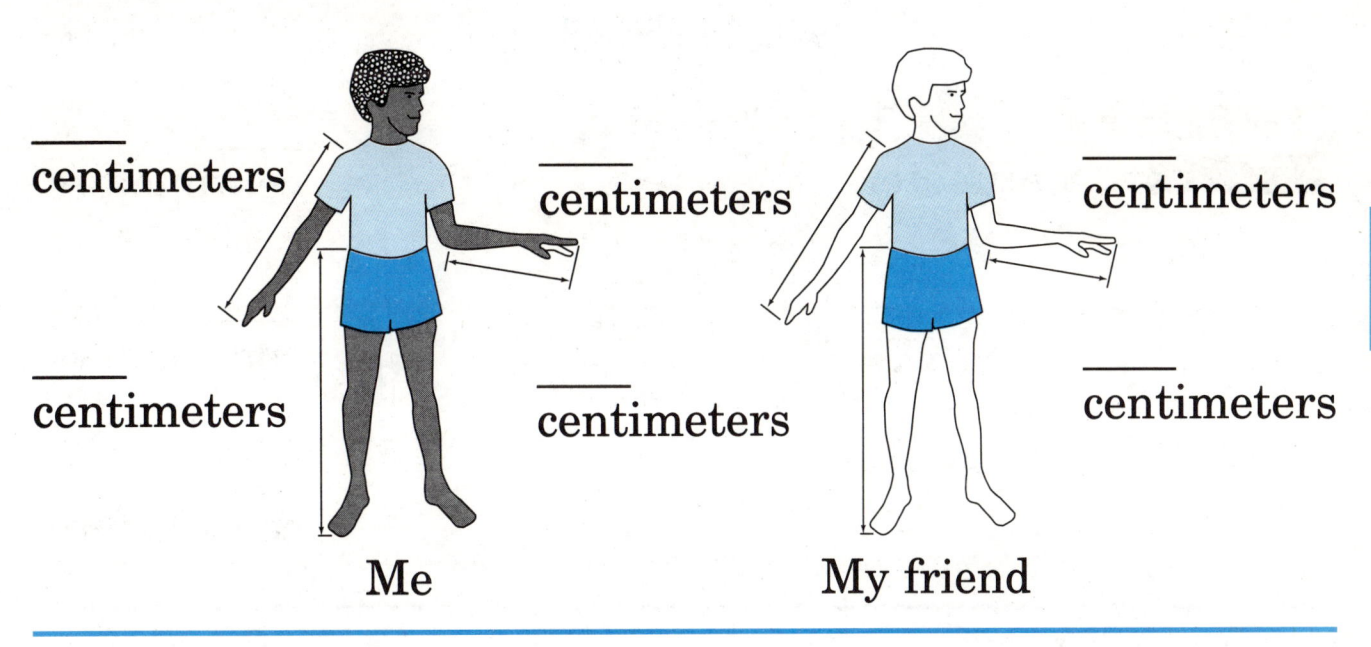

___ centimeters
___ centimeters
___ centimeters
___ centimeters
___ centimeters
___ centimeters

Me

My friend

Use an inch ruler.
Measure each other.

___ inches
___ inches
___ inches
___ inches

Me

My friend

Number Correct
LESSON FOLLOW-UP AND ERROR ANALYSIS
9–10: After students record their measurements, have them compare and decide who wears the longer and shorter shoes.
7–8: Review with students exactly what objects they are to measure with the centimeter ruler and inch ruler.
Less than 7: Remind students to start their measuring at the beginning of the ruler, not with the number 1.

Lesson 9 Measuring

Work with a friend.

Use a centimeter ruler.

Measure these things found in your classroom.

Answers will vary.

____ centimeters

____ centimeters

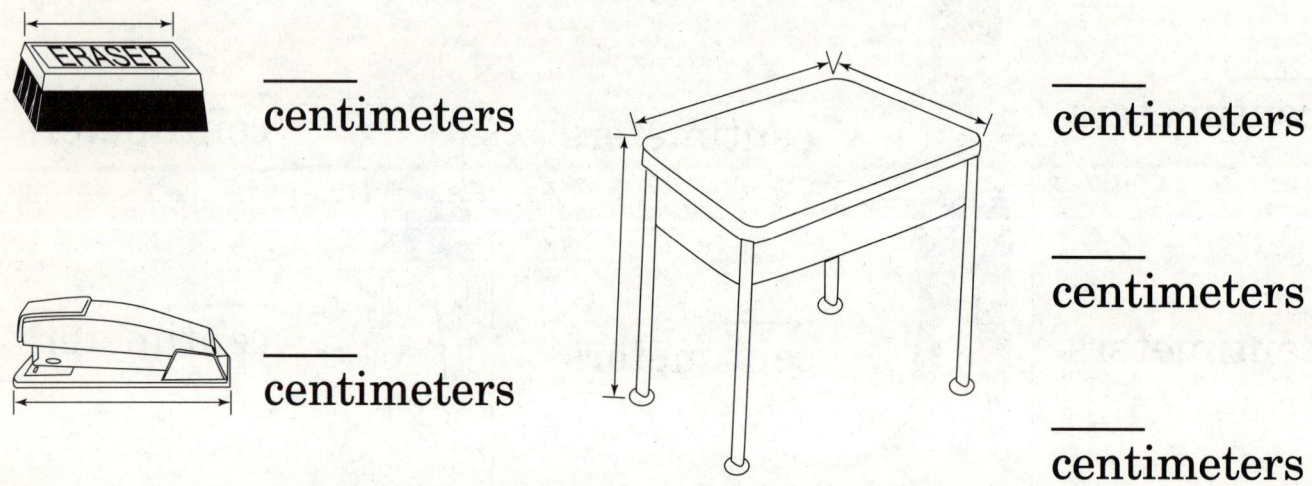

____ centimeters

____ centimeters

____ centimeters

Use an inch ruler.

Measure these things found in your classroom.

____ inches

____ inches

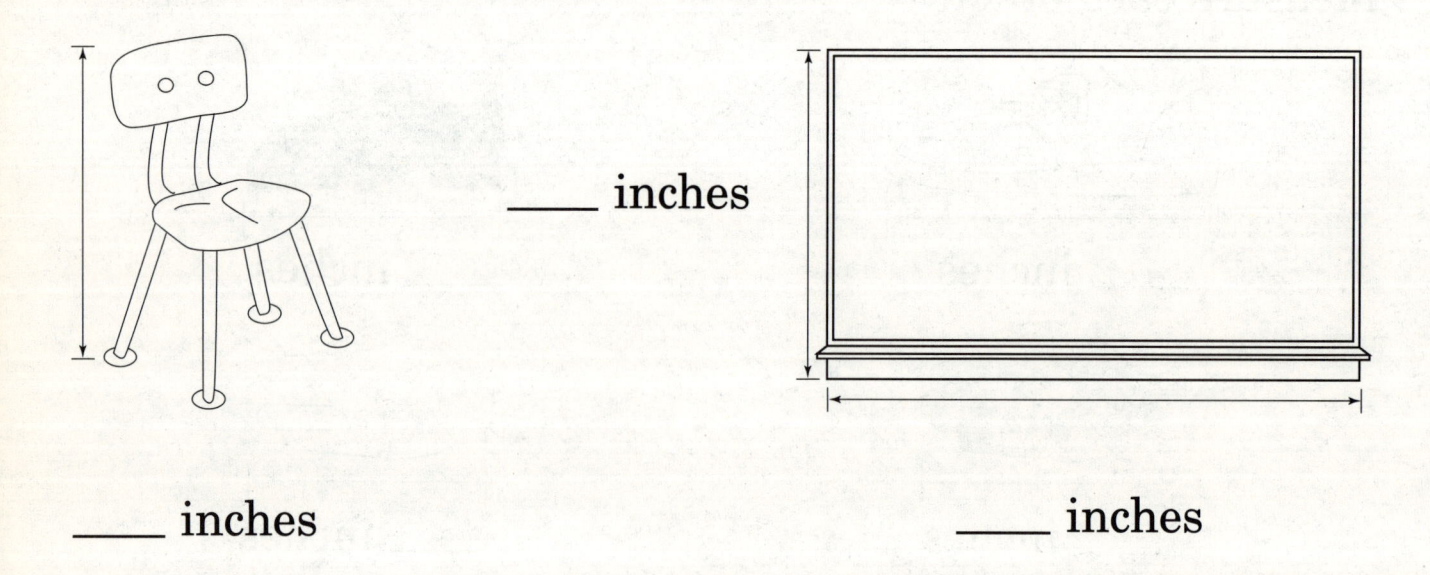

____ inches

CHAPTER 6
Measurement

94

Lesson 9
Measuring

For further evaluation, use the Chapter Test on page 170.
For maintaining skills, use the Cumulative Review on page 158.

Possible Score: 8
Time Frame: 10 minutes

CHAPTER 6 PRACTICE TEST
Measurement

Write the time for each clock.

7:30

__seven__thirty

5 : 30

1 : 30

Use a centimeter ruler.

How long is each object?

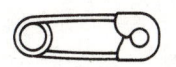

__2__ centimeters

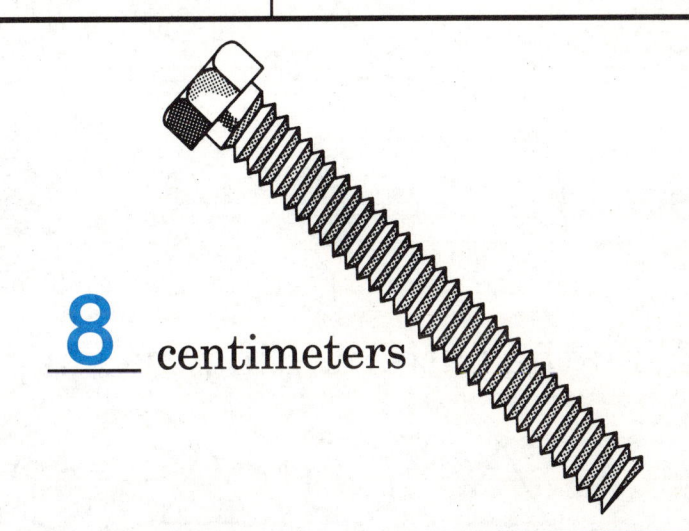

__8__ centimeters

Use an inch ruler.

How long is each object?

__4__ inches

__1__ inch

__2__ inches

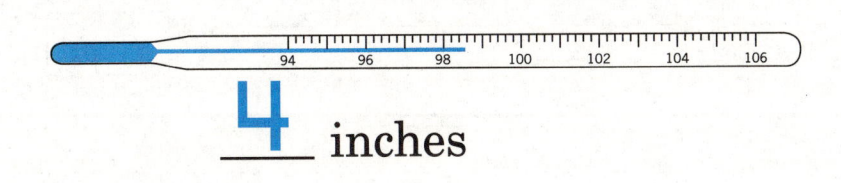

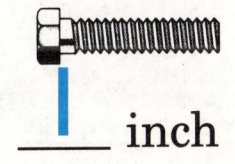

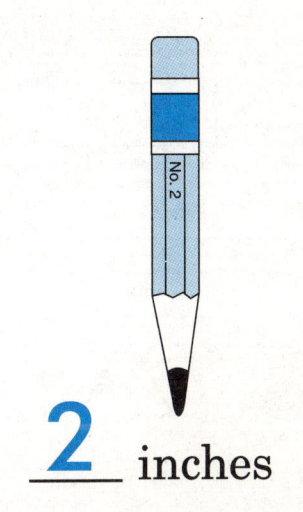

Number Correct	LESSON FOLLOW-UP AND ERROR ANALYSIS	Spectrum Software Measurement 1–5
7–8:	Have students ring the longest object they measured on the page and □ the shortest object.	
5–6:	Remind students that objects are measured from the beginning of a ruler, not the 1.	
Less than 5:	Determine whether students are having trouble understanding time or length and review the concepts.	

Math Intervention: Reading a Graph, Gold Book, pages 65–72.
Real World Problem Solving practice: Gold Book, pages 75–76.

CHAPTER 7 PRETEST
Geometry

Ring the shape.

square

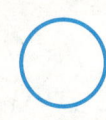

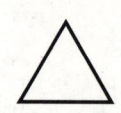

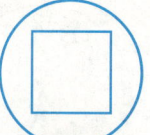

cube

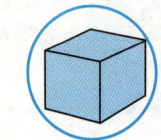

circle

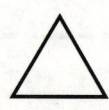

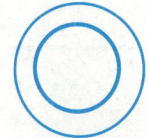

sphere

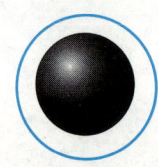

Find the pattern. Ring the shape that comes next.

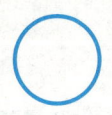

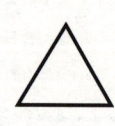

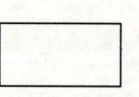

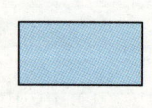

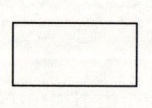

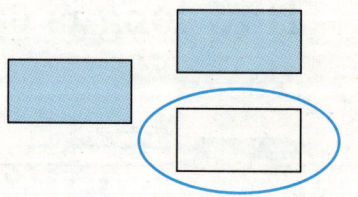

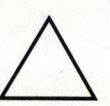

CHAPTER 7
Geometry
96

CHAPTER 7 PRETEST

Prerequisite Skills: color recognition

Lesson Focus: identifying plane figures
Possible Score: 11
Time Frame: 10–15 minutes

Lesson 1 Plane Figures

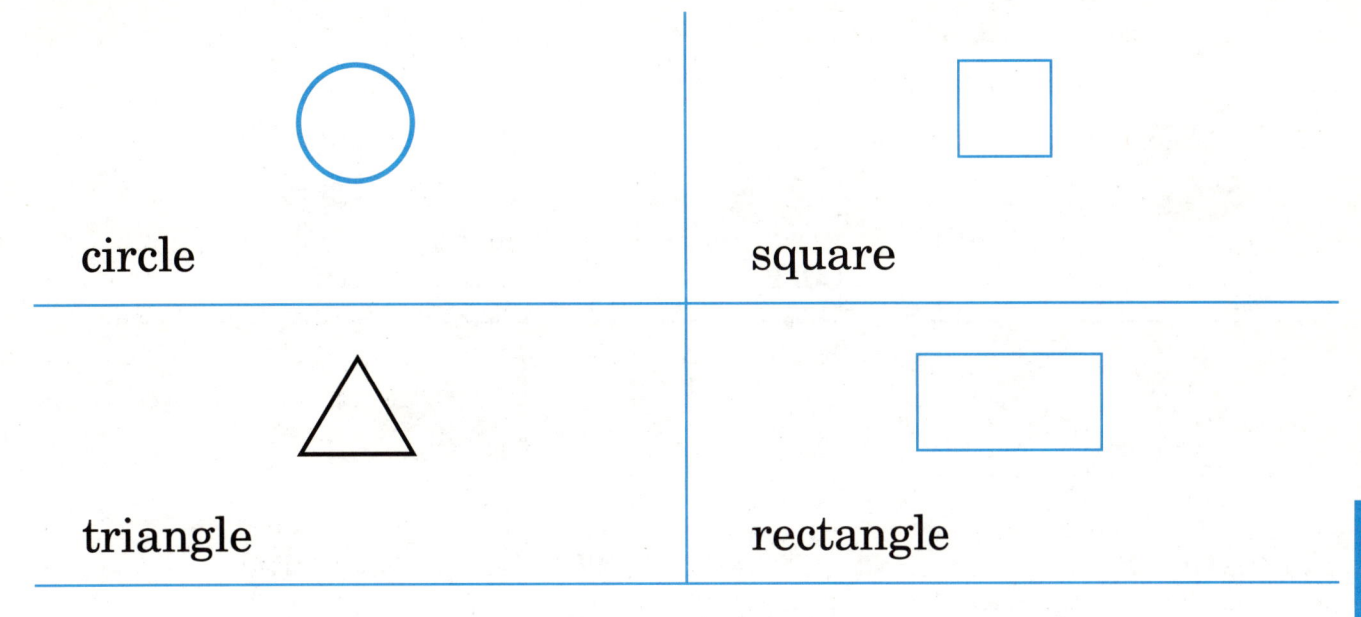

circle

square

triangle

rectangle

Color all circles blue. Color all squares red. Color all triangles green. Color all rectangles yellow.

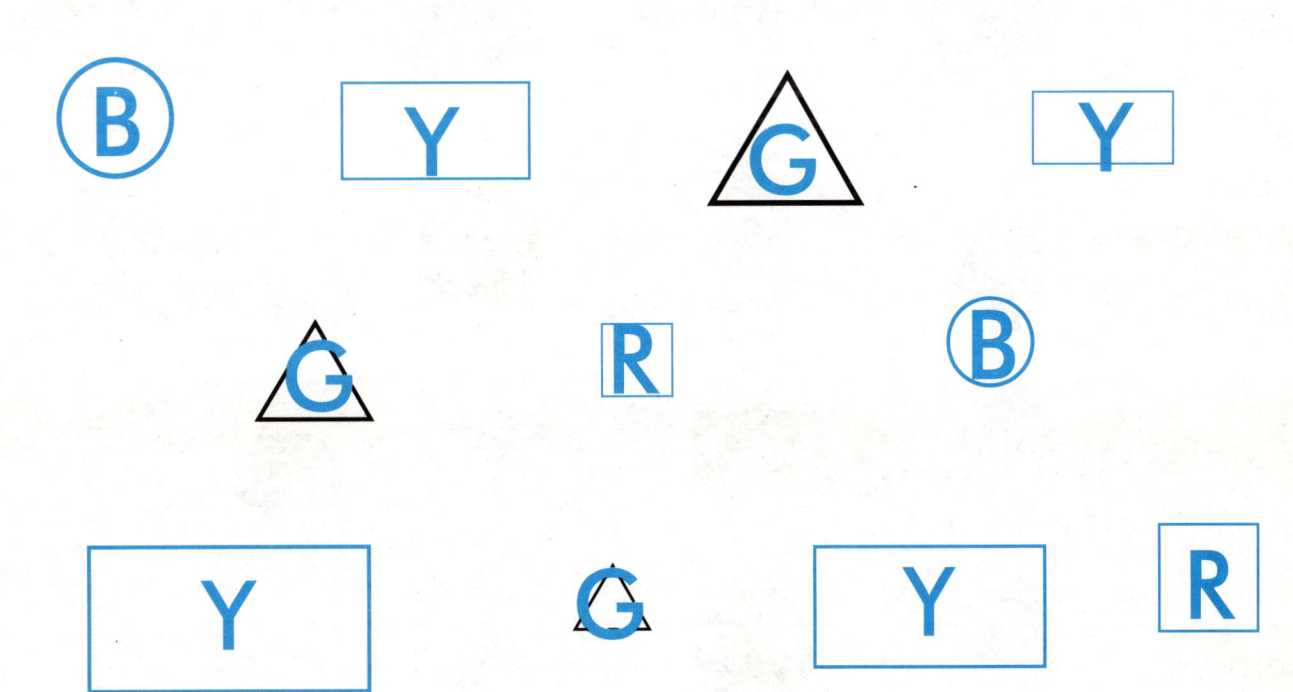

Ⓑ ▢Y △G ▭Y

　　△G ▢R Ⓑ

▭Y △G ▭Y ▢R

Number Correct

LESSON FOLLOW-UP AND ERROR ANALYSIS

8–11: Have students draw their own circle, square, triangle, and rectangle.
7–8: Have students write the name of the figure inside of it before coloring it.
Less than 7: Have students cut out one of each of the figures and compare the cutout figures to the ones on the page.

Prerequisite Skills: plane figure recognition

Lesson Focus: identifying plane figures
Possible Score: 21
Time Frame: 15–20 minutes

Lesson 2 Solid Figures

sphere

cone

cube

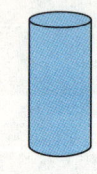

cylinder

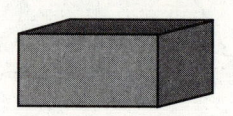

rectangular solid

Ring the shape.

sphere

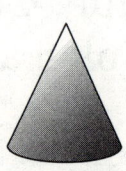

cylinder

rectangular solid

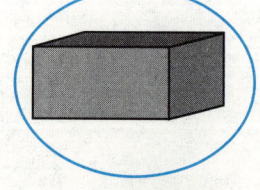

cone

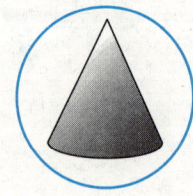

Number Correct	LESSON FOLLOW-UP AND ERROR ANALYSIS
17–21:	Have students draw one of each of the five figures on their own.
12–16:	Have students write the name of the figure inside of it before coloring it.
Less than 12:	Have students cut out a copy of each figure and use the cutout figures to identify the ones on the page.

98

Lesson 2 Solid Figures

Color all cubes blue. Color all cones red. Color all spheres green. Color all rectangular solids yellow. Color all cylinders purple.

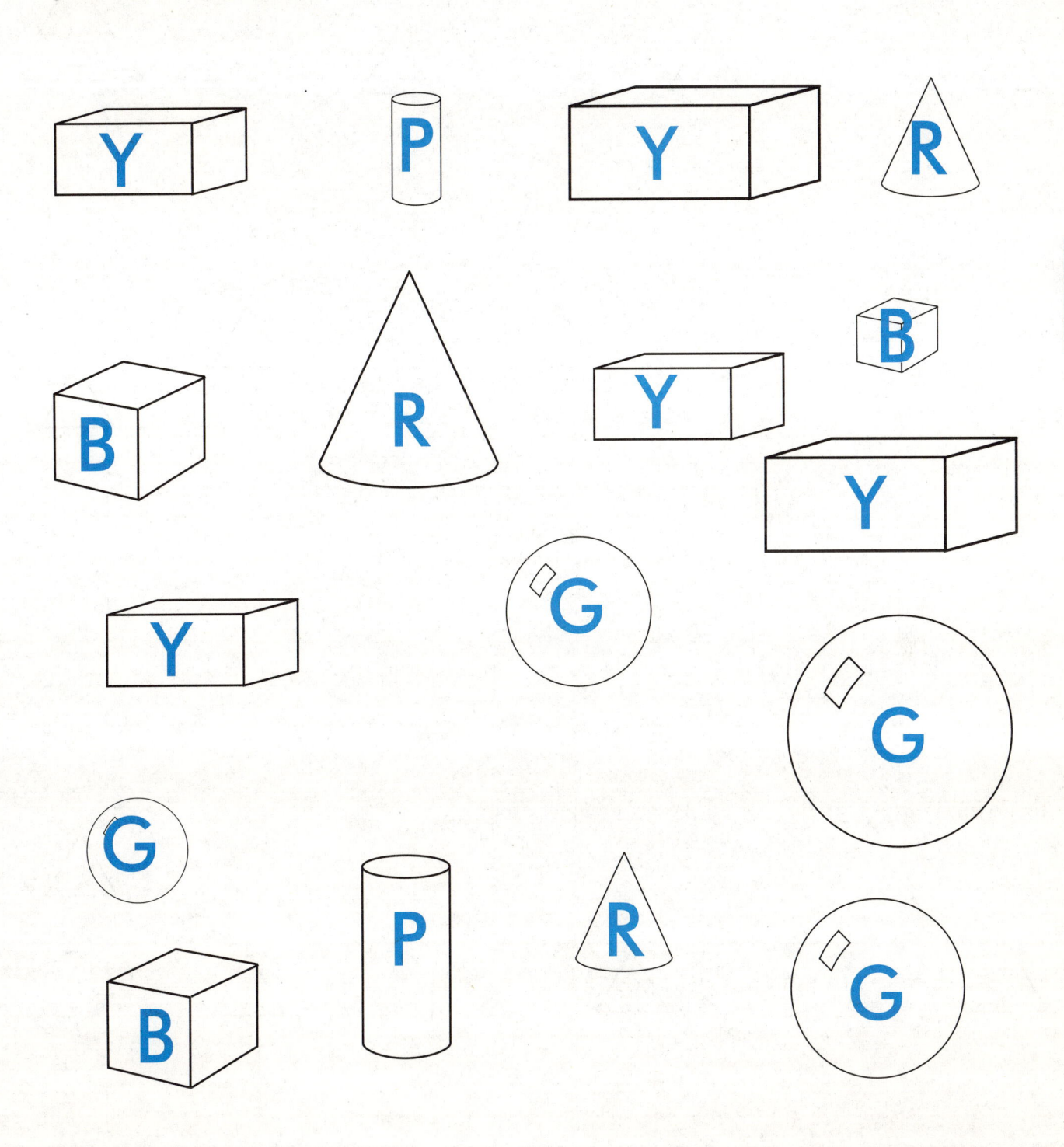

CHAPTER 7
Geometry

Lesson 2
Solid Figures

99

Prerequisite Skills: pattern recognition

Lesson Focus: pattern recognition
Possible Score: 4
Time Frame: 5–10 minutes

Lesson 3 Geometric Patterns

Find the pattern. Ring the shape that comes next.

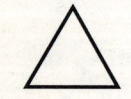

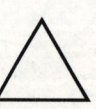

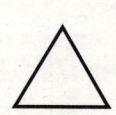

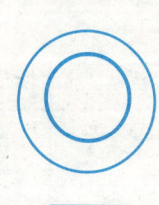

LESSON FOLLOW-UP AND ERROR ANALYSIS

Number Correct
- **4:** Have students make up their own pattern.
- **3:** Have students write out the pattern in words.
- **Less than 3:** Have students draw figures to continue the pattern.

100

Prerequisite Skills: pattern recognition

Lesson Focus: pattern recognition
Possible Score: 4
Time Frame: 5–10 minutes

Lesson 4 Geometric Patterns

Find the pattern. Ring the shape that comes next.

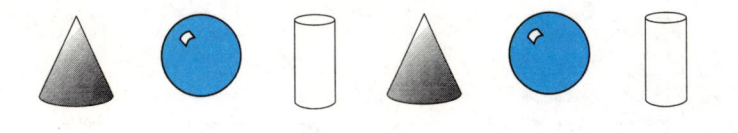

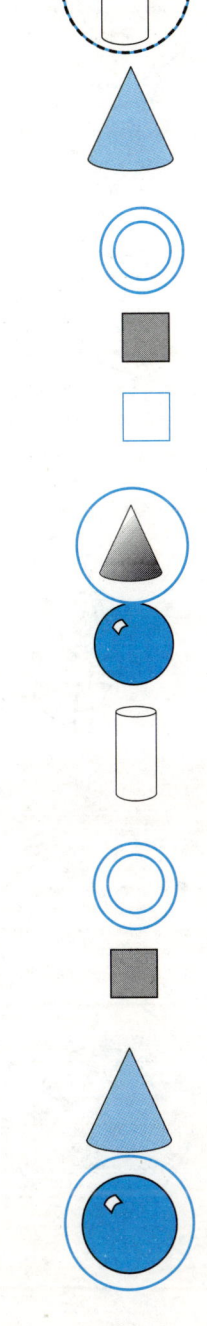

LESSON FOLLOW-UP AND ERROR ANALYSIS

Number Correct
- **4:** Have students make up their own pattern.
- **3:** Have students write out the pattern in words.
- **Less than 2:** Have students draw figures to continue the pattern.

101

Prerequisite Skills: recognizing congruent shapes

Lesson Focus: line symmetry
Possible Score: 7
Time Frame: 5–10 minutes

Lesson 5 Symmetry

Ring the pictures that match when folded on the line.

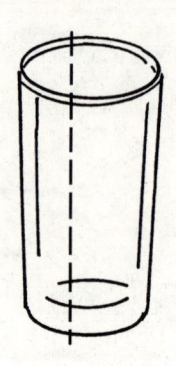

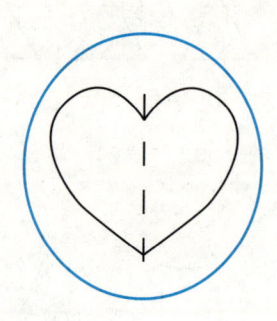

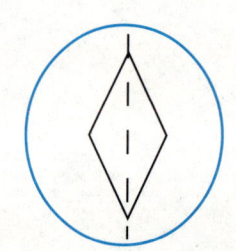

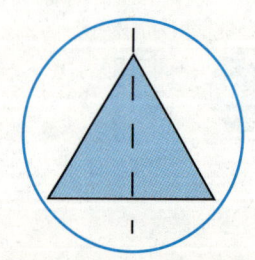

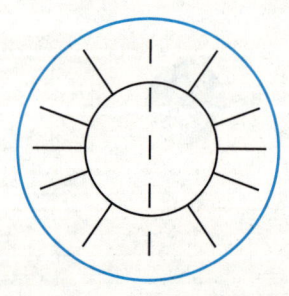

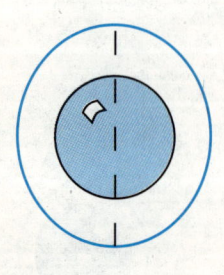

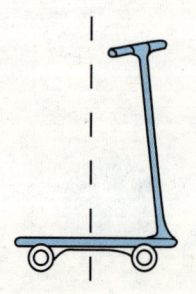

LESSON FOLLOW-UP AND ERROR ANALYSIS

Number Correct

7: Have students draw shapes of their own that have line symmetry.
6: Have students rework the problems they missed and tell why they missed each problem.
Less than 5: Have students cut out each shape and fold it along the line to determine if the shapes match.

For further evaluation, copy the Chapter Test on page 171.
For maintaining skills, use the Cumulative Review on page 159.

Possible Score: 6
Time Frame: 5–10 minutes

CHAPTER 7 PRACTICE TEST
Geometry

Ring the shape.

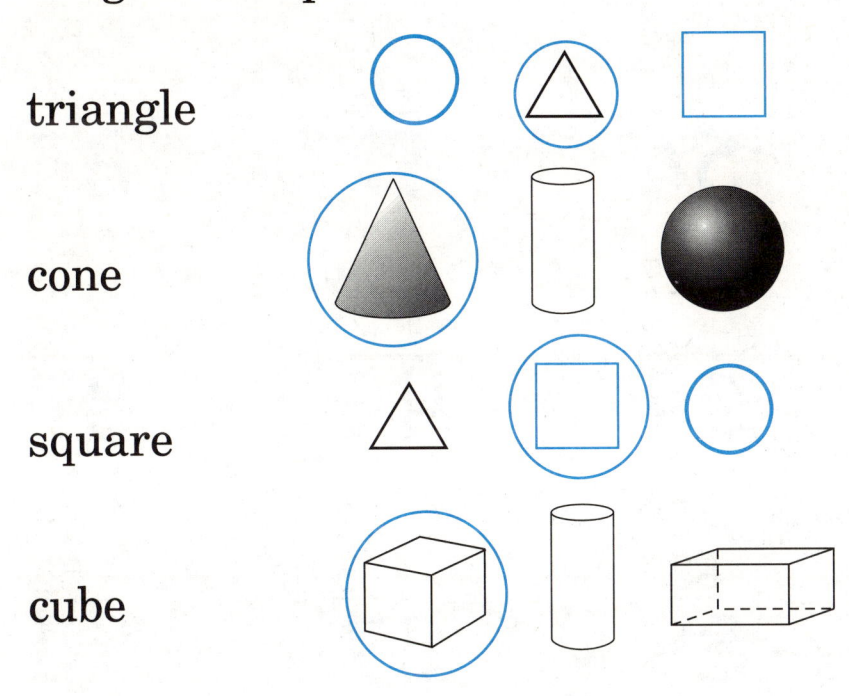

triangle

cone

square

cube

Ring the pictures that match when folded on the line.

Number Correct — LESSON FOLLOW-UP AND ERROR ANALYSIS
- **6:** Have students draw shapes that have lines of symmetry.
- **4–5:** Have students draw an example of each type of plane and solid figure and compare those to the shapes.
- **Less than 4:** Have students rework the problems they missed.

Math Intervention: 2-digit Addition, Gold Book, pages 77–84.
Real World Problem Solving practice: Gold Book, pages 85–86.

CHAPTER 8 PRETEST
Addition and Subtraction (2-digit with no renaming)

Add.

50 +30 **80**	26 + 3 **29**	44 +12 **56**	13 +54 **67**	60 +25 **85**
24 +62 **86**	41 +37 **78**	27 +32 **59**	38 +10 **48**	42 +45 **87**
78 +20 **98**	42 +33 **75**	52 +32 **84**	62 +25 **87**	46 +52 **98**

Subtract.

60 −30 **30**	38 − 4 **34**	37 −10 **27**	26 −12 **14**	47 −31 **16**
28 − 6 **22**	56 −35 **21**	68 −33 **35**	29 −12 **17**	58 −21 **37**
67 −20 **47**	73 −21 **52**	48 −24 **24**	39 −15 **24**	95 −62 **33**

CHAPTER 8
Addition and Subtraction (2-digit with no renaming)

Prerequisite Skills: adding and subtracting through 10

Lesson Focus: adding and subtracting
Possible Score: 66
Time Frame: 15–20 minutes

Lesson 1 Addition and Subtraction Facts

Add.

5	7	3	2	6	3
+2	+1	+7	+2	+3	+2
7	8	10	4	9	5

1	3	1	2	3	5
+8	+1	+1	+8	+4	+4
9	4	2	10	7	9

2	5	9	2	4	10
+1	+5	+1	+6	+4	+0
3	10	10	8	8	10

Subtract.

8	9	6	7	4	10
−1	−9	−3	−0	−2	−3
7	0	3	7	2	7

10	9	7	10	5	9
−9	−6	−6	−8	−4	−2
1	3	1	2	1	7

5	8	10	6	9	7
−3	−5	−6	−4	−8	−4
2	3	4	2	1	3

CHAPTER 8

Number Correct

LESSON FOLLOW-UP AND ERROR ANALYSIS

Spectrum Software Addition 4–5; Subtraction 4–5

56–66: Have students color the remainder of page 106 with a color of their choice.
43–55: If students have not performed the correct operations on page 106, have them rework each incorrect answer.
Less than 43: Have students use manipulatives to rework each incorrect answer.

105

Lesson 1 Addition and Subtraction Facts

Add or subtract. If you get 5, color that part green. Check students' work before they color.

$\begin{array}{r}10\\-4\\\hline 6\end{array}$

$\begin{array}{r}4\\+1\\\hline 5\end{array}$

$\begin{array}{r}4\\+2\\\hline 6\end{array}$

$\begin{array}{r}9\\-3\\\hline 6\end{array}$ $\begin{array}{r}5\\+5\\\hline 10\end{array}$ $\begin{array}{r}6\\-0\\\hline 6\end{array}$ $4 + 4 = \underline{\ 8\ }$

$\begin{array}{r}8\\-4\\\hline 4\end{array}$

$\begin{array}{r}3\\+5\\\hline 8\end{array}$ $7 - 3 = \underline{\ 4\ }$ $\begin{array}{r}8\\-3\\\hline 5\end{array}$

$\begin{array}{r}9\\-4\\\hline 5\end{array}$ $\begin{array}{r}2\\+7\\\hline 9\end{array}$ $\begin{array}{r}1\\+4\\\hline 5\end{array}$ $\begin{array}{r}5\\-0\\\hline 5\end{array}$ $\begin{array}{r}3\\+2\\\hline 5\end{array}$ $\begin{array}{r}3\\+3\\\hline 6\end{array}$

$\begin{array}{r}10\\-5\\\hline 5\end{array}$ $\begin{array}{r}5\\+0\\\hline 5\end{array}$

$\begin{array}{r}8\\-3\\\hline 5\end{array}$ $\begin{array}{r}6\\-1\\\hline 5\end{array}$

$\begin{array}{r}2\\+3\\\hline 5\end{array}$

$\begin{array}{r}0\\+5\\\hline 5\end{array}$ $\begin{array}{r}7\\-2\\\hline 5\end{array}$ $\begin{array}{r}9\\-4\\\hline 5\end{array}$ $\begin{array}{r}4\\+6\\\hline 10\end{array}$

$\begin{array}{r}6\\+1\\\hline 7\end{array}$ $\begin{array}{r}4\\+5\\\hline 9\end{array}$ $\begin{array}{r}8\\-6\\\hline 2\end{array}$

$9 - 7 = \underline{\ 2\ }$

CHAPTER 8
Addition and Subtraction (2-digit with no renaming)

Prerequisite Skills: adding and subtracting through 9; understanding of "tens"

Lesson Focus: adding and subtracting tens
Possible Score: 31
Time Frame: 10–15 minutes

Lesson 2 Adding and Subtracting Tens

```
  2 tens        2 0        8 tens        8 0
+ 6 tens      + 6 0      – 6 tens      – 6 0
  8 tens        8 0        2 tens         20
```

Add.   **Subtract.**

```
  4 tens        4 0        9 tens        9 0
+ 5 tens      + 5 0      – 5 tens      – 5 0
  9 tens        90         4 tens         40

  1 ten         1 0        6 tens        6 0
+ 5 tens      + 5 0      – 5 tens      – 5 0
  6 tens        60         1 ten          10
```

```
  30    80    60      50    60    90
 +40   +10   +30     –40   –20   –30
  70    90    90      10    40    60

  20    40    10      20    90    30
 +30   +40   +70     –10   –70   –20
  50    80    80      10    20    10

  50    60    30      80    70    90
 +20   +10   +30     –30   –40   –60
  70    70    60      50    30    30
```

Number Correct

LESSON FOLLOW-UP AND ERROR ANALYSIS

Spectrum Software Addition 6; Subtraction 6

27–31: Have students choose one problem on page 108 and write their own problem it would solve.
20–26: Encourage students to use manipulatives when adding/subtracting the tens column.
Less than 20: Remind students that *more* means "add" and *use, spent,* and *left,* can mean "subtract."

107

Lesson 2 Problem Solving

Solve each problem.

There are 90 ⬭.
40 are used.
How many are not used?

$$\begin{array}{r} 90 \\ -40 \\ \hline 50 \end{array}$$

You have 20 ✏️.
You buy 30 more.
Now how many do you have?

$$\begin{array}{r} 20 \\ +30 \\ \hline 50 \end{array}$$

Gina had 60 ¢.
She spent 40 ¢.
How many ¢ does she have left?

$$\begin{array}{r} 60 \\ -40 \\ \hline 20 \end{array}$$

Zach found 10.
Then he found 20 more.
Now how many does he have?

$$\begin{array}{r} 10 \\ +20 \\ \hline 30 \end{array}$$

There were 80.
60 ran away.
Then how many were left?

$$\begin{array}{r} 80 \\ -60 \\ \hline 20 \end{array}$$

CHAPTER 8
Addition and Subtraction (2-digit with no renaming)

Lesson 2
Adding and Subtracting Tens

Prerequisite Skills: adding through sums of 9; understanding of "tens" and "ones"

Lesson Focus: adding 2-digit numbers
Possible Score: 24
Time Frame: 10–15 minutes

Lesson 3   Addition (2-digit)

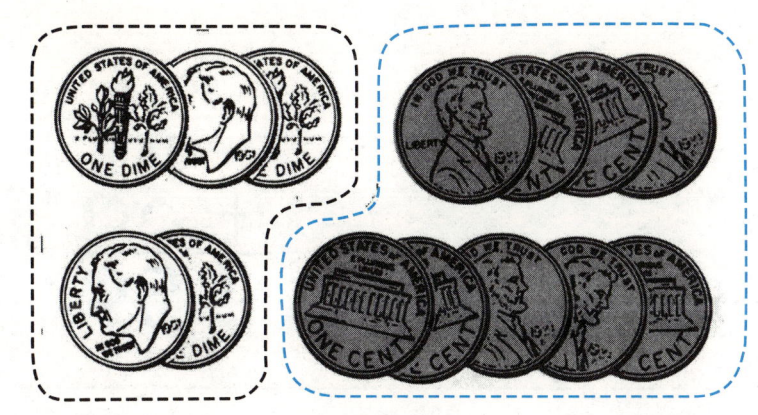

Join the pennies.
Add the ones.

Join the dimes.
Add the tens.

$$\begin{array}{r}34\\+25\\\hline 9\end{array} \Rightarrow \begin{array}{r}34\\+25\\\hline 59\end{array}$$

Add.

$$\begin{array}{r}47\\+2\\\hline 49\end{array}$$ ← Add the ones. / Add the tens.

$$\begin{array}{r}52\\+44\\\hline 96\end{array} \quad \begin{array}{r}84\\+10\\\hline 94\end{array} \quad \begin{array}{r}26\\+13\\\hline 39\end{array}$$

$$\begin{array}{r}11\\+14\\\hline 25\end{array} \quad \begin{array}{r}31\\+12\\\hline 43\end{array} \quad \begin{array}{r}12\\+1\\\hline 13\end{array} \quad \begin{array}{r}78\\+11\\\hline 89\end{array} \quad \begin{array}{r}43\\+10\\\hline 53\end{array}$$

$$\begin{array}{r}50\\+18\\\hline 68\end{array} \quad \begin{array}{r}18\\+50\\\hline 68\end{array} \quad \begin{array}{r}81\\+5\\\hline 86\end{array} \quad \begin{array}{r}75\\+23\\\hline 98\end{array} \quad \begin{array}{r}54\\+42\\\hline 96\end{array}$$

$$\begin{array}{r}43\\+16\\\hline 59\end{array} \quad \begin{array}{r}22\\+26\\\hline 48\end{array} \quad \begin{array}{r}43\\+2\\\hline 45\end{array} \quad \begin{array}{r}33\\+54\\\hline 87\end{array} \quad \begin{array}{r}31\\+26\\\hline 57\end{array}$$

Number Correct

LESSON FOLLOW-UP AND ERROR ANALYSIS

Spectrum Software Addition 7

20–24: To reinforce place value, have students ring the greatest number on the page and □ the least number.
16–19: Discuss how the ones column is like adding pennies and the tens column is like adding dimes.
Less than 16: Using manipulatives, have students practice joining sets of ones and sets of tens.

CHAPTER 8

Lesson 3 Problem Solving

Solve each problem.

There are 24 🌳.

35 more are planted.

Now how many are there?

$$\begin{array}{r}24\\+35\\\hline 59\end{array}$$

Al had 27 🏴.

He bought 12 more.

Now how many does he have?

$$\begin{array}{r}27\\+12\\\hline 39\end{array}$$

Ima has 54 .

Max has 34 .

How many do they have in all?

$$\begin{array}{r}54\\+34\\\hline 88\end{array}$$

You found 82 ●.

Then you find 7 more.

Now how many do you have?

$$\begin{array}{r}82\\+7\\\hline 89\end{array}$$

20 ✿ are blue.

79 ✿ are white.

How many ✿ and ✿ are there in all?

$$\begin{array}{r}20\\+79\\\hline 99\end{array}$$

CHAPTER 8
Addition and Subtraction (2-digit with no renaming)

Lesson 3
Addition (2-digit)

Prerequisite Skills: adding through sums of 9

Lesson Focus: adding 2-digit numbers
Possible Score: 36
Time Frame: 10–15 minutes

Lesson 4   Addition (2-digit)

Add.

24	75	50	62	46
+13	+ 4	+27	+15	+23
37	**79**	**77**	**77**	**69**

52	96	73	38	35
+34	+ 2	+16	+40	+21
86	**98**	**89**	**78**	**56**

10	14	12	33	13
+21	+ 5	+34	+53	+11
31	**19**	**46**	**86**	**24**

24	57	60	12	71
+21	+ 2	+33	+43	+26
45	**59**	**93**	**55**	**97**

16	28	51	40	63
+52	+ 1	+27	+45	+16
68	**29**	**78**	**85**	**79**

22	64	24	41	31
+67	+ 4	+72	+38	+56
89	**68**	**96**	**79**	**87**

CHAPTER 8

Number Correct
- **30–36:** Have students change the prices for one problem on page 112 and rework the problem.
- **23–29:** Be sure students have transferred the correct amount from the top of the page to the work area.
- **Less than 23:** Using manipulatives, have students practice joining sets of ones and sets of tens.

LESSON FOLLOW-UP AND ERROR ANALYSIS

Spectrum Software Addition 7

Lesson 4 Problem Solving

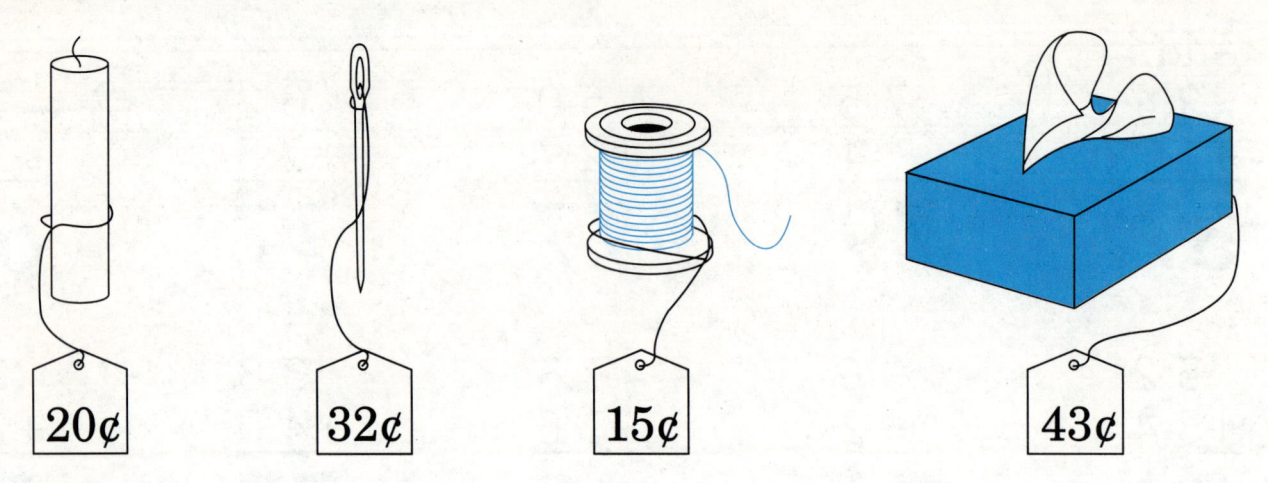

Candle 20¢   Needle 32¢   Spool 15¢   Tissues 43¢

Solve each problem.

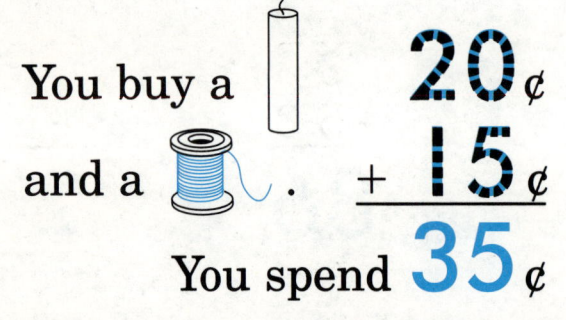

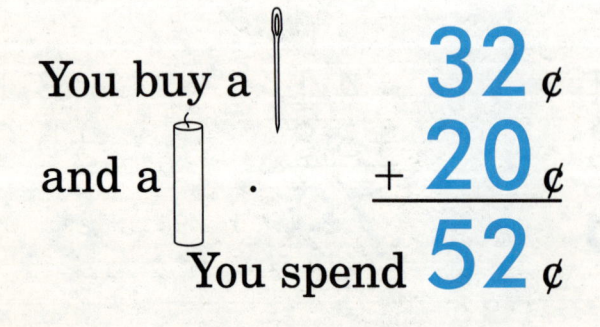

You buy a 🕯 and a 🧵.
20¢
+15¢
You spend 35¢

You buy a 🧵 and a 🪡.
15¢
+32¢
You spend 47¢

You buy a 📦 and a 🧵.
43¢
+15¢
You spend 58¢

You buy a 🕯 and a 📦.
20¢
+43¢
You spend 63¢

You buy a 🪡 and a 🕯.
32¢
+20¢
You spend 52¢

You buy a 📦 and a 🪡.
43¢
+32¢
You spend 75¢

CHAPTER 8
Addition and Subtraction (2-digit with no renaming)

Lesson 4
Addition (2-digit)

Prerequisite Skills: subtracting through 9

Lesson Focus: subtracting 2-digit numbers
Possible Score: 24
Time Frame: 10–15 minutes

Lesson 5 Subtraction (2-digit)

Take away 4 pennies.
Subtract the ones.

$$\begin{array}{r}36\\-24\\\hline 2\end{array}$$

Take away 2 dimes.
Subtract the tens.

$$\begin{array}{r}36\\-24\\\hline 12\end{array}$$

Subtract.

$$\begin{array}{r}78\\-6\\\hline 72\end{array}\qquad\begin{array}{r}69\\-47\\\hline 22\end{array}\qquad\begin{array}{r}28\\-15\\\hline 13\end{array}\qquad\begin{array}{r}45\\-32\\\hline 13\end{array}$$

↰ Subtract the ones.
  Subtract the tens.

$$\begin{array}{r}59\\-45\\\hline 14\end{array}\qquad\begin{array}{r}98\\-43\\\hline 55\end{array}\qquad\begin{array}{r}17\\-5\\\hline 12\end{array}\qquad\begin{array}{r}57\\-43\\\hline 14\end{array}\qquad\begin{array}{r}48\\-34\\\hline 14\end{array}$$

$$\begin{array}{r}58\\-17\\\hline 41\end{array}\qquad\begin{array}{r}85\\-25\\\hline 60\end{array}\qquad\begin{array}{r}87\\-7\\\hline 80\end{array}\qquad\begin{array}{r}96\\-80\\\hline 16\end{array}\qquad\begin{array}{r}66\\-51\\\hline 15\end{array}$$

$$\begin{array}{r}94\\-41\\\hline 53\end{array}\qquad\begin{array}{r}39\\-22\\\hline 17\end{array}\qquad\begin{array}{r}33\\-2\\\hline 31\end{array}\qquad\begin{array}{r}65\\-22\\\hline 43\end{array}\qquad\begin{array}{r}78\\-65\\\hline 13\end{array}$$

Number Correct
- **20–24:** Have students change the numbers for one problem on page 114 and rework the problem.
- **16–19:** Be sure students have arranged the numbers correctly when completing page 114.
- **Less than 16:** Have students use manipulatives to subtract the ones column first, then the tens column.

LESSON FOLLOW-UP AND ERROR ANALYSIS

Spectrum Software Subtraction 7; Word Problems 11 and 12

Lesson 5 Problem Solving

Solve each problem.

There are 54 🌹.
32 were picked.
How many are left?

$$\begin{array}{r}54\\-32\\\hline 22\end{array}$$

You have 48 ⬜.
35 are blue.
The rest are white.
How many white ones are there?

$$\begin{array}{r}48\\-35\\\hline 13\end{array}$$

A store has 99 🔨.
The store sold 73.
How many 🔨 does the store have now?

$$\begin{array}{r}99\\-73\\\hline 26\end{array}$$

Yoko has 23 ✉.
Neal has 12 ✉.
How many more ✉ does Yoko have?

$$\begin{array}{r}23\\-12\\\hline 11\end{array}$$

To build a 🏠 you need 48 🔩.
You have 28 🔩.
How many more 🔩 do you need?

$$\begin{array}{r}48\\-28\\\hline 20\end{array}$$

CHAPTER 8
Addition and Subtraction (2-digit with no renaming)

Lesson 5
Subtraction (2-digit)

Prerequisite Skills: subtracting through 9

Lesson Focus: subtracting 2-digit numbers
Possible Score: 36
Time Frame: 15–20 minutes

Lesson 6 Subtraction (2-digit)

Subtract.

75	67	30	48	55
−34	− 4	−20	−30	−32
41	**63**	**10**	**18**	**23**

78	56	98	86	98
−67	− 3	−86	−15	−48
11	**53**	**12**	**71**	**50**

95	84	65	79	84
−31	− 2	−45	−48	−50
64	**82**	**20**	**31**	**34**

42	39	89	67	66
−10	− 6	−42	−21	−36
32	**33**	**47**	**46**	**30**

98	72	43	57	69
−73	− 2	−13	−32	−15
25	**70**	**30**	**25**	**54**

32	97	78	99	87
−11	− 5	−22	−16	−47
21	**92**	**56**	**83**	**40**

CHAPTER 8

Number Correct
- **30–36:** Have students create their own problems using the objects on the page 116.
- **23–29:** Be sure students have copied the cost of each item correctly on page 116.
- **Less than 23:** Have students use manipulatives to subtract the ones column first, then the tens column.

LESSON FOLLOW-UP AND ERROR ANALYSIS

Spectrum Software Subtraction 7; Word Problems 13

Lesson 6 Problem Solving

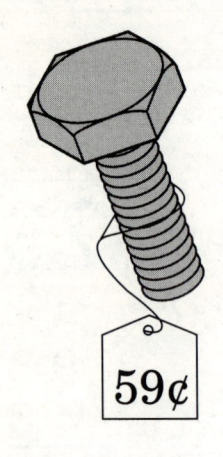

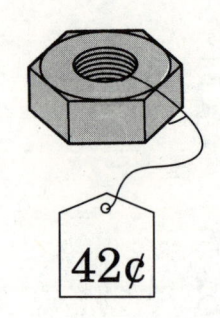

| | 59¢ | 15¢ | 42¢ | 30¢ |

Solve each problem.

You have	6 2¢
You buy a 🔩	−42¢
You have left	20¢

You have	5 0¢
You buy a 🔩	−30¢
You have left	20¢

You have	5 3¢
You buy a 🔩	−30¢
You have left	23¢

You have	9 9¢
You buy a 🔩	−59¢
You have left	40¢

You have	7 6¢
You buy a ⭕	−15¢
You have left	61¢

You have	4 5¢
You buy a 🔩	−42¢
You have left	3¢

CHAPTER 8
Addition and Subtraction (2-digit with no renaming)

Lesson 6
Subtraction (2-digit)

Prerequisite Skills: adding 2-digit numbers

Lesson Focus: adding three 2-digit numbers
Possible Score: 18
Time Frame: 15–20 minutes

Lesson 7 Adding 3 Numbers

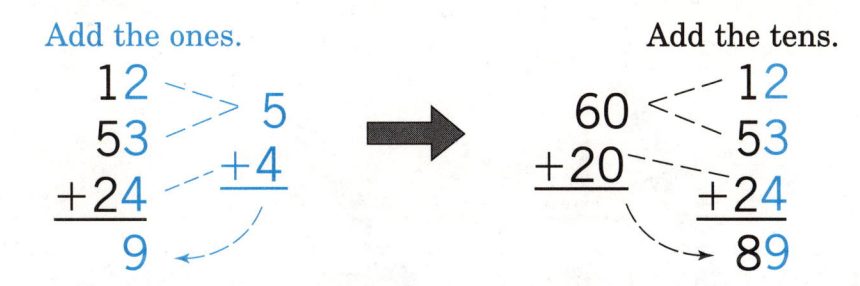

Add the ones.
```
  12 ⟶ 5
  53
 +24 +4
   9
```

⟶

Add the tens.
```
  60 ⟵ 12
       53
 +20  +24
       89
```

Add.

```
  45          32          35          47
  33          37          21          20
 +10         +20         +11         +22
  88          89          67          89
```
↑ Add the ones.
└── Add the tens.

```
  24          31          40          54          25
  24          23          13          10          33
 +21         +31         +11         +23         +20
  69          85          64          87          78
```

```
  61          30          36          31          44
  12          24          32          20          20
 +24         +15         +31         +24         +34
  97          69          99          75          98
```

Number Correct

LESSON FOLLOW-UP AND ERROR ANALYSIS

Spectrum Software Addition 8–11

15–18: Have students change the order of the addends in one problem and see whether they get the same sum.
12–14: Check to see that students have copied the numbers correctly on page 118.
Less than 12: Have students explain why it is important to line up ones under ones and tens under tens on page 118.

Lesson 7   Problem Solving

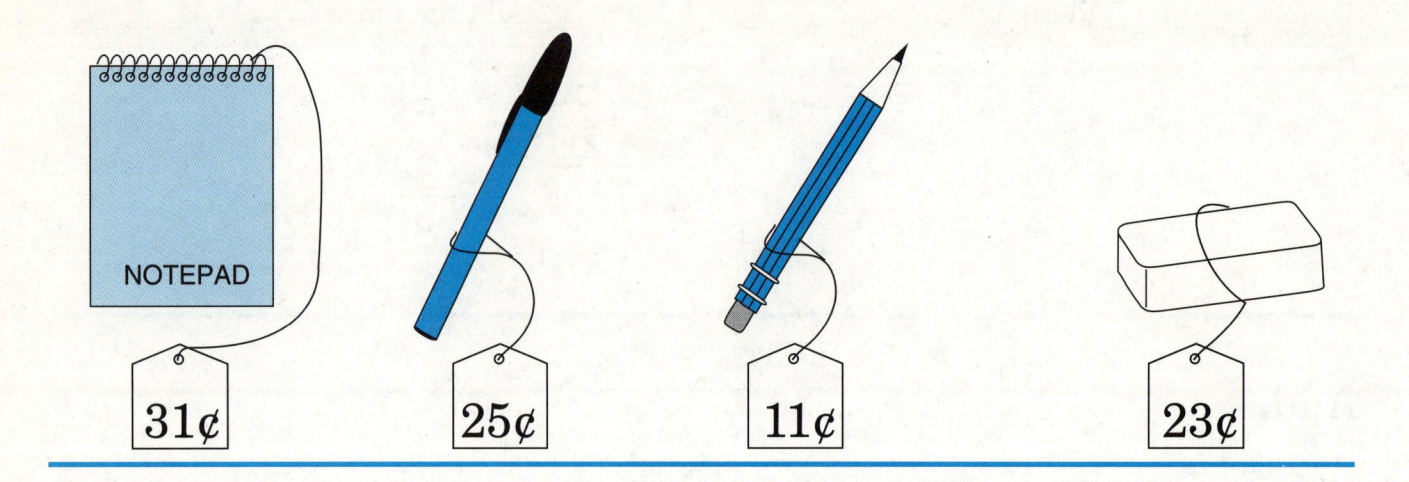

NOTEPAD 31¢   25¢   11¢   23¢

Solve each problem.

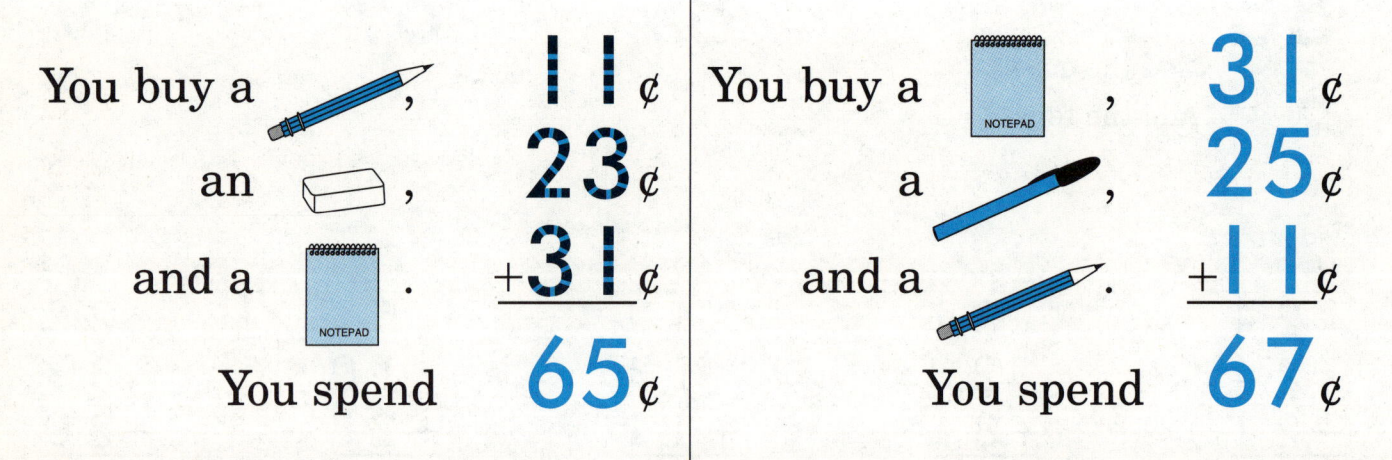

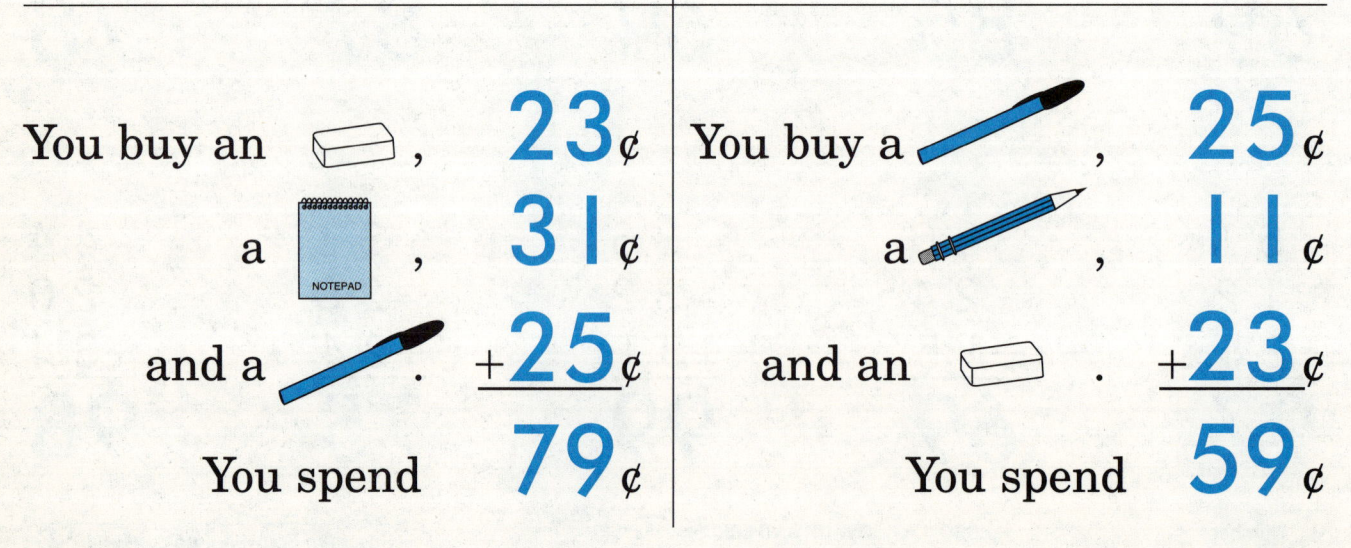

You buy a ✏️,   11¢
an ▭,   23¢
and a 📓.   +31¢
You spend   65¢

You buy a 📓,   31¢
a 🖊,   25¢
and a ✏️.   +11¢
You spend   67¢

You buy an ▭,   23¢
a 📓,   31¢
and a 🖊.   +25¢
You spend   79¢

You buy a 🖊,   25¢
a ✏️,   11¢
and an ▭.   +23¢
You spend   59¢

CHAPTER 8
Addition and Subtraction (2-digit with no renaming)
118

Lesson 7
Adding 3 Numbers

Prerequisite Skills: adding and subtracting through 18

Lesson Focus: adding and subtracting 2-digit numbers
Possible Score: 30
Time Frame: 10–15 minutes

Lesson 8 Addition and Subtraction

Add or subtract. STOP! Watch the + and − !

```
  32        57        82        92        42
 +34       −25       − 2       −61       +57
  66        32        80        31        99

  86        15        40        31        73
 −52       +62       + 7       +15       −13
  34        77        47        46        60

  69        34        87        84        40
 +30       −12       − 6       +14       +35
  99        22        81        98        75

  95        86        77        61        59
 −25       −43       + 2       +17       −44
  70        43        79        78        15

  39        68        55        88        96
 +60       −67       + 4       −83       −81
  99         1        59         5        15
```

CHAPTER 8

| Number Correct | LESSON FOLLOW-UP AND ERROR ANALYSIS | Spectrum Software Addition 7; Subtraction 7; Word Problems 14 and 15 |

26–30: To reinforce place value, have students ring each answer greater than 75 and □ each answer less than 25.
20–25: If students have not performed the correct operation, have them rework the answer.
Less than 20: Have students use manipulatives to redo each incorrect answer.

119

Lesson 8 **Problem Solving**

Solve each problem.

There are 43 white ⚪.

There are 45 blue 🔵.

How many more blue 🔵 than white ⚪ are there?

$$\begin{array}{r}45\\-43\\\hline 2\end{array}$$

There are 19 🐦.

30 more come.

How many are there now?

$$\begin{array}{r}19\\+30\\\hline 49\end{array}$$

---

34 🥛 are on the table.

2 are broken.

How many are not broken?

$$\begin{array}{r}34\\-2\\\hline 32\end{array}$$

You need 19 📎.

You have 7 📎.

How many more do you need?

$$\begin{array}{r}19\\-7\\\hline 12\end{array}$$

You have 32 🪙.

You get 57 more.

Now how many do you have?

$$\begin{array}{r}32\\+57\\\hline 89\end{array}$$

CHAPTER 8
Addition and Subtraction (2-digit with no renaming)

Lesson 8
Addition and Subtraction

Prerequisite Skills: adding and subtracting through 18

Lesson Focus: adding and subtracting 2-digit numbers
Possible Score: 50
Time Frame: 10–15 minutes

Lesson 9 Addition and Subtraction

Add or subtract. STOP! Watch the + and − !

If you get 56, color the box.
Check students' work before they color.

22 +34 **56**	78 −24 **54**	59 − 3 **56**	75 −11 **64**	15 +41 **56**
96 −40 **56**	15 +62 **77**	50 + 6 **56**	61 +15 **76**	67 −11 **56**
69 −13 **56**	78 −22 **56**	57 − 1 **56**	84 +14 **98**	40 +16 **56**
97 −41 **56**	86 −32 **54**	54 + 2 **56**	61 +17 **78**	99 −43 **56**
31 +25 **56**	68 −67 **1**	52 + 4 **56**	88 −83 **5**	79 −23 **56**

Number Correct LESSON FOLLOW-UP AND ERROR ANALYSIS
42–50: To reinforce place value, have students ring every answer greater than 56.
35–41: If students have not performed the correct operation, have them rework the answer.
Less than 35: Have students use manipulatives to rework each incorrect answer.

Spectrum Software Addition 7; Subtraction 7; Word Problems 16

CHAPTER 8

121

Lesson 9 Addition and Subtraction

Add or subtract. **STOP!** Watch the + and – !

If you get 75, color the box.
Check students' work before they color.

71 + 4 **75**	83 +14 **97**	44 +34 **78**	63 +12 **75**	73 + 2 **75**
70 + 5 **75**	32 +43 **75**	97 −22 **75**	44 +31 **75**	76 − 1 **75**
87 −12 **75**	90 + 7 **97**	85 −22 **63**	61 +25 **86**	79 − 4 **75**
95 −20 **75**	78 − 3 **75**	85 −10 **75**	61 +14 **75**	50 +25 **75**
72 + 3 **75**	85 +10 **95**	51 −20 **31**	67 −30 **37**	95 −20 **75**

CHAPTER 8
Addition and Subtraction (2-digit with no renaming)

Lesson 9
Addition and Subtraction

For further evaluation, copy the Chapter Test on page 172.
For maintaining skills, use the Cumulative Review on page 160.

Extending the Chapter: *Spectrum Software* Addition 15–20; Subtraction 9–11
Possible Score: 25
Time Frame: 10–15 minutes

CHAPTER 8 PRACTICE TEST
Addition and Subtraction (2-digit with no renaming)

Add.

$$\begin{array}{r} 30 \\ +50 \\ \hline 80 \end{array} \qquad \begin{array}{r} 34 \\ +5 \\ \hline 39 \end{array} \qquad \begin{array}{r} 61 \\ +24 \\ \hline 85 \end{array} \qquad \begin{array}{r} 18 \\ +31 \\ \hline 49 \end{array} \qquad \begin{array}{r} 50 \\ +36 \\ \hline 86 \end{array}$$

$$\begin{array}{r} 45 \\ +21 \\ \hline 66 \end{array} \qquad \begin{array}{r} 92 \\ +7 \\ \hline 99 \end{array} \qquad \begin{array}{r} 73 \\ +13 \\ \hline 86 \end{array} \qquad \begin{array}{r} 54 \\ +24 \\ \hline 78 \end{array} \qquad \begin{array}{r} 82 \\ +17 \\ \hline 99 \end{array}$$

$$\begin{array}{r} 35 \\ +12 \\ \hline 47 \end{array} \qquad \begin{array}{r} 60 \\ +8 \\ \hline 68 \end{array} \qquad \begin{array}{r} 30 \\ 40 \\ +10 \\ \hline 80 \end{array} \qquad \begin{array}{r} 51 \\ 16 \\ +12 \\ \hline 79 \end{array} \qquad \begin{array}{r} 26 \\ 21 \\ +12 \\ \hline 59 \end{array}$$

Subtract.

$$\begin{array}{r} 70 \\ -40 \\ \hline 30 \end{array} \qquad \begin{array}{r} 85 \\ -2 \\ \hline 83 \end{array} \qquad \begin{array}{r} 54 \\ -30 \\ \hline 24 \end{array} \qquad \begin{array}{r} 97 \\ -35 \\ \hline 62 \end{array} \qquad \begin{array}{r} 74 \\ -54 \\ \hline 20 \end{array}$$

$$\begin{array}{r} 28 \\ -18 \\ \hline 10 \end{array} \qquad \begin{array}{r} 78 \\ -4 \\ \hline 74 \end{array} \qquad \begin{array}{r} 46 \\ -23 \\ \hline 23 \end{array} \qquad \begin{array}{r} 89 \\ -33 \\ \hline 56 \end{array} \qquad \begin{array}{r} 93 \\ -62 \\ \hline 31 \end{array}$$

CHAPTER 8

Number Correct — LESSON FOLLOW-UP AND ERROR ANALYSIS

Spectrum Software Addition 4–11; Subtraction 4–7; Word Problems 11–16

21–25: Have students choose one addition answer and write a different problem that will add up to the same sum.
16–20: If students have not performed the correct operation, have them rework the answer.
Less than 16: Have students use manipulatives to rework each incorrect answer.

Math Intervention: Addition and Subtraction Facts, Gold Book, pages 87–94.
Real World Problem Solving practice: Gold Book, pages 95–96.

CHAPTER 9 PRETEST
Addition and Subtraction (facts through 18)

Add.

8	7	7	6	9	7
+9	+5	+7	+5	+6	+9
17	**12**	**14**	**11**	**15**	**16**

6	8	9	4	8	9
+7	+4	+2	+9	+8	+5
13	**12**	**11**	**13**	**16**	**14**

7	5	6	8	9	9
+4	+9	+8	+5	+4	+8
11	**14**	**14**	**13**	**13**	**17**

Subtract.

11	17	14	13	13	19
−4	−8	−8	−5	−4	−14
7	**9**	**6**	**8**	**9**	**5**

13	12	11	13	16	14
−6	−4	−2	−9	−8	−5
7	**8**	**9**	**4**	**8**	**9**

17	16	14	15	12	11
−9	−9	−7	−6	−5	−5
8	**7**	**7**	**9**	**7**	**6**

Prerequisite Skills: adding and subtracting through 10

Lesson Focus: adding and subtracting through 11
Possible Score: 33
Time Frame: 15–20 minutes

Lesson 1 Facts for 11

Add or subtract.

$$\begin{array}{r}8\\+3\\\hline 11\end{array}\qquad\begin{array}{r}3\\+8\\\hline 11\end{array}\qquad\begin{array}{r}11\\-8\\\hline 3\end{array}\qquad\begin{array}{r}11\\-3\\\hline 8\end{array}$$

$$\begin{array}{r}9\\+2\\\hline 11\end{array}\qquad\begin{array}{r}2\\+9\\\hline 11\end{array}\qquad\begin{array}{r}11\\-9\\\hline 2\end{array}\qquad\begin{array}{r}11\\-2\\\hline 9\end{array}$$

$$\begin{array}{r}6\\+5\\\hline 11\end{array}\qquad\begin{array}{r}5\\+6\\\hline 11\end{array}\qquad\begin{array}{r}11\\-6\\\hline 5\end{array}\qquad\begin{array}{r}11\\-5\\\hline 6\end{array}$$

$$\begin{array}{r}7\\+4\\\hline 11\end{array}\qquad\begin{array}{r}4\\+7\\\hline 11\end{array}\qquad\begin{array}{r}11\\-7\\\hline 4\end{array}\qquad\begin{array}{r}11\\-4\\\hline 7\end{array}$$

$$\begin{array}{r}7\\+4\\\hline 11\end{array}\quad\begin{array}{r}6\\+5\\\hline 11\end{array}\quad\begin{array}{r}3\\+8\\\hline 11\end{array}\quad\begin{array}{r}11\\-6\\\hline 5\end{array}\quad\begin{array}{r}11\\-9\\\hline 2\end{array}\quad\begin{array}{r}11\\-7\\\hline 4\end{array}$$

$$\begin{array}{r}11\\+0\\\hline 11\end{array}\quad\begin{array}{r}9\\+2\\\hline 11\end{array}\quad\begin{array}{r}5\\+6\\\hline 11\end{array}\quad\begin{array}{r}11\\-2\\\hline 9\end{array}\quad\begin{array}{r}11\\-0\\\hline 11\end{array}\quad\begin{array}{r}11\\-8\\\hline 3\end{array}$$

Number Correct
LESSON FOLLOW-UP AND ERROR ANALYSIS
Spectrum Software Addition 12–14; Subtraction 4–8; Word Problems 17

28–33: Ask students to see if they can name two numbers whose sum is 11 but are not shown on the page. (10 + 1)
21–27: Help students make the connection between the dots on the dominoes and the problems shown vertically.
Less than 21: Help students translate the problems on page 126 to vertical addition.

Lesson 1 Problem Solving

Solve each problem.

   8 crayons in a box
+ 3 more crayons
  11 crayons in all

   6 birds on a wire
+ 5 birds coming
  11 birds in all

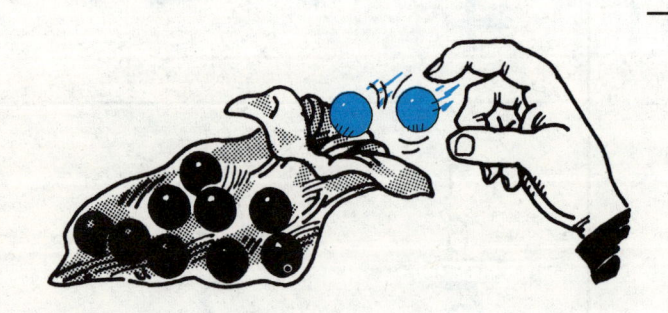

   5 black hats
+ 7 blue hats
  12 hats in all

   9 marbles in a bag
+ 2 marbles are put in
  11 marbles in all

   5 ants on a hill
+ 6 ants coming
  11 ants in all

CHAPTER 9
Addition and Subtraction (facts through 18)

Lesson 1
Facts for 11

Prerequisite Skills: adding and subtracting through 11

Lesson Focus: adding and subtracting through 12
Possible Score: 31
Time Frame: 15–20 minutes

Lesson 2 Facts for 12

Add or subtract.

8 +4 --- 12		4 +8 --- 12	12 −8 --- 4		12 −4 --- 8
9 +3 --- 12		3 +9 --- 12	12 −9 --- 3		12 −3 --- 9
7 +5 --- 12		5 +7 --- 12	12 −7 --- 5		12 −5 --- 7
6 +6 --- 12			12 −6 --- 6		

| 9
+3
---
12 | 5
+7
---
12 | 12
+0
---
12 | 12
−6
---
6 | 12
−0
---
12 | 12
−8
---
4 |
| 6
+6
---
12 | 4
+8
---
12 | 7
+5
---
12 | 12
−5
---
7 | 12
−9
---
3 | 12
−4
---
8 |

Number Correct   LESSON FOLLOW-UP AND ERROR ANALYSIS   *Spectrum Software* Addition 12–14, Subtraction 4–8; Word Problems 18

26–31: Ask students to draw their own picture story using addition or subtraction.
20–25: Check to see that students have copied the exercises on page 128 correctly.
Less than 20: Have students count the dots on the dominoes aloud as they rework each incorrect answer.

127

Lesson 2 Problem Solving

Solve each problem.

$$\begin{array}{r} 12 \\ -4 \\ \hline 8 \end{array}$$ birds in all
birds flying away
birds stay

$$\begin{array}{r} 11 \\ -2 \\ \hline 9 \end{array}$$ cars in all
cars leaving
cars stay

$$\begin{array}{r} 12 \\ -3 \\ \hline 9 \end{array}$$ flowers in all
blue flowers
white flowers

$$\begin{array}{r} 7 \\ +4 \\ \hline 11 \end{array}$$ blue buttons
black buttons
buttons in all

$$\begin{array}{r} 12 \\ -5 \\ \hline 7 \end{array}$$ berries in all
berries falling
berries not falling

CHAPTER 9
Addition and Subtraction (facts through 18)
128

Lesson 2
Facts for 12

Prerequisite Skills: adding and subtracting through 12

Lesson Focus: adding and subtracting through 12
Possible Score: 41
Time Frame: 10–15 minutes

Lesson 3 Facts through 12

Add.

8	7	6	3	9	6
+4	+4	+6	+9	+2	+5
12	11	12	12	11	11

5	7	9	4	5	3
+5	+5	+1	+8	+7	+8
10	12	10	12	12	11

4	2	8	4	9	5
+6	+9	+3	+7	+3	+6
10	11	11	11	12	11

Subtract.

12	11	12	11	12	11
− 8	− 9	− 5	− 4	− 6	− 0
4	2	7	7	6	11

12	12	10	11	10	11
− 3	− 7	− 3	− 8	− 6	− 5
9	5	7	3	4	6

12	11	10	12	11	12
− 0	− 2	− 8	− 4	− 7	− 9
12	9	2	8	4	3

CHAPTER 9

Number Correct
LESSON FOLLOW-UP AND ERROR ANALYSIS
Spectrum Software Addition 12–14; Subtraction 4–8

35–41: Have students draw one addition and one subtraction picture story using 12.
27–34: Check to see that students have copied the numbers correctly and used the correct operation on page 130.
Less than 27: Have students use manipulatives to rework each incorrect answer.

Lesson 3   Problem Solving

Solve each problem.

$$\begin{array}{r} 7 \\ +5 \\ \hline 12 \end{array}$$ books on top shelf
books on bottom shelf
books in all

$$\begin{array}{r} 12 \\ -6 \\ \hline 6 \end{array}$$ cars in all
cars going
cars still parked

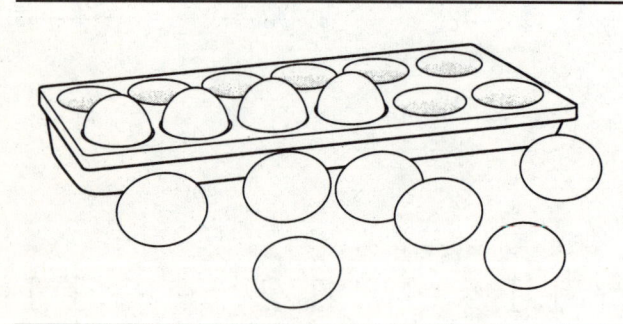

$$\begin{array}{r} 4 \\ +7 \\ \hline 11 \end{array}$$ eggs in the carton
eggs on the table
eggs in all

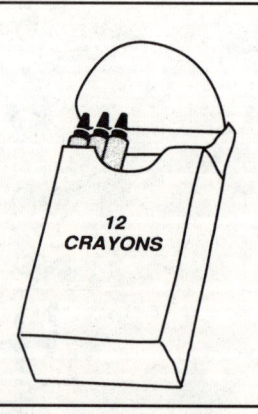

$$\begin{array}{r} 12 \\ -3 \\ \hline 9 \end{array}$$ crayons that can be in the box
crayons in the box
crayons needed to fill the box

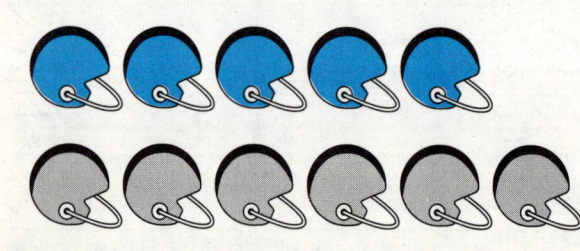

$$\begin{array}{r} 5 \\ +6 \\ \hline 11 \end{array}$$ blue football helmets
gray football helmets
helmets in all

CHAPTER 9
Addition and Subtraction (facts through 18)

Lesson 3
Facts through 12

Prerequisite Skills: adding and subtracting through 13

Lesson Focus: adding and subtracting through 14
Possible Score: 28
Time Frame: 5–10 minutes

Lesson 4 Facts for 13

Add or subtract.

$$\begin{array}{r}7\\+6\\\hline 13\end{array} \qquad \begin{array}{r}6\\+7\\\hline 13\end{array} \qquad \begin{array}{r}13\\-7\\\hline 6\end{array} \qquad \begin{array}{r}13\\-6\\\hline 7\end{array}$$

$$\begin{array}{r}8\\+5\\\hline 13\end{array} \qquad \begin{array}{r}5\\+8\\\hline 13\end{array} \qquad \begin{array}{r}13\\-8\\\hline 5\end{array} \qquad \begin{array}{r}13\\-5\\\hline 8\end{array}$$

$$\begin{array}{r}9\\+4\\\hline 13\end{array} \qquad \begin{array}{r}4\\+9\\\hline 13\end{array} \qquad \begin{array}{r}13\\-9\\\hline 4\end{array} \qquad \begin{array}{r}13\\-4\\\hline 9\end{array}$$

$$\begin{array}{r}5\\+8\\\hline 13\end{array} \quad \begin{array}{r}9\\+4\\\hline 13\end{array} \quad \begin{array}{r}7\\+6\\\hline 13\end{array} \quad \begin{array}{r}13\\-5\\\hline 8\end{array} \quad \begin{array}{r}13\\-7\\\hline 6\end{array} \quad \begin{array}{r}13\\-9\\\hline 4\end{array}$$

$$\begin{array}{r}6\\+7\\\hline 13\end{array} \quad \begin{array}{r}8\\+5\\\hline 13\end{array} \quad \begin{array}{r}4\\+9\\\hline 13\end{array} \quad \begin{array}{r}13\\-4\\\hline 9\end{array} \quad \begin{array}{r}13\\-8\\\hline 5\end{array} \quad \begin{array}{r}13\\-6\\\hline 7\end{array}$$

Number Correct — **LESSON FOLLOW-UP AND ERROR ANALYSIS** — *Spectrum Software* Addition 12–14; Subtraction 4–8

20–24: In the last two rows, have students ring two addition problems that use the same numbers but in a different order.
16–19: Have students draw dots to help them rework addition and subtraction problems.
Less than 16: Discuss that 13 is used in all the subtraction problems. Have students cover the dots taken away.

Prerequisite Skills: adding and subtracting through 13

Lesson Focus: adding and subtracting through 14
Possible Score: 28
Time Frame: 5–10 minutes

Lesson 5 Facts for 14

Add or subtract.

$\begin{array}{r}9\\+5\\\hline 14\end{array}$ $\quad$ $\begin{array}{r}5\\+9\\\hline 14\end{array}$ $\quad$ $\begin{array}{r}14\\-9\\\hline 5\end{array}$ $\quad$ $\begin{array}{r}14\\-5\\\hline 9\end{array}$

$\begin{array}{r}8\\+6\\\hline 14\end{array}$ $\quad$ $\begin{array}{r}6\\+8\\\hline 14\end{array}$ $\quad$ $\begin{array}{r}14\\-8\\\hline 6\end{array}$ $\quad$ $\begin{array}{r}14\\-6\\\hline 8\end{array}$

$\begin{array}{r}7\\+7\\\hline 14\end{array}$ $\quad$ $\begin{array}{r}14\\-7\\\hline 7\end{array}$

$\begin{array}{r}8\\+6\\\hline 14\end{array}$ $\quad$ $\begin{array}{r}7\\+7\\\hline 14\end{array}$ $\quad$ $\begin{array}{r}6\\+6\\\hline 12\end{array}$ $\quad$ $\begin{array}{r}14\\-8\\\hline 6\end{array}$ $\quad$ $\begin{array}{r}12\\-7\\\hline 5\end{array}$ $\quad$ $\begin{array}{r}14\\-5\\\hline 9\end{array}$

$\begin{array}{r}9\\+4\\\hline 13\end{array}$ $\quad$ $\begin{array}{r}5\\+9\\\hline 14\end{array}$ $\quad$ $\begin{array}{r}7\\+4\\\hline 11\end{array}$ $\quad$ $\begin{array}{r}14\\-7\\\hline 7\end{array}$ $\quad$ $\begin{array}{r}13\\-8\\\hline 5\end{array}$ $\quad$ $\begin{array}{r}14\\-6\\\hline 8\end{array}$

$\begin{array}{r}9\\+5\\\hline 14\end{array}$ $\quad$ $\begin{array}{r}6\\+7\\\hline 13\end{array}$ $\quad$ $\begin{array}{r}6\\+8\\\hline 14\end{array}$ $\quad$ $\begin{array}{r}11\\-8\\\hline 3\end{array}$ $\quad$ $\begin{array}{r}14\\-9\\\hline 5\end{array}$ $\quad$ $\begin{array}{r}12\\-4\\\hline 8\end{array}$

Number Correct

LESSON FOLLOW-UP AND ERROR ANALYSIS

Spectrum Software Addition 12–14; Subtraction 4–8

24–28: Have students draw a picture story using an addition or subtraction fact for 14.
18–23: Have students draw dots to help them rework addition and subtraction problems.
Less than 18: Have students use manipulatives to rework each incorrect answer and explain each step.

Prerequisite Skills: adding and subtracting through 14

Lesson Focus: adding and subtracting through 14
Possible Score: 41
Time Frame: 10–15 minutes

Lesson 6 Facts through 14

Add.

| 9
+4
13 | 7
+7
14 | 6
+5
11 | 8
+4
12 | 5
+9
14 | 4
+7
11 |

| 5
+6
11 | 9
+5
14 | 5
+7
12 | 8
+5
13 | 7
+6
13 | 6
+8
14 |

| 3
+8
11 | 7
+5
12 | 8
+6
14 | 5
+8
13 | 4
+9
13 | 6
+6
12 |

Subtract.

| 12
− 5
7 | 13
− 7
6 | 14
− 5
9 | 11
− 3
8 | 14
− 7
7 | 13
− 6
7 |

| 13
− 8
5 | 12
− 9
3 | 14
− 6
8 | 11
− 5
6 | 14
− 9
5 | 12
− 6
6 |

| 11
− 7
4 | 11
− 9
2 | 13
− 4
9 | 12
− 8
4 | 13
− 9
4 | 14
− 8
6 |

Number Correct

LESSON FOLLOW-UP AND ERROR ANALYSIS

Spectrum Software Addition 12–14; Subtraction 4–8

35–41: Have students write a picture story illustrating a subtraction fact for 14.
27–34: Check to see that students have copied the numbers correctly on page 134.
Less than 27: Have students count the objects aloud as they write the numbers on page 134.

Lesson 6 Problem Solving

Solve each problem.

$$\begin{array}{r} 8 \\ +6 \\ \hline 14 \end{array}$$ trucks in a box
other trucks
trucks in all

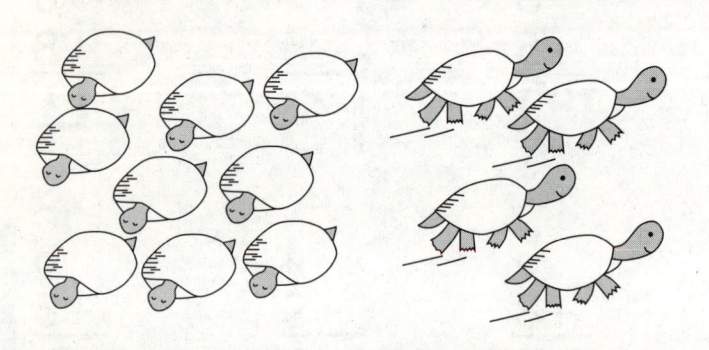

$$\begin{array}{r} 13 \\ -4 \\ \hline 9 \end{array}$$ turtles in all
turtles going away
turtles stay

$$\begin{array}{r} 9 \\ +5 \\ \hline 14 \end{array}$$ candles on the cake
other candles
candles in all

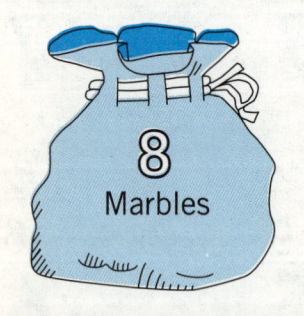

$$\begin{array}{r} 8 \\ +5 \\ \hline 13 \end{array}$$ marbles in a bag
more marbles
marbles in all

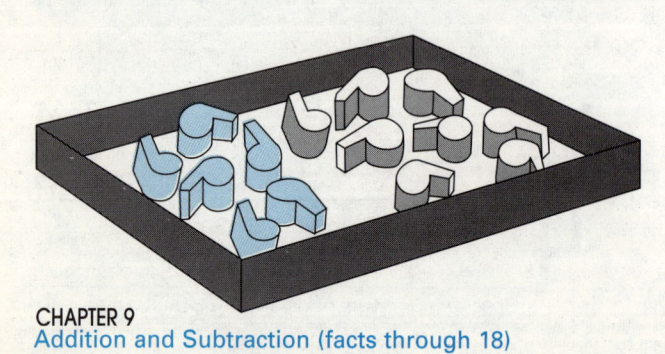

$$\begin{array}{r} 14 \\ -8 \\ \hline 6 \end{array}$$ whistles in the box
white whistles
blue whistles

Prerequisite Skills: adding and subtracting through 14

Lesson Focus: adding and subtracting through 15
Possible Score: 26
Time Frame: 5–10 minutes

Lesson 7 Facts for 15

Add or subtract.

✶✶✶✶ ✶✶✶✶
✶✶✶✶ ✶✶✶

```
  8      7     15     15
 +7     +8     -7     -8
 15     15      8      7
```

✶✶✶✶✶ ✶✶✶
✶✶✶✶ ✶✶✶

```
  9      6     15     15
 +6     +9     -6     -9
 15     15      9      6
```

```
  6      7      8     14     15     13
 +9     +8     +6     -9     -8     -7
 15     15     14      5      7      6

  6      9      8     15     14     15
 +8     +5     +7     -9     -6     -7
 14     14     15      6      8      8

  8      9      7     13     15     14
 +5     +6     +7     -8     -6     -5
 13     15     14      5      9      9
```

Number Correct
22–26: Have students connect problems that use the same numbers (such as 6 + 9 = 15 and 15 − 9 = 6).
17–21: Have students count the black and blue stars aloud as they rework each incorrect answer in the top two rows.
Less than 17: Have students use manipulatives as they rework each incorrect answer.

LESSON FOLLOW-UP AND ERROR ANALYSIS

Spectrum Software Addition 12–14; Subtraction 4–8

135

Prerequisite Skills: adding and subtracting through 15

Lesson Focus: adding and subtracting through 16
Possible Score: 24
Time Frame: 5–10 minutes

Lesson 8 Facts for 16

Add or subtract.

```
   9        7      1 6      1 6
  +7       +9      − 7      − 9
  ──       ──      ───      ───
  16       16       9        7
```

```
   8              1 6
  +8              − 8
  ──              ───
  16               8
```

8 +7 ── 15	9 +7 ── 16	7 +8 ── 15	1 6 − 9 ─── 7	1 5 − 7 ─── 8	1 4 − 5 ─── 9
8 +8 ── 16	5 +9 ── 14	7 +7 ── 14	1 4 − 9 ─── 5	1 5 − 6 ─── 9	1 6 − 8 ─── 8
7 +9 ── 16	6 +8 ── 14	9 +6 ── 15	1 4 − 8 ─── 6	1 6 − 7 ─── 9	1 5 − 9 ─── 6

Number Correct

LESSON FOLLOW-UP AND ERROR ANALYSIS

Spectrum Software Addition 12–14; Subtraction 4–8

20–24: Have students connect problems that use the same numbers (such as 9 + 7 = 16 and 16 − 9 = 7).
16–19: Have students count the buttons aloud as they rework each incorrect answer to the top six problems.
Less than 16: Have students use manipulatives as they rework each incorrect answer.

136

Prerequisite Skills: adding and subtracting through 16

Lesson Focus: adding and subtracting through 16
Possible Score: 41
Time Frame: 10–15 minutes

Lesson 9 Facts through 16

Add.

7	6	5	8	7	6
+8	+6	+9	+4	+7	+9
15	12	14	12	14	15

8	9	7	8	7	8
+8	+4	+6	+6	+9	+3
16	13	13	14	16	11

5	8	9	8	6	9
+6	+7	+7	+5	+8	+6
11	15	16	13	14	15

Subtract.

14	15	16	13	14	12
−7	−6	−7	−8	−5	−9
7	9	9	5	9	3

12	14	11	16	11	15
−6	−6	−9	−8	−3	−9
6	8	2	8	8	6

15	13	16	14	15	14
−7	−9	−9	−9	−8	−8
8	4	7	5	7	6

LESSON FOLLOW-UP AND ERROR ANALYSIS

Spectrum Software Addition 12–14; Subtraction 4–8

Number Correct
- **35–41:** Have students draw a picture story for 9 + 7 = 16 and for 16 − 8 = 8.
- **27–34:** Have students count the objects aloud on page 138 as they rework each incorrect answer.
- **Less than 27:** Have students use manipulatives to rework each incorrect answer.

Lesson 9 Problem Solving

Solve each problem.

$$\begin{array}{r}16\\-8\\\hline 8\end{array}$$ balloons in all
balloons broken
balloons not broken

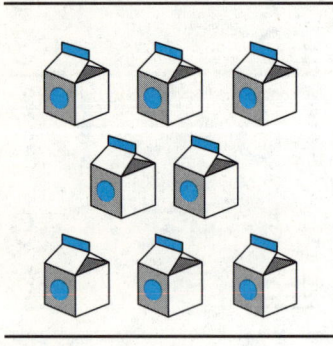

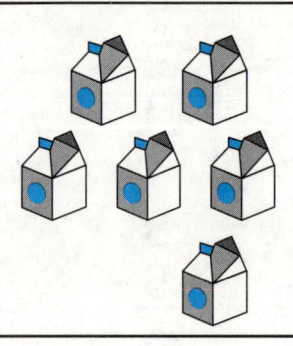

$$\begin{array}{r}14\\-6\\\hline 8\end{array}$$ cartons in all
cartons open
cartons closed

$$\begin{array}{r}8\\+7\\\hline 15\end{array}$$ books in a box
books in a pile
books in all

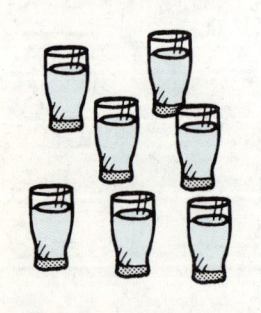

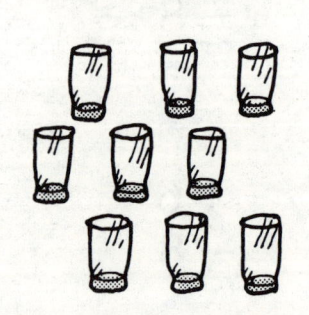

$$\begin{array}{r}16\\-7\\\hline 9\end{array}$$ glasses in all
glasses filled
glasses empty

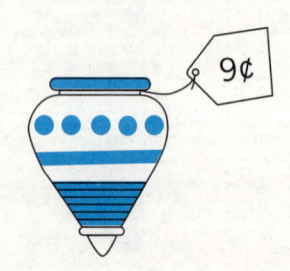

$$\begin{array}{r}7¢\\+9¢\\\hline 16¢\end{array}$$ for a yo-yo
for a top
for both

CHAPTER 9
Addition and Subtraction (facts through 18)
138

Lesson 9
Facts through 16

Prerequisite Skills: adding and subtracting through 16

Lesson Focus: adding and subtracting through 18
Possible Score: 29
Time Frame: 10–15 minutes

Lesson 10 Facts through 18
Add or subtract.

$$\begin{array}{r}9\\+8\\\hline 17\end{array} \qquad \begin{array}{r}8\\+9\\\hline 17\end{array} \qquad \begin{array}{r}17\\-8\\\hline 9\end{array} \qquad \begin{array}{r}17\\-9\\\hline 8\end{array}$$

$$\begin{array}{r}9\\+9\\\hline 18\end{array} \qquad\qquad \begin{array}{r}18\\-9\\\hline 9\end{array}$$

6 +8 = 14	8 +8 = 16	8 +9 = 17	17 −8 = 9	15 −7 = 8	16 −9 = 7
7 +9 = 16	8 +7 = 15	9 +6 = 15	14 −7 = 7	18 −9 = 9	16 −8 = 8
9 +8 = 17	8 +8 = 16	9 +9 = 18	15 −6 = 9	17 −9 = 8	16 −7 = 9

Number Correct
25–29: Have students draw a picture story for 8 + 9 = 17 and for 18 − 9 = 9.
18–24: Have students use manipulatives to rework each incorrect answer.
Less than 18: Have students count the objects aloud on page 140 as they rework each incorrect answer.

LESSON FOLLOW-UP AND ERROR ANALYSIS

Spectrum Software Addition 12–14; Subtraction 4–8

Lesson 10 Problem Solving

Solve each problem.

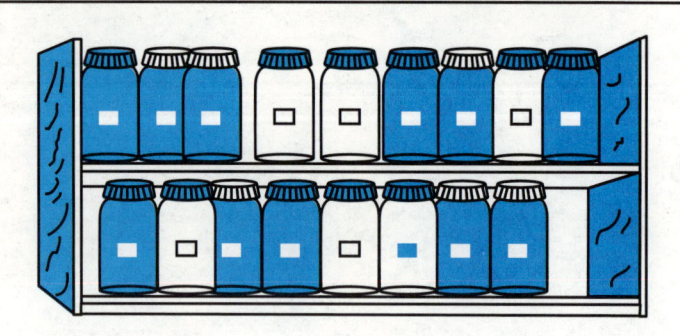

17 balls in all
− 8 small balls
9 large balls

9 jars on top shelf
+ 8 jars on bottom shelf
17 jars in all

9 pencils in a box
+ 9 more pencils
18 pencils in all

8 big stars
+ 9 small stars
17 stars in all

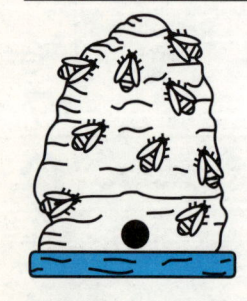

18 bees in all
− 9 bees go away
9 bees stay

Prerequisite Skills: adding through sums of 18

Lesson Focus: adding through sums of 18
Possible Score: 62
Time Frame: 10–15 minutes

Lesson 11   Addition Facts through 18

Add.

5 +7 **12**	7 +5 **12**	2 +9 **11**	9 +2 **11**	5 +8 **13**	8 +5 **13**
6 +4 **10**	4 +6 **10**	9 +4 **13**	4 +9 **13**	6 +8 **14**	8 +6 **14**
7 +8 **15**	8 +7 **15**	4 +8 **12**	8 +4 **12**	9 +6 **15**	6 +9 **15**
7 +7 **14**	5 +6 **11**	6 +5 **11**	5 +9 **14**	9 +5 **14**	8 +8 **16**
5 +5 **10**	7 +6 **13**	6 +7 **13**	9 +8 **17**	8 +9 **17**	6 +6 **12**
7 +9 **16**	9 +7 **16**	4 +8 **12**	8 +3 **11**	7 +3 **10**	9 +9 **18**

Number Correct
- **53–62:** To reinforce numeration, have students ring each answer of 13 on page 141.
- **40–52:** Discuss that students may have to ring more than one fact in each problem.
- **Less than 40:** Students may first cross out facts that are not correct, then ring the correct facts.

LESSON FOLLOW-UP AND ERROR ANALYSIS

Spectrum Software Addition 12–14

141

Lesson 11 Addition Facts through 18

Ring each fact for the number in the ⬤.

11
- 4 + 8
- (9 + 2)
- (5 + 6)
- 6 + 6
- (4 + 7)
- (8 + 3)

12
- 3 + 8
- (3 + 9)
- (6 + 6)
- 6 + 7
- (8 + 4)
- (7 + 5)
- 5 + 8
- 5 + 6

13
- (8 + 5)
- (7 + 6)
- 6 + 8
- 9 + 5
- (9 + 4)
- (6 + 7)
- 4 + 8

14
- (8 + 6)
- (9 + 5)
- 6 + 7
- (7 + 7)
- (6 + 8)
- 8 + 8

15
- 7 + 7
- (9 + 6)
- (8 + 7)
- (6 + 9)
- (7 + 8)
- 5 + 9

16
- 6 + 9
- 5 + 7
- (9 + 7)
- 8 + 7
- (7 + 9)
- (8 + 8)

17
- 9 + 9
- (8 + 9)
- 8 + 8
- 6 + 9
- 8 + 7
- (9 + 8)

18
- 5 + 8
- 4 + 6
- (9 + 9)
- 8 + 7
- 6 + 9

CHAPTER 9
Addition and Subtraction (facts through 18)
142

Prerequisite Skills: subtracting from 18

Lesson Focus: subtracting through 18
Possible Score: 78
Time Frame: 15–20 minutes

Lesson 12   Subtraction Facts through 18

Subtract.

15 − 7 = **8**	15 − 8 = **7**	13 − 9 = **4**	13 − 4 = **9**	12 − 8 = **4**	12 − 4 = **8**
14 − 6 = **8**	14 − 8 = **6**	11 − 7 = **4**	11 − 4 = **7**	10 − 7 = **3**	10 − 3 = **7**
15 − 6 = **9**	15 − 9 = **6**	14 − 9 = **5**	14 − 5 = **9**	17 − 8 = **9**	17 − 9 = **8**
16 − 8 = **8**	16 − 7 = **9**	16 − 9 = **7**	13 − 5 = **8**	13 − 8 = **5**	14 − 7 = **7**
12 − 6 = **6**	11 − 3 = **8**	11 − 8 = **3**	13 − 7 = **6**	13 − 6 = **7**	10 − 5 = **5**
10 − 8 = **2**	10 − 2 = **8**	12 − 5 = **7**	12 − 7 = **5**	18 − 9 = **9**	15 − 7 = **8**

CHAPTER 9

Number Correct
66–78: Have students choose one word from the page and write different subtraction facts that will spell out the same word.
51–65: Students may have figured out the answers without doing all of the subtraction, so have them show their work.
Less than 51: Have students use manipulatives to rework each incorrect answer.

LESSON FOLLOW-UP AND ERROR ANALYSIS

Spectrum Software Subtraction 4–8

143

Lesson 12 Subtraction Facts through 18

How many subtraction facts do you know?

0	1	2	3	4	5	6	7	8	9
R	I	U	Y	E	K	O	V	W	N

Check students' work before they write the code.
Subtract. Then write the letter that goes with the answer.

11 − 8 = 3 Y
15 − 9 = 6 O
10 − 8 = 2 U
14 − 9 = 5 K
16 − 7 = 9 N
14 − 8 = 6 O
15 − 7 = 8 W

7 − 3 = 4 E
9 − 2 = 7 V
8 − 4 = 4 E
9 − 9 = 0 R
10 − 7 = 3 Y
11 − 5 = 6 O
11 − 2 = 9 N
13 − 9 = 4 E

12 − 9 = 3 Y
13 − 7 = 6 O
11 − 9 = 2 U
16 − 8 = 8 W
10 − 9 = 1 I
18 − 9 = 9 N

CHAPTER 9
Addition and Subtraction (facts through 18)

For further evaluation, copy the Chapter Test on page 173.
For maintaining skills, use the Cumulative Review on pages 161–162.

Possible Score: 40
Time Frame: 5–10 minutes

CHAPTER 9 PRACTICE TEST
Addition and Subtraction (facts through 18)
For assessment of Chapters 1–9, use the Final Test on pages 149–152.

Add.

9 +8 = **17**	5 +7 = **12**	8 +6 = **14**	7 +5 = **12**	4 +9 = **13**	5 +6 = **11**
7 +6 = **13**	8 +8 = **16**	5 +9 = **14**	9 +9 = **18**	7 +8 = **15**	6 +6 = **12**
4 +7 = **11**	9 +2 = **11**	7 +7 = **14**	8 +4 = **12**	9 +6 = **15**	7 +9 = **16**

Subtract.

13 −6 = **7**	14 −7 = **7**	15 −6 = **9**	11 −3 = **8**	12 −8 = **4**	16 −9 = **7**
13 −8 = **5**	12 −9 = **3**	11 −5 = **6**	17 −8 = **9**	18 −9 = **9**	15 −7 = **8**
14 −8 = **6**	11 −7 = **4**	12 −6 = **6**	14 −5 = **9**	11 −9 = **2**	17 −9 = **8**

Number Correct   LESSON FOLLOW-UP AND ERROR ANALYSIS   *Spectrum Software* Addition 12–14; Subtraction 4–8; Word Problems 17 and 18

- **34–40:** Have students draw picture stories showing addition and subtraction using the same numbers.
- **26–33:** Have students count the objects aloud as they write the numbers vertically.
- **Less than 26:** Have students use manipulatives to rework each incorrect answer.

145

CHAPTER 9 PRACTICE TEST
Problem Solving

Solve each problem.

   8 closed boxes
+ 6 open boxes
14 boxes in all

  12 candles in all
− 3 blue candles
   9 white candles

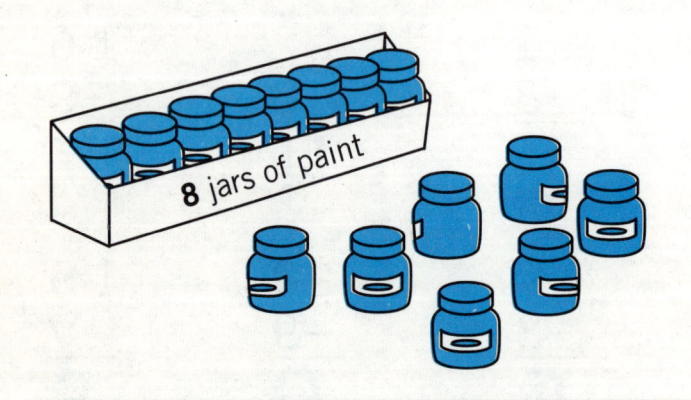

   8 jars in a box
+ 7 other jars
15 jars in all

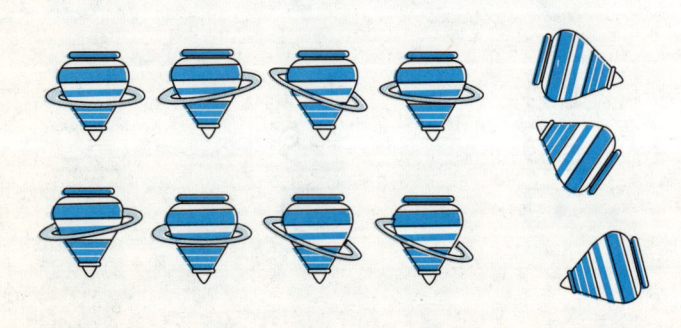

8 jars of paint

  11 tops in all
− 3 tops not spinning
   8 tops spinning

CHAPTER 9
Addition and Subtraction (facts through 18)

MID-TEST Chapters 1-4

Ring the numeral.

0 1 (2) 3	4 (5) 6 7	7 8 9 (10)
(2¢) 5¢ 6¢	1¢ 5¢ (10¢)	4¢ (8¢) 9¢

Ring the ☐ in the place named.

fourth

third

Add.

5	3	4	3	2	3
+5	+6	+3	+1	+6	+3
10	9	7	4	8	6

Subtract.

9	7	10	9	10	5
−7	−5	−4	−9	−9	−2
2	2	6	0	1	3

SPECTRUM MATHEMATICS
Gold Book

MID-TEST
Chapters 1–4

147

MID-TEST   Chapters 1-4 (continued)

Add or subtract.   STOP!   Watch the + and − signs!

```
  4        6        4       1 0       1        8
 +6       −1       +4       −5       +8       −7
 ──       ──       ──       ──       ──       ──
 10        5        8        5        9        1
```

Solve each problem.

TICKET 6¢   TICKET 3¢   1¢ TICKET

I buy [TICKET]   3¢   I have   9¢
and [TICKET]   +1¢   I buy [TICKET]   −6¢
I spent   ──   I have left   ──
                         4¢   3¢

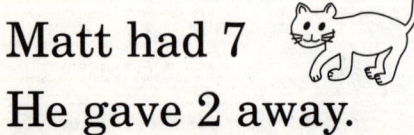

Matt had 7 🐱.   7
He gave 2 away.   −2
How many does he have now?   ──
                                            5

There are 6 blue 🌼.   6
There are 3 white 🌼.   +3
How many are there in all?   ──
                                            9

STOP
MID-TEST
Chapters 1–4

SPECTRUM MATHEMATICS
Gold Book
148

FINAL TEST Chapters 1-9

Tell how many cents.

__6__ ¢   __30__  ¢   __42__ ¢

Name the numbers in order.

56, 57, 58, __59__, __60__, __61__, __62__

Write the time for each clock.

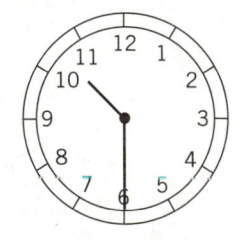

__10__:__30__ 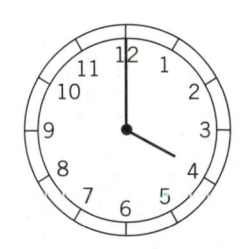   __4__:__00__ 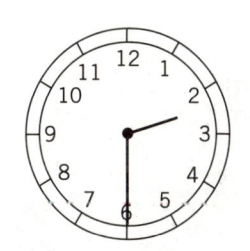   __2__:__30__

Automobiles

How many  🚗 ? __2__

How many 🚚 ? __4__

How many 🚌 ? __3__

SPECTRUM MATHEMATICS
Gold Book

FINAL TEST   Chapters 1–9 (continued)

How long is each object?

Use a centimeter ruler.

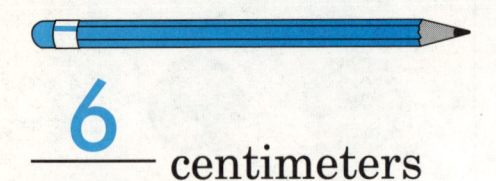

__6__ centimeters

__3__ centimeters

Use an inch ruler.

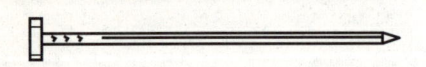

__2__ inches

__4__ inches

Add.

```
   3        6        4        0        4
 + 1      + 4      + 5      + 7      + 4
   4       10        9        7        8

  20       71       21       42       12
 +14      + 3      +25      +15      +67
  34       74       46       57       79
```

Subtract.

```
   5        7       10        9        8
 - 3      - 1      - 4      - 7      - 5
   2        6        6        2        3

  68       72       39       84       57
 -48      -50      - 4      -41      -52
  20       22       35       43        5
```

SPECTRUM MATHEMATICS
Gold Book
150

GO
FINAL TEST
Chapters 1–9

FINAL TEST   Chapters 1-9 (continued)

Add or subtract. STOP!   **Watch the + and − signs.**

10 − 2 **8**	5 +5 **10**	7 +2 **9**	7 −3 **4**	10 −7 **3**
51 +27 **78**	69 −10 **59**	43 + 2 **45**	87 −17 **70**	76 −62 **14**

Add.

3 +8 **11**	7 +7 **14**	8 + 4 **12**	9 +9 **18**	8 +8 **16**
8 +7 **15**	4 +9 **13**	7 + 6 **13**	6 +8 **14**	8 +9 **17**

Subtract.

12 − 6 **6**	14 − 7 **7**	11 − 8 **3**	15 − 9 **6**	17 − 8 **9**
13 − 9 **4**	15 − 8 **7**	16 − 7 **9**	14 − 6 **8**	18 − 9 **9**

FINAL TEST   Chapters 1-9 (continued)

Ring the shape.

square   ○   △   ⊡

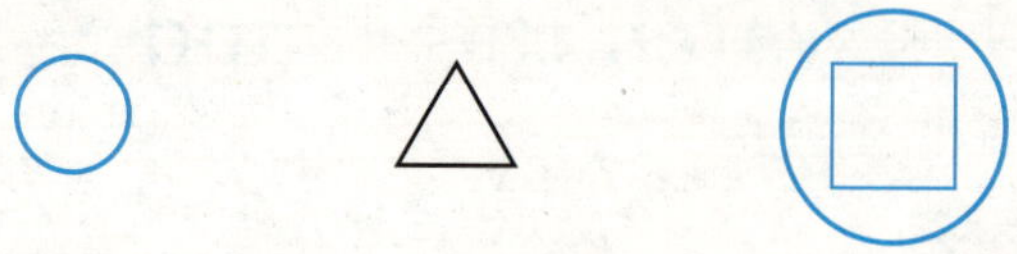

cylinder   △   Ⓘ   ●

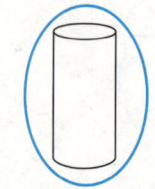

Solve each problem.

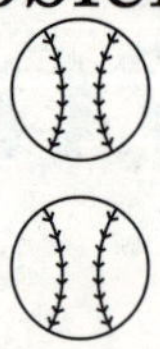

Sara has 2 ⚾.
Ryan has 6 ⚾.

How many do they have in all?

$$\begin{array}{r} 2 \\ +6 \\ \hline 8 \end{array}$$

You had 38¢.
You spent 23¢.

How much do you have left?

$$\begin{array}{r} 38¢ \\ -23¢ \\ \hline 15¢ \end{array}$$

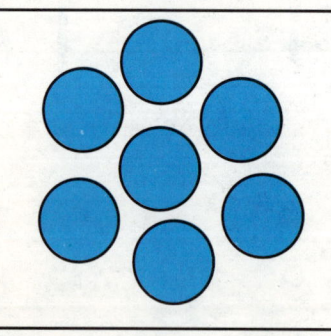

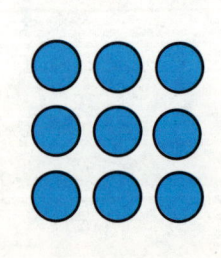

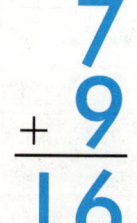

$$\begin{array}{r} 7 \text{ large balls} \\ +9 \text{ small balls} \\ \hline 16 \text{ balls in all} \end{array}$$

$$\begin{array}{r} 13 \text{ cars in all} \\ -7 \text{ black cars} \\ \hline 6 \text{ white cars} \end{array}$$

STOP

FINAL TEST
Chapters 1-9

152

CHAPTER 1   CUMULATIVE REVIEW

Work each problem.
Find the correct answer.
Mark the space for the answer.

Part 1 Concepts

Tell how many.

1.
- A 5
- ✓ B 6
- C 7
- D 8

2.
- F 6
- G 7
- H 8
- ✓ J 9

3.
- A 3
- ✓ B 4
- C 5
- D 6

Part 2 Computation

What numeral goes in the ☐ to finish the pattern?

4. 1 2 ☐ 4 5
- F 6
- ✓ H 3
- G 7
- J 8

5. 4 5 6 ☐ 8
- ✓ A 7
- C 9
- B 8
- D 10

Part 3 Applications

6. Name the place of the ringed box.

- F first
- G second
- ✓ H third
- J fourth

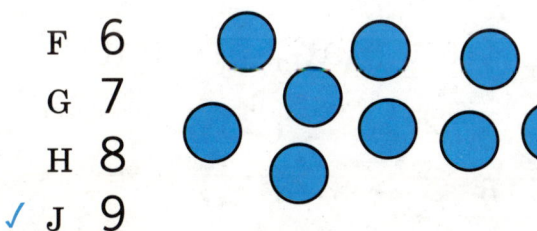

ANSWER ROW
1 Ⓐ ● Ⓒ Ⓓ   3 Ⓐ ● Ⓒ Ⓓ   5 ● Ⓑ Ⓒ Ⓓ
2 Ⓕ Ⓖ Ⓗ ●   4 Ⓕ Ⓖ ● Ⓙ   6 Ⓕ Ⓖ ● Ⓙ

CHAPTER 1
CUMULATIVE REVIEW
153

CHAPTER 2 CUMULATIVE REVIEW

Work each problem.
Find the correct answer.
Mark the space for the answer.

Part 1 Concepts

1. Tell how many. 
   - A 5
   - B 6
   - ✓ C 7
   - D 8

2. Finish the pattern. What number goes in the ☐?

   2 3 ☐ 5 6
   - ✓ F 4
   - G 5
   - H 6
   - J 7

Part 2 Computation

3. Add.   3
              +1
   - A 1
   - B 2
   - C 3
   - ✓ D 4

4. Subtract.   4
              −3
   - ✓ F 1
   - G 2
   - H 3
   - J 4

Part 3 Applications

5. There are 5 ✈. 
   2 fly away.
   How many are left?
   - A 2
   - ✓ B 3
   - C 6
   - D 7

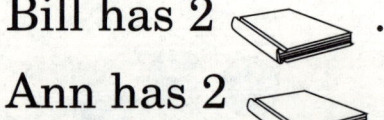

6. Bill has 2 📕.
   Ann has 2 📕.
   How many in all?
   - ✓ F 4
   - G 5
   - H 3
   - J 2

ANSWER ROW
1 Ⓐ Ⓑ ●C Ⓓ   3 Ⓐ Ⓑ Ⓒ ●D   5 Ⓐ ●B Ⓒ Ⓓ
2 ●F Ⓖ Ⓗ Ⓙ   4 ●F Ⓖ Ⓗ Ⓙ   6 ●F Ⓖ Ⓗ Ⓙ

CHAPTER 3   CUMULATIVE REVIEW

Work each problem.
Find the correct answer.
Mark the space for the answer.

Part 1   Concepts

1. Tell how many.

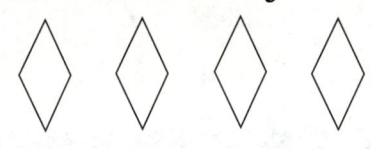

- A 3
- ✓ B 4
- C 5
- D 6

2. Name the place of the ringed ball.

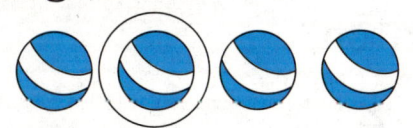

- F first
- ✓ G second
- H third
- J fourth

Part 2   Computation

3. Add.   4
            +3

- A 6
- ✓ B 7
- C 8
- D 9

4. Subtract.   8
                 −6

- F 1
- ✓ G 2
- H 3
- J 4

Part 3   Applications

5. There are 4 🎈. 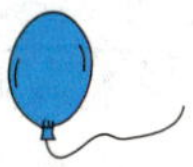
There are 3 🎈. 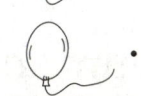
How many in all?

- A 4
- B 5
- C 6
- ✓ D 7

6. There are 3 🐱. 
5 more come.
How many in all?

- F 6
- G 7
- H 2
- ✓ J 8

ANSWER ROW
1 Ⓐ ●B Ⓒ Ⓓ   3 Ⓐ ●B Ⓒ Ⓓ   5 Ⓐ Ⓑ Ⓒ ●D
2 Ⓕ ●G Ⓗ Ⓙ   4 Ⓕ ●G Ⓗ Ⓙ   6 Ⓕ Ⓖ Ⓗ ●J

CHAPTER 4 CUMULATIVE REVIEW

Work each problem.
Find the correct answer.
Mark the space for the answer.

Part 1 Concepts

1. Tell how many.
   - A four
   - ✓ B five
   - C six
   - D seven

2. Count forward. What numeral goes in the ☐?

   1 2 3 ☐ 5 6

   - F 3
   - ✓ G 4
   - H 5
   - J 6

Part 2 Computation

3. Add.   6
              +4

   - A 7
   - B 8
   - C 9
   - ✓ D 10

4. Subtract.   9
               −2

   - F 5
   - G 6
   - ✓ H 7
   - J 8

Part 3 Applications

5. There were 9 🍎.
   6 were eaten.
   How many were not eaten?
   - A 2
   - ✓ B 3
   - C 4
   - D 5

6. I have 5 📦.
   I find 4 more.
   Now how many in all?
   - F 7
   - G 8
   - ✓ H 9
   - J 10

STOP

ANSWER ROW   1 Ⓐ ●B Ⓒ Ⓓ   3 Ⓐ Ⓑ Ⓒ ●D   5 Ⓐ ●B Ⓒ Ⓓ
             2 Ⓕ ●G Ⓗ Ⓙ   4 Ⓕ Ⓖ ●H Ⓙ   6 Ⓕ Ⓖ ●H Ⓙ

CHAPTER 5   CUMULATIVE REVIEW

Work each problem.
Find the correct answer.
Mark the space for the answer.

Part 1   Concepts

Complete.

1. 1 ten 6 ones = _____

   ✓ A 16
   B 15
   C 51
   D 61

2. 4 tens 8 ones = _____

   F 47
   ✓ G 48
   H 78
   J 87

Part 2   Computation

3. Add.   2
              +8

   A 7
   B 8
   C 9
   ✓ D 10

4. Subtract.   9
                 −6

   F 2   H 4
   ✓ G 3   J 5

Part 3   Applications

5. There were 6 🐟.

   4 swam away.

   How many were left?

   ✓ A 2
   B 3
   C 4
   D 5

6. There are 8 🌼.

   Nick finds 2 more.

   Now how many in all?

   F 7
   G 8
   H 9
   ✓ J 10

ANSWER ROW
1 Ⓐ Ⓑ Ⓒ Ⓓ   3 Ⓐ Ⓑ Ⓒ Ⓓ   5 Ⓐ Ⓑ Ⓒ Ⓓ
2 Ⓕ Ⓖ Ⓗ Ⓙ   4 Ⓕ Ⓖ Ⓗ Ⓙ   6 Ⓕ Ⓖ Ⓗ Ⓙ

CHAPTER 6 CUMULATIVE REVIEW

Work each problem.
Find the correct answer.
Mark the space for the answer.

Part 1 Concepts

1. Complete.

    5 tens 2 ones = _____

    A 25   ✓ C 52
    B 26   D 62

2. Count by 2s. What number goes in the ___?

    6, 8, __, 12, 14

    F 12   H 4
    ✓ G 10   J 16

Part 2 Computation

3. Add.   7
                      +2

    A 7
    B 8
    ✓ C 9
    D 10

4. Subtract.   10
                      −3

    F 5
    G 6
    ✓ H 7
    J 8

Part 3 Applications

5. What time is on the clock?

    A 4:00
    B 6:00
    ✓ C 4:30
    D 5:30

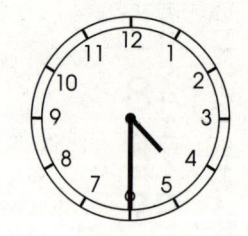

6. How long is the pencil?

    F 4 centimeters
    G 5 centimeters
    ✓ H 6 centimeters
    J 7 centimeters

STOP

ANSWER ROW
1 Ⓐ Ⓑ ● Ⓓ   3 Ⓐ Ⓑ ● Ⓓ   5 Ⓐ Ⓑ ● Ⓓ
2 Ⓕ ● Ⓗ Ⓙ   4 Ⓕ Ⓖ ● Ⓙ   6 Ⓕ Ⓖ ● Ⓙ

CHAPTER 6
CUMULATIVE REVIEW

CHAPTER 7 CUMULATIVE REVIEW

Work each problem.
Find the correct answer.
Mark the space for the answer.

Part 1 Concepts

1. Which number is the greatest?

   34   40   8   22

   A 34
   ✓ B 40
   C 8
   D 22

2. Count by 5s. What number goes in the ___?

   5, 10, 15, __, 25

   F 15
   ✓ G 20
   H 25
   J 30

Part 2 Computation

3. Add.   6
          +2

   A 6
   B 7
   ✓ C 8
   D 9

4. Subtract.   9
               −4

   F 4
   ✓ G 5
   H 6
   J 7

Part 3 Applications

5. What time is on the clock?

   4:30

   A two-thirty
   B three-thirty
   ✓ C four-thirty
   D five-thirty

6. Which shape is shown?

   △

   F circle
   G rectangle
   H square
   ✓ J triangle

ANSWER ROW   1 Ⓐ ● Ⓒ Ⓓ   3 Ⓐ Ⓑ ● Ⓓ   5 Ⓐ Ⓑ ● Ⓓ
             2 Ⓕ ● Ⓗ Ⓙ   4 Ⓕ ● Ⓗ Ⓙ   6 Ⓕ Ⓖ Ⓗ ●

CHAPTER 7
CUMULATIVE REVIEW
159

CHAPTER 8 CUMULATIVE REVIEW

Work each problem.
Find the correct answer.
Mark the space for the answer.

Part 1 Concepts

1. Tell how many.

    A 15
    ✓ B 16
    C 17
    D 18

2. Count by 10s. What number goes in the ___?

    20, 30, 40, __, 60

    F 30
    G 40
    ✓ H 50
    J 60

Part 2 Computation

3. Add.   40
         +32

    A 62
    ✓ B 72
    C 82
    D 92

4. Subtract.   39
              −24

    F 5
    ✓ G 15
    H 25
    J 35

Part 3 Applications

5. Which shape is shown?

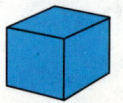

    A cone
    ✓ B cube
    C cylinder
    D sphere

6. How long is the crayon?

    ✓ F 4 inches
    G 5 inches
    H 6 inches
    J 7 inches

ANSWER ROW
1 Ⓐ ●B Ⓒ Ⓓ   3 Ⓐ ●B Ⓒ Ⓓ   5 Ⓐ ●B Ⓒ Ⓓ
2 Ⓕ Ⓖ ●H Ⓙ   4 Ⓕ ●G Ⓗ Ⓙ   6 ●F Ⓖ Ⓗ Ⓙ

CHAPTER 8
CUMULATIVE REVIEW

160

CHAPTER 9   **CUMULATIVE REVIEW**

Work each problem.
Find the correct answer.
Mark the space for the answer.

Part 1 Concepts

1. Tell how many.

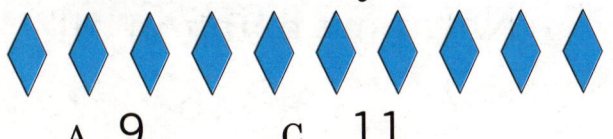

◆◆◆◆◆◆◆◆◆◆

   A 9   C 11
✓B 10   D 12

2. Which number is the greatest?

5   2   12   10

   F 5
   G 2
✓H 12
   J 10

3. Count by 2s. What number goes in the ___?

24, 26, ___, 30, 32

   A 27
✓B 28
   C 29
   D 30

Part 2 Computation

4. Add.   7
     +6

   F 12
✓G 13
   H 14
   J 15

5. Subtract.   15
         −8

   A 5
   B 6
✓C 7
   D 8

6. Add.   9
     +6

   F 12
   G 13
   H 14
✓J 15

GO

ANSWER ROW   1 Ⓐ ●Ⓒ Ⓓ   3 Ⓐ ● Ⓒ Ⓓ   5 Ⓐ Ⓑ ● Ⓓ
             2 Ⓕ Ⓖ ● Ⓙ   4 Ⓕ ● Ⓗ Ⓙ   6 Ⓕ Ⓖ Ⓗ ●

CHAPTER 9   CUMULATIVE REVIEW (continued)

7. Subtract.   12
                  −3

- A 7
- B 8
- ✓ C 9
- D 10

8. Add.   54
             +12

- ✓ F 66
- G 56
- H 46
- J 36

9. Subtract.   49
                  −13

- A 16
- B 26
- ✓ C 36
- D 46

Part 3 Applications

10. There are 6 🍁.

I find 8 more.

Now how many in all?

- F 7
- ✓ G 14
- H 16
- J 18

11. Which shape is shown?

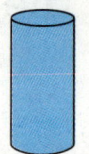

- A cone
- B cube
- ✓ C cylinder
- D rectangular solid

12. How long is the ribbon?

- F 2 centimeters
- ✓ G 3 centimeters
- H 4 centimeters
- J 5 centimeters

STOP

ANSWER ROW
7 Ⓐ Ⓑ ●C Ⓓ   9 Ⓐ Ⓑ ●C Ⓓ   11 Ⓐ Ⓑ ●C Ⓓ
8 ●F Ⓖ Ⓗ Ⓙ   10 Ⓕ ●G Ⓗ Ⓙ   12 Ⓕ ●G Ⓗ Ⓙ

Spectrum Math Assessment

INFORMAL ASSESSMENT

✓ Daily Lessons

Performance on the daily lessons is informal assessment to chart progress and understanding. The daily lesson scores can be averaged over the course of a grading period to provide one part of a student's evaluation.

✓ Lesson Follow-up

Suggestions for addressing student performance on the daily lesson can be found at the end of each lesson in the Teacher's Edition.

✓ Problem Solving

The problem solving exercises that follow the daily lessons provide specific insight into whether students can apply the skill they have just practiced. The ability to apply the skill in another context is a clear sign of understanding.

✓ Achieve Key Skills and Strategies

The skill lessons and problem solving activities provide further insight into student understanding of important math concepts.

FORMAL ASSESSMENT

✓ Readiness Check

The Readiness Checks at the beginning of **Levels Red–Purple** offer insight into student skill level and placement.

✓ Chapter Pretests

The Chapter Pretest at the beginning of each chapter provides insight so teachers can plan their instruction according to the needs of the student.

✓ Chapter Tests

The Chapter Tests in blackline master form in the back of each Teacher's Edition provide for a formal assessment of each chapter's content.

- Using the **Chapter Tests**
  Administer the Chapter Test after students complete the Cumulative Review at the end of each chapter. Record the scores as part of the math evaluation.

ASSESSMENT

Spectrum Math Assessment

SELF ASSESSMENT

✓ Chapter Practice Tests

Gives students an opportunity to evaluate their knowledge of the chapter content before taking the Chapter Test. Students can record the scores on the Chapter Practice Test chart as part of their math evaluation.

✓ Self Assessment

The students can keep track of their progress by recording their scores from the Chapter Practice Tests on the chart located on the inside back cover.

✓ Cumulative Review

The Cumulative Review for each chapter in the Student Edition offers insight into student ability to maintain skills taught from the beginning of the book.

✓ Spectrum Math Software

The Teacher Manager in the Spectrum Math Software program records each student's progress through the lessons. A quick look at the Class Record will show what scores students achieved on each lesson completed. Extra practice pages can be printed for students who need additional work.

ASSESSMENT

CHAPTER 1 TEST

NAME _____

Tell how many.

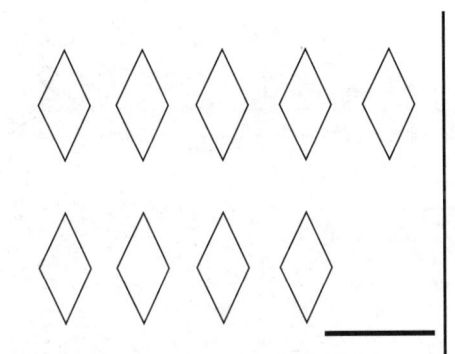

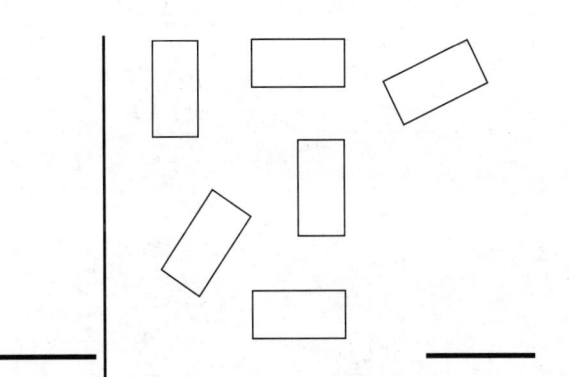

_____   _____   _____

Read the numeral. Draw that many ◯s.

7   4   3

Write a numeral in each ☐ to finish the pattern.

4   5   ☐   7   8

3   ☐   5   6   7

Ring the fourth ball.

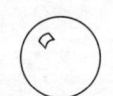

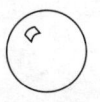

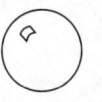

CHAPTER 2 TEST

Add.

2	5	1	2	0	1
+1	+0	+4	+2	+1	+2

2	3	4	1	4	2
+0	+1	+0	+3	+1	+3

1	0	3	0	4	1
+0	+2	+2	+5	+0	+2

Subtract.

4	5	4	5	3	5
−2	−0	−1	−2	−1	−1

4	3	5	5	3	2
−0	−2	−4	−2	−3	−1

5	2	2	3	4	4
−5	−2	−0	−1	−3	−4

SPECTRUM MATHEMATICS
Gold Book

NAME _____

CHAPTER 3 TEST

Add.

3	4	6	2	6
+4	+4	+0	+5	+1

1	1	2	7	6
+5	+7	+4	+0	+2

Subtract.

8	6	7	8	6
−3	−4	−1	−7	−0

8	6	6	8	7
−6	−5	−3	−4	−5

Add or subtract. STOP! Watch the + and −.

3	7	7	3	4
+4	−4	−0	+3	+3

7	7	2	8	5
−3	−2	+6	−2	+2

SPECTRUM MATHEMATICS
Gold Book

CHAPTER 3 TEST

167

CHAPTER 4 TEST

Add.

2	3	8	1	4
+8	+6	+2	+8	+5

5	2	0	6	0
+5	+7	+8	+4	+9

Subtract.

9	9	10	9	9
−3	−1	−1	−7	−0

10	10	9	9	9
−5	−6	−6	−2	−4

Add or subtract. STOP! **Watch the + and −.**

10	9	3	9	10
−3	−6	+7	+1	−4

9	7	6	9	2
−0	+3	+4	−5	+6

CHAPTER 5 TEST

Complete.

5 tens 2 ones = _____   4 tens 6 ones = _____

4 tens 3 ones = _____   6 tens 1 one = _____

5 tens 0 ones = _____   3 tens 4 ones = _____

Name the numbers in order for each row.

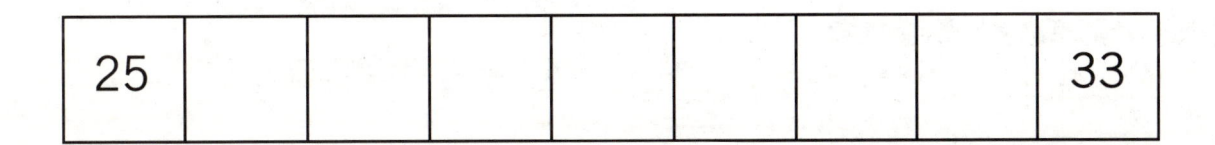

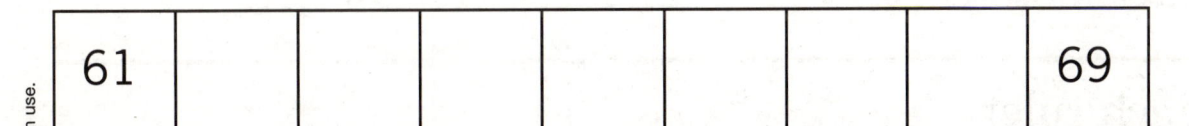

| 25 | | | | | | | 33 |

| 61 | | | | | | | 69 |

Ring the number that is greater.

25   28 | 55   52 | 93   90

Count by 2s. Write the missing numbers.

6, 8, ____, 12, ____, 16

30, 32, 34, ____, 38, ____, 42

SPECTRUM MATHEMATICS
Gold Book

NAME _____

CHAPTER 6 TEST

Write the time for each clock.

_____ thirty

_____ : _____

_____ : _____

Use a centimeter ruler.
How long is each object?

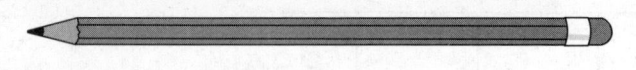

_____ centimeters

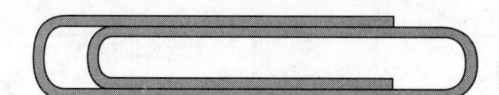

_____ centimeters

Use an inch ruler.
How long is each object?

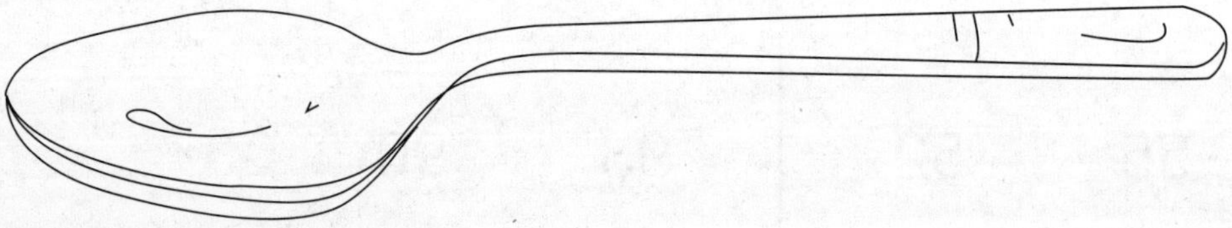

_____ inches

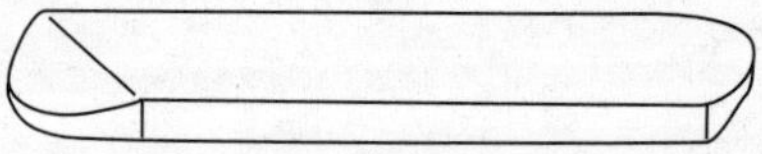

_____ inches

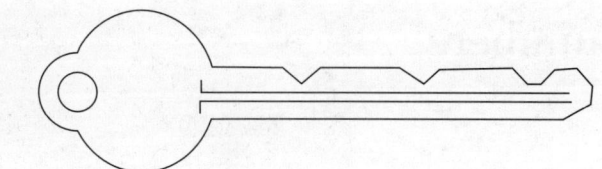

_____ inches

SPECTRUM MATHEMATICS
Gold Book

CHAPTER 6 TEST

NAME _____

CHAPTER 7 TEST

Ring the shape.

circle

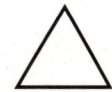

cube

triangle

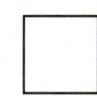

sphere

Ring the shapes that match when folded on the line.

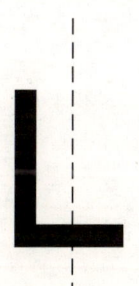

SPECTRUM MATHEMATICS
Gold Book

CHAPTER 7 TEST

171

CHAPTER 8 TEST

Add.

24 + 3	23 +51	56 +32	60 +16	32 +14

48 +31	43 +25	61 +25	52 +41	25 +43

44 +20	43 +43	51 +42	37 +22	42 +54

Subtract.

44 −31	35 −15	48 −24	29 −15	77 −46

49 −16	76 −15	69 −33	63 −42	67 −56

89 −56	67 −32	49 −32	77 −35	76 −62

SPECTRUM MATHEMATICS
Gold Book

CHAPTER 9 TEST

Add.

7 +7	6 +5	7 +9	9 +6	9 +8	7 +4

5 +9	6 +8	9 +2	8 +4	9 +4	8 +5

8 +9	7 +5	4 +9	8 +8	9 +5	6 +7

Subtract.

13 −6	12 −4	13 −5	13 −4	14 −5	11 −5

14 −9	17 −8	14 −8	11 −2	14 −7	15 −6

12 −5	16 −9	13 −9	16 −8	17 −9	11 −4

SPECTRUM MATHEMATICS
Gold Book

CHAPTER 9 TEST

CHAPTER 1 TEST

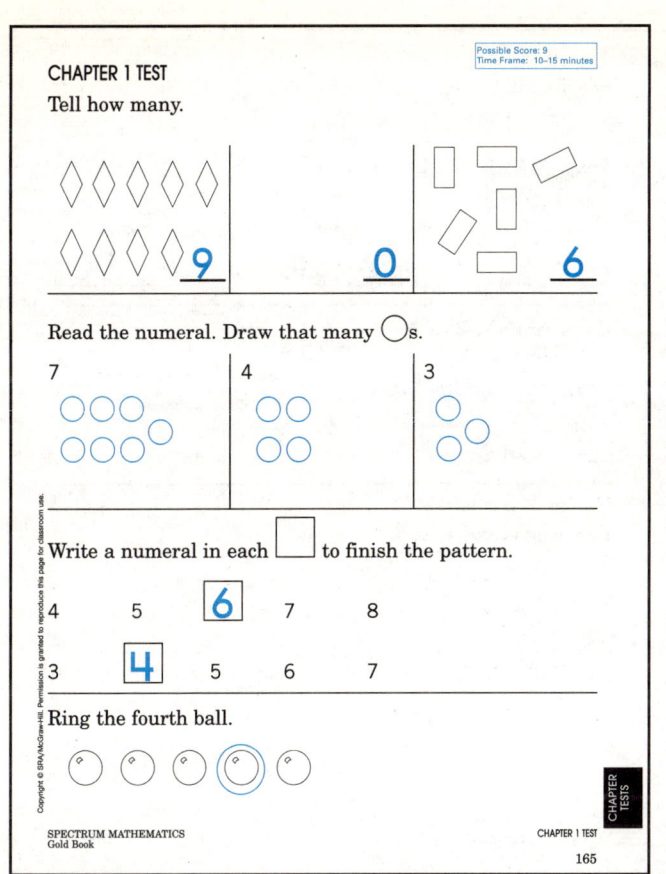

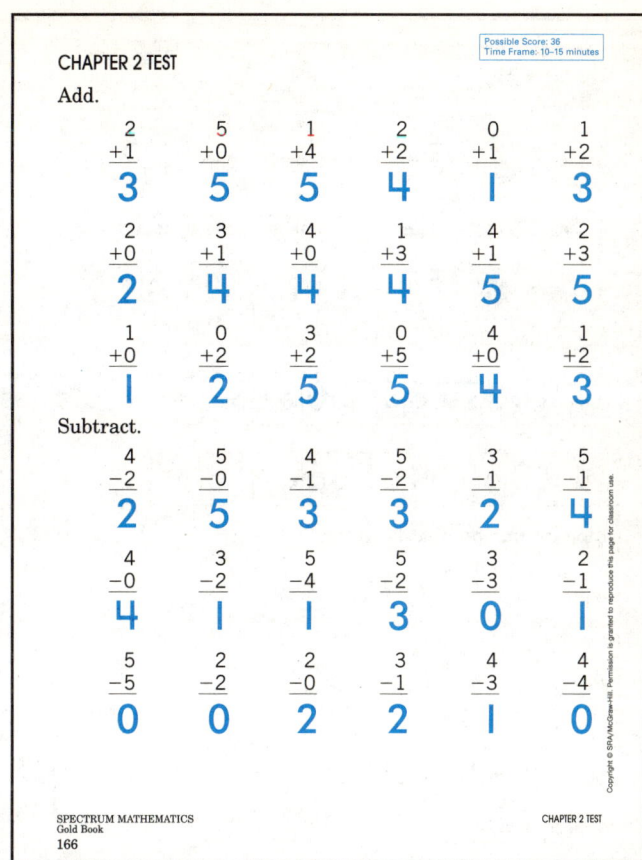

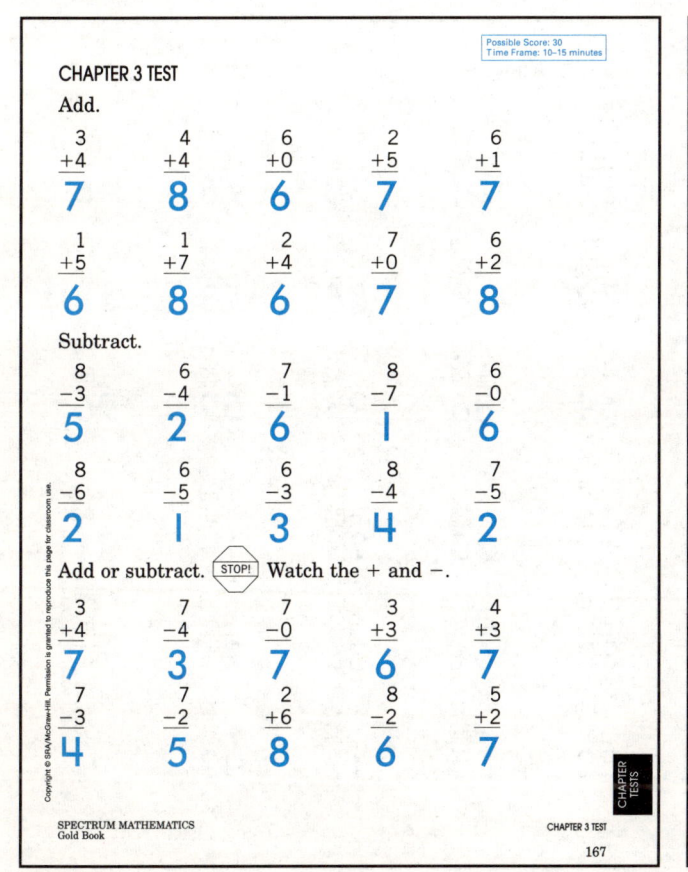

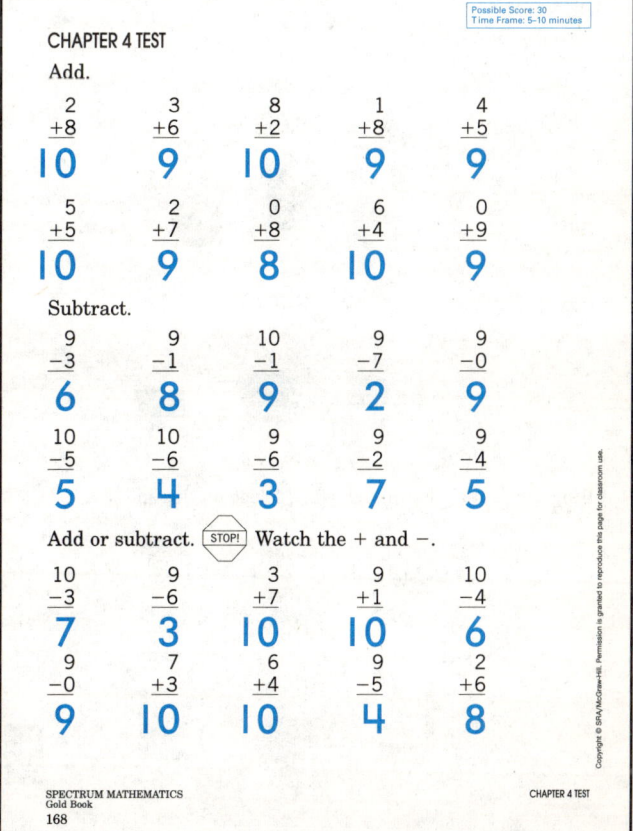

Possible Score: 9
Time Frame: 10–15 minutes

Tell how many.

◇◇◇◇
◇◇◇◇◇ **9**   □ **0**   ▭▭▭▭▭▭ **6**

Read the numeral. Draw that many ◯s.

7 ◯◯◯◯◯◯◯   4 ◯◯◯◯   3 ◯◯◯

Write a numeral in each ☐ to finish the pattern.

4   5   **6**   7   8
3   **4**   5   6   7

Ring the fourth ball.

◯ ◯ ◯ ⊛ ◯

CHAPTER 1 TEST
165

CHAPTER 2 TEST

Possible Score: 36
Time Frame: 10–15 minutes

Add.

2	5	1	2	0	1
+1	+0	+4	+2	+1	+2
3	**5**	**5**	**4**	**1**	**3**

2	3	4	1	4	2
+0	+1	+0	+3	+1	+3
2	**4**	**4**	**4**	**5**	**5**

1	0	3	0	4	1
+0	+2	+2	+5	+0	+2
1	**2**	**5**	**5**	**4**	**3**

Subtract.

4	5	4	5	3	5
−2	−0	−1	−2	−1	−1
2	**5**	**3**	**3**	**2**	**4**

4	3	5	5	3	2
−0	−2	−4	−2	−3	−1
4	**1**	**1**	**3**	**0**	**1**

5	2	2	3	4	4
−5	−2	−0	−1	−3	−4
0	**0**	**2**	**2**	**1**	**0**

CHAPTER 2 TEST
166

CHAPTER 3 TEST

Possible Score: 30
Time Frame: 10–15 minutes

Add.

3	4	6	2	6
+4	+4	+0	+5	+1
7	**8**	**6**	**7**	**7**

1	1	2	7	6
+5	+7	+4	+0	+2
6	**8**	**6**	**7**	**8**

Subtract.

8	6	7	8	6
−3	−4	−1	−7	−0
5	**2**	**6**	**1**	**6**

8	6	6	8	7
−6	−5	−3	−4	−5
2	**1**	**3**	**4**	**2**

Add or subtract. 🛑 Watch the + and −.

3	7	7	3	4
+4	−4	−0	+3	+3
7	**3**	**7**	**6**	**7**

7	7	2	8	5
−3	−2	+6	−2	+2
4	**5**	**8**	**6**	**7**

CHAPTER 3 TEST
167

CHAPTER 4 TEST

Possible Score: 30
Time Frame: 5–10 minutes

Add.

2	3	8	1	4
+8	+6	+2	+8	+5
10	**9**	**10**	**9**	**9**

5	2	0	6	0
+5	+7	+8	+4	+9
10	**9**	**8**	**10**	**9**

Subtract.

9	9	10	9	9
−3	−1	−1	−7	−0
6	**8**	**9**	**2**	**9**

10	10	9	9	9
−5	−6	−6	−2	−4
5	**4**	**3**	**7**	**5**

Add or subtract. 🛑 Watch the + and −.

10	9	3	9	10
−3	−6	+7	+1	−4
7	**3**	**10**	**10**	**6**

9	7	6	9	2
−0	+3	+4	−5	+6
9	**10**	**10**	**4**	**8**

CHAPTER 4 TEST
168

SPECTRUM MATHEMATICS
Gold Book

CHAPTER TEST
Answers

175

CHAPTER 5 TEST

Possible Score: 27
Time Frame: 5–10 minutes

Complete.

5 tens 2 ones = **52**   4 tens 6 ones = **46**

4 tens 3 ones = **43**   6 tens 1 one = **61**

5 tens 0 ones = **50**   3 tens 4 ones = **34**

Name the numbers in order for each row.

| 25 | **26** | **27** | **28** | **29** | **30** | **31** | **32** | 33 |

| 61 | **62** | **63** | **64** | **65** | **66** | **67** | **68** | 69 |

Ring the number that is greater.

25 (28) | (55) 52 | (93) 90

Count by 2s. Write the missing numbers.

6, 8, **10**, 12, **14**, 16

30, 32, 34, **36**, 38, **40**, 42

SPECTRUM MATHEMATICS
Gold Book
CHAPTER 5 TEST
169

CHAPTER 6 TEST

Possible Score: 8
Time Frame: 10–15 minutes

Write the time for each clock.

five thirty   **2** : **30**   **8** : **00**

Use a centimeter ruler. How long is each object?

8 centimeters   **6** centimeters

Use an inch ruler. How long is each object?

5 inches

2 inches

3 inches

SPECTRUM MATHEMATICS
Gold Book
CHAPTER 6 TEST
170

CHAPTER 7 TEST

Possible Score: 5
Time Frame: 5–10 minutes

Ring the shape.

circle — (○) △ □

cube — (■) cylinder sphere

triangle — (△) □ ○

sphere — cube (●) rectangle

Ring the shapes that match when folded on the line.

(crown)   flower

L   (T)

SPECTRUM MATHEMATICS
Gold Book
CHAPTER 7 TEST
171

CHAPTER 8 TEST

Possible Score: 30
Time Frame: 10–15 minutes

Add.

```
 24      23      56      60      32
+ 3     +51     +32     +16     +14
 27      74      88      76      46

 48      43      61      52      25
+31     +25     +25     +41     +43
 79      68      86      93      68

 44      43      51      37      42
+20     +43     +42     +22     +54
 64      86      93      59      96
```

Subtract.

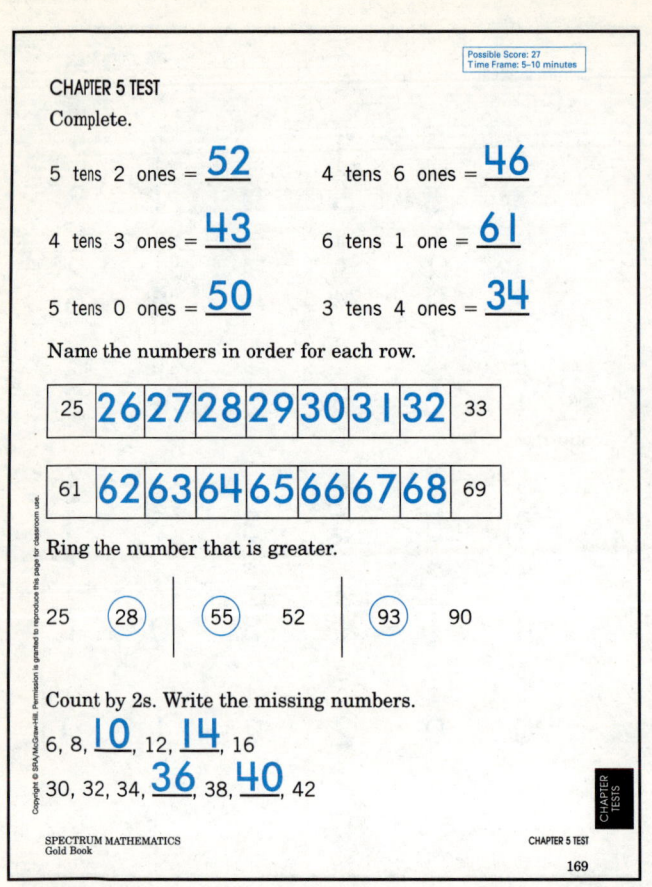

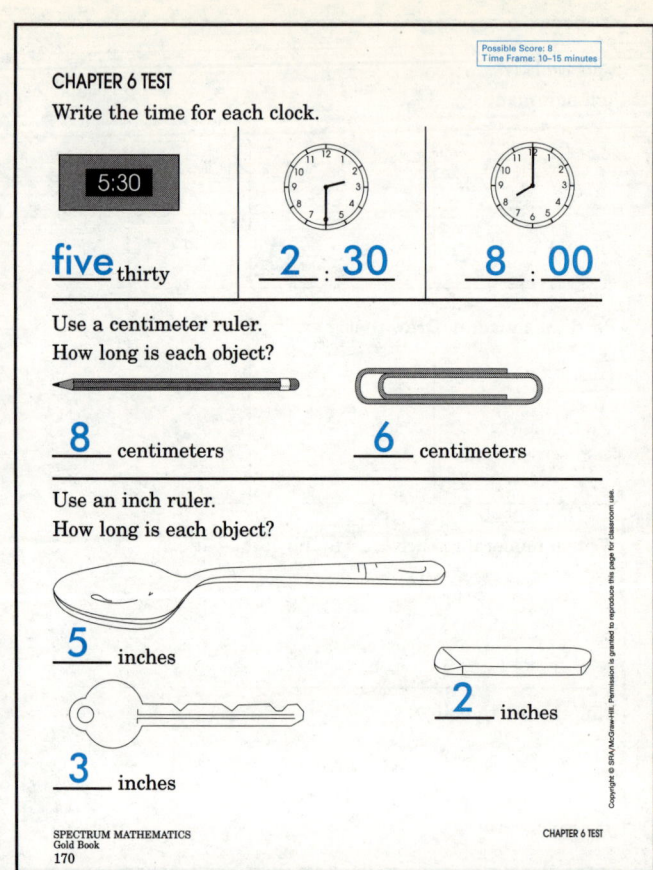

```
 44      35      48      29      77
-31     -15     -24     -15     -46
 13      20      24      14      31

 49      76      69      63      67
-16     -15     -33     -42     -56
 33      61      36      21      11

 89      67      49      77      76
-56     -32     -32     -35     -62
 33      35      17      42      14
```

SPECTRUM MATHEMATICS
Gold Book
CHAPTER 8 TEST
172

SPECTRUM MATHEMATICS
Gold Book

CHAPTER TEST
Answers

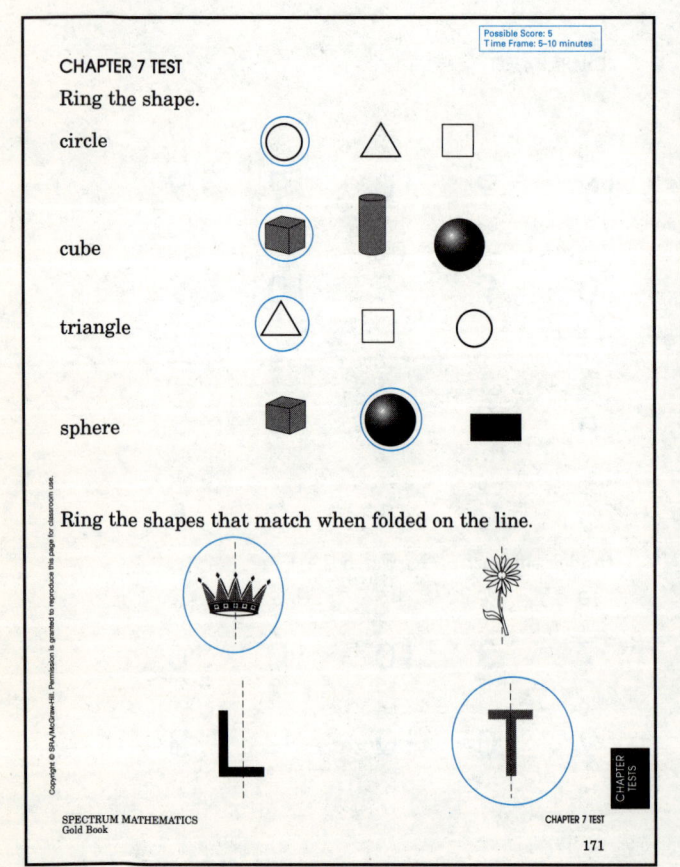

176

CHAPTER 9 TEST

Possible Score: 36
Time Frame: 5–10 minutes

Add.

7	6	7	9	9	7
+7	+5	+9	+6	+8	+4
14	11	16	15	17	11

5	6	9	8	9	8
+9	+8	+2	+4	+4	+5
14	14	11	12	13	13

8	7	4	8	9	6
+9	+5	+9	+8	+5	+7
17	12	13	16	14	13

Subtract.

13	12	13	13	14	11
−6	−4	−5	−4	−5	−5
7	8	8	9	9	6

14	17	14	11	14	15
−9	−8	−8	−2	−7	−6
5	9	6	9	7	9

12	16	13	16	17	11
−5	−9	−9	−8	−9	−4
7	7	4	8	8	7

SRA SPECTRUM MATH

Program Evaluation

As part of SRA's interest in updating and improving our curricula, we ask that you take a few moments to complete this questionnaire and return it to us. Feel free to add any additional comments on another sheet of paper.
Please return to:

SRA/McGraw-Hill – Editorial
8787 Orion Place
Columbus, Ohio 43240-4027

We look forward to your comments and suggestions.

Sincerely,
SRA/McGraw-Hill

Your name _____ Date _____

School _____

Address _____

City _____ State _____ Zip _____

What grade level do you teach? _____

What levels of **Spectrum Math** do you use? (Please check as many as apply.)

_____ Gold (1)   _____ Brown (2)   _____ Red (3)   _____ Orange (4)

_____ Yellow (5)   _____ Green (6)   _____ Blue (7)   _____ Purple (8)

What components of **Spectrum Math** do you use?

_____ Student Edition   _____ Teacher's Guide

_____ Spanish Edition   _____ CD-ROM (software)

_____ Achieve: Key Skills and Strategies

How long have you been using **Spectrum Math?** _____

For what purpose(s) do you use **Spectrum Math?** _____

With what size group do you use **Spectrum Math?** _____

What do you consider to be **Spectrum Math's** strongest features? _____

_____

_____

_____

SPECTRUM MATHEMATICS
Gold Book

EVALUATION

What do you consider to be *Spectrum Math's* weakest feature? _____
_____
_____
_____

Rank how this level of *Spectrum Math* covers the following content areas.
(**W** = Weak, **A** = Adequate, **T** = Thorough, **N** = Not Applicable)

_____ Addition	_____ Averages	_____ Patterns
_____ Subtraction	_____ Algebra	_____ Fractions
_____ Multiplication	_____ Decimals	_____ Rounding
_____ Division	_____ Measurement	_____ Geometry
_____ Real-world word problems	_____ Graphing	_____ Estimating
_____ Problem Solving Strategies	_____ Probability	

Are there any topics that should be added to this level of *Spectrum Math?*
_____
_____

Are the Problem Solving Strategy Lessons in the Student Edition valuable and appropriate for this grade level? _____
_____

Are the Cumulative Reviews useful in helping students become familiar with Standardized Tests?
_____

What specific changes, if any, would you like to see in the next edition of *Spectrum Math?*
_____

Additional Comments
_____
_____
_____
_____
_____
_____
_____

SPECTRUM MATHEMATICS
Gold Book